Just Business
Arguments in Business Ethics

Martin E. Sandbu

Prentice Hall

Boston   Columbus   Indianapolis   New York   San Francisco   Upper Saddle River
Amsterdam   Cape Town   Dubai   London   Madrid   Milan   Munich   Paris   Montreal   Toronto
Delhi   Mexico City   São Paulo   Sydney   Hong Kong   Seoul   Singapore   Taipei   Tokyo

Editorial Director: Craig Campanella
Editor in Chief: Dickson Musslewhite
Publisher: Nancy Roberts
Editorial Project Manager: Kate Fernandes
Editorial Assistant: Nart Varoqua
Director of Marketing: Brandy Dawson
Marketing Manager: Laura Lee Manley
Managing Editor: Maureen Richardson
Project Manager: Annemarie Franklin
Media Editor: Rachel Comerford
Operations Specialist: Christina Amato
Cover Design Manager: Jayne Conte
Cover Designer: Suzanne Duda
Cover Photo: Xaq Pitkow
Full-Service Project Management: Chitra Ganesan/PreMediaGlobal
Composition: PreMediaGlobal
Printer/Binder: STP Courier
Cover Printer: STP Courier
Text Font: Palatino

Library of Congress Cataloging-in-Publication Data

Sandbu, Martin E.
   Just business : arguments in business ethics/Martin E. Sandbu.—1st ed.
     p. cm.
   Includes bibliographical references and index.
   ISBN-13: 978-0-205-69775-5 (alk. paper)
   ISBN-10: 0-205-69775-5 (alk. paper)
 1. Business ethics.   I. Title.
   HF5387.S263 2012
   174'.4—dc22

                                                                2010049762

10 9 8 7 6 5 4 3 2 1

Prentice Hall
is an imprint of

www.pearsonhighered.com

ISBN 10:   0-205-69775-5
ISBN 13: 978-0-205-69775-5

For my teachers; for my students

CONTENTS

INTRODUCTION

The Purpose of This Book

For being an intellectual discipline, business ethics is embarrassingly undisciplined in its sprawl. The range and variety of research published in academic journals, or of courses taught in universities under the label of business ethics or similar-sounding monikers, cohabit uneasily, inspired and shaped as they are by widely different academic origins. Add to this the confusions arising from the communicative gap between scholars and practitioners, and everything conspires to make it quite unclear what is meant when someone says they teach, or study, or write about business ethics. Although it indisputably presents a challenge for the discipline, this sprawl need not be a shortcoming. Thomas Dunfee and Thomas Donaldson are quite right, for example, to argue that a comprehensive theory of business ethics must find a way to combine philosophical theory and empirical social science to have any hope of being true, let alone useful.[i] However, more than perhaps any other discipline, business ethics lacks both an obvious core body of knowledge and a unifying methodology. That is one reason why this book, although it is written with students or other newcomers to formal ethical argument in mind, is not conceived as a textbook in the ordinary sense. Any attempt at "covering the field" even at an introductory level—and certainly in a single volume of comfortable length—is doomed to fail.

Nevertheless, there are some features that any intellectual approach to business ethics—especially any academic course on the subject—must display. What sets it apart from other sorts of business studies is its normativity. Ethics, after all, is about how one ought to act, and any enquiry into ethics must be, at least in part, a study of practical reasons as Kant understood that term: an analysis of reasons for acting in some ways rather than others, including, importantly, reasons that are *intrinsically* and not merely instrumentally normative. Without delving into the tradition of thought that takes such reasons as its subject—moral philosophy, that is—one cannot do business ethics well, whatever plausible approach one otherwise takes to it.

This book, then, is an attempt to work through the basic contributions that Western moral philosophy (its non-religious strands) makes to thinking about ethics in

---

[i] In their *Ties that Bind: A Social Contracts Approach to Business Ethics* (Boston, MA: Harvard Business School Press, 1999).

business. In that sense, it is a textbook or an introductory philosophy book; although how I have chosen to resolve the questions inevitably thrown up by such a project has taken it some distance from conventions about what textbooks are supposed to do. Since these choices shape how the book may perhaps best be used in a classroom, it is worth describing them at some length here.

The first and most fundamental is that the book, as I put it above, *works through* rather than "presents" moral philosophy's relevance to business. Too many have suffered a first encounter with philosophy consisting of an "exposition" of what different theories have to say about a subject and have been left with an impression that the task philosophy teaches one to master is to regurgitate a laundry list of those theories. But philosophical reasoning—and moral reasoning most of all—is something one learns *to do*, not primarily something one learns *about*. While this book certainly does visit the main mileposts of the Western moral canon, it tries to show that these theories are part of the canon because they are solutions to problems we face, rather than the other way round. It does so by developing them as the positions a reflective person may naturally arrive at when reasoning in good faith about moral problems. It also, in a departure from conventional textbooks, takes a view. (The view it develops is an argument broadly in favor of a social-contract approach to business ethics). This is inevitable given the goal of engaging the reader in the *process* of moral reasoning and not merely its product. It is also desirable. For *doing* moral philosophy and not merely learning about it requires passing judgment on different claims, rather than adopting a stance of neutrality to which many textbooks aspire. Therefore, this text is written in the hope that it will prompt readers to engage in moral reasoning of their own—though not, of course, in the expectation that all or even most readers will agree with its arguments. Indeed I expect many of them not to, and I trust that any instructors who find the book useful will emphasize problems with and counter-arguments to its reasoning. It is precisely because they will disagree with many of the arguments presented here that readers may find themselves genuinely engaging with them; that, at least, is a test of whether the book succeeds.

The second choice is to introduce and develop ethical thinking in a very general sense, rather than to approach normative business ethics as the specialty it in fact is in the academe. The book makes fewer references than some other academic introductions to business ethics to work being done by business ethics researchers today or to most current scholarly debates in the field. It also does not go very far in an applied direction and eschews detailed (let alone "solved") case studies. The focus is instead on the basic arguments in moral philosophy that seem to this author most relevant to business practice: the possibility of reasoned argument about ethics at all (Chapters 1 and 2); whether moral questions can be satisfactorily answered with reference to the virtues, social roles, and cultural conventions (Chapters 3 and 4); the claim that consequences—in particular for people's well-being—are all that matter morally (Chapters 5 to 7); and the disputed need for rights and how to justify and specify them (Chapters 8 to 12, which include discussions of distributive justice and social contract theory). These arguments are "basic" in both senses of that word: "basic" as general and introductory; and "basic" as foundational. The double meaning goes a long way to justify the choice. Just as in economics, a critical examination of the First Theorem of Welfare Economics or of principal-agent theory presupposes a view of the principles of utility maximization or the expected utility hypothesis, so in ethics, one cannot critically evaluate a proposed social contract theory without a theory of rights or a principle of autonomy in the background. Any serious intellectual engagement with either the moral issues at stake in detailed real-world cases or specialized discussions in philosophical theory must be preceded by a "working out" of the broad questions of general principle that this book addresses.

Thirdly, it is of course cases, examples, and thought experiments that bring moral philosophy to life and illustrate the analytical power and sheer joy that philosophical reasoning has to offer. Conventional textbooks, accordingly, are either plain anthologies or are at least full of lengthy case studies. Although this book is not lacking in examples, it does, again, choose a different approach from the textbook norm by weaving cases and examples into the text in a rather summary fashion. This choice should not be taken to play down the indisputable need for case studies. In fact the text grew in large part from attempts to distill discussions of concrete cases in order to show that what the canonical theories in moral philosophy do is to formalize and systematize the intuitions that real-world dilemmas trigger. But to belabor a point, business ethics is a sprawling discipline, and there will only be minimal overlap between the sets of case studies (and other material) that those using this book as a course text consider useful. It seems wiser, then, to offer a short book on normative reasoning that can organize thoughts and intuitions brought forth by a variety of possible cases than add to the existing shelf of anthologies and case compendia. This is an all the more natural choice to make as technology is quickly rendering obsolete the massive textbook containing everything that might (but often turns out not to) be relevant for a course. (This obsolescence is a development we may well cheer: Mammoth textbooks have drained the wallets and pained the backs of many a student.)

Just Business is therefore not a stand-alone course text, but it I hope it may be found suitable as the core treatment of moral reasoning around which a business ethics course can be built. To facilitate this use, each chapter ends with a short section entitled "Summary of the argument in this chapter." Readers may want to start the book by reading all these summary sections consecutively; they give a roadmap to the book and enable instructors to judge whether to use the book in its entirety or excerpt individual parts. If used as the moral philosophy core of a class course, every chapter contributes a theoretical development of ideas that are predictably generated by class discussions of cases. The book may therefore fruitfully be interwoven with case readings, with each chapter read or assigned after such case discussions. There are various cases covered briefly in the text itself; many instructors will have their won favorite cases and there is no reason why they should not use them instead. The appendix gives further references and suggestions for supplementary material to match the text. The publisher, moreover, has paired the book with an associated Web site offering ample access to case studies and other related material (http://MyEthicsKit.com). This model—pairing a core text with an online library of texts from which to select—allows instructors and students to get by with only one short physical book by downloading other material as and when necessary. Like every intellectual endeavor, of course, it benefits from collaboration, and any suggestions for material to add to the Web site will be received with gratitude.

ACKNOWLEDGMENTS

The old joke has it that business ethics is an oxymoron: You can have business or ethics but not both. If that were true, there would be no point to this book. But there is another sense in which business ethics does indeed bring together two opposites—or must do so if it is to be successful. I think of the two intellectual disciplines of moral philosophy and economics: It is far too rare for scholars in the two fields to learn from each other, let alone to attempt to master both. If there is anything useful in this book for those who think about ethics in business, it reflects the rare but important efforts to bridge the two disciplines that I have been privileged to benefit from since as far back as my undergraduate days.

I am indebted to the Philosophy, Politics, and Economics programme at Oxford University and Balliol College, where my teachers—whether economists or philosophers—demonstrated the sort of respect and interest for each other's way of thinking that distinguishes practical wisdom from mere theoretical cleverness. During my doctoral studies at Harvard University I had the fortune of finding continued intellectual support for crossing disciplinary boundaries. A fellowship at the Harvard Center for Ethics and the Professions gave me not only good colleagues but friends. And though Harvard sits atop an academic world that respects fences between disciplines more than it encourages one to jump them, it also houses thinkers who care more about lifting the constraints on our minds than about navigating those of academia. My doctoral committee chair Amartya Sen's influence on both my thinking and my own professional ethics endures to this day—an inspiration I hope comes across in this book.

I also had the good fortune to work for three years at the Wharton School's Department for Legal Studies and Business Ethics, home to the world's best group of scholars dedicated to applying philosophical thinking to business issues. I am thankful for the institutional support I received from the Wharton School's Zicklin Center for Business Ethics Research during the time it took to write the book and for the opportunity to try out material that later made it into the book at the Norwegian School of Economics and Business Administration in Bergen. My latest professional home, *The Financial Times*, has granted me a ringside seat to the recent upheavals in the economic and business worlds—and beaten out of me some of the leadenness that passes for writing in academia. Among the teachers and colleagues whose insights I enjoyed at these institutions and elsewhere, I would like to name and thank Arthur Applbaum, Christopher Avery, Michael Bacharach, Alexander Cappelen, Thomas Donaldson, Thomas Dunfee, Andrew Graham, Jerry Green, Louis-Philippe Hodgson,

Nien-Hê Hsieh, Macartan Humphreys, Waheed Hussain, William Laufer, Stephen Marglin, Eric Maskin, Martin O'Neill, Philip Nichols, Eric Orts, Matthew Price, Sanjay Reddy, Michael Sandel, Andrea Sangiovanni-Vincentelli, Tim Scanlon, Richard Shell, Annie Stilz, Alan Strudler, Adam Swift, Richard Tuck, David Vines, and Richard Zeckhauser.

A number of people have helped me with the practical challenges I have faced from the book's conception to its printing. I am grateful to Tamara English, Lauretta Tomasco, Gale Wilson, and Cherly Vaughn-Curry at the Wharton School for all their smiling help; to Jacobia Dahm, for explaining to me the secrets of publishing; to Dave Repetto, Nancy Roberts, Kate Fernandes, Annemarie Franklin, Chitra Ganesan, Wendy Guarino, and everybody else at Pearson for making the book a tangible reality. I also owe my agent, Michael Snell, thanks for his advice and help in finding a home for the book.

All teachers know that the best way to master a subject is to have to teach it. That is doubly true for the work that went into this book, which is largely based on the course I taught to Wharton undergraduates between 2005 and 2008. Presenting my thinking to them, answering their questions, and observing their own intellectual journey into moral philosophy all helped me improve and sharpen my own views. I am grateful to the hundreds of students at Harvard and Wharton that I have had the privilege to teach. This book is dedicated to them, as well as to those who have taught me.

It is lonely work to write a book. My greatest thanks go to two wonderful friends who were always there to fuel my efforts with new energy. Xaq Pitkow, who somehow manages to be at the same time my best listener and my best critic (and who designed the book cover). And my beloved Ana, who gives me the strength to find my own ways.

Martin E. Sandbu

London, November 2010

SUPPORT FOR INSTRUCTORS AND STUDENTS

- **myethicskit** is an online resource that offers a wealth of tools to help student learning and comprehension, including practice quizzes, videos, primary source readings and more. MyEthicsKit also includes a rich array of interactive tools enhanced with audio and video to engage students in learning. Please see your Pearson sales representative for more information or visit www.myethicskit.com.
- Instructor's Manual with Tests (0-205-69777-1): For each chapter in the text, this valuable resource provides a detailed outline, list of objectives, discussion questions, and suggested readings and videos. In addition, test questions in multiple-choice, true/false, fill-in-the-blank, and short answer formats are available for each chapter; the answers are page-referenced to the text. For easy access, this manual is available at www.pearsonhighered.com/irc.
- MyTest Test Generator (0-205-00927-1): This computerized software allows instructors to create their own personalized exams, edit any or all of the existing test questions, and add new questions. Other special features of this program include random generation of test questions, creation of alternate versions of the same test, scrambling question sequence, and test preview before printing. For easy access, this software is available at www.pearsonhighered.com/irc.
- PowerPoint Presentation Slides for Just Business: Arguments in Business Ethics (0-205-00926-3): These PowerPoint slides combine text and graphics for each chapter to help instructors convey philosophical principles in a clear and engaging way. For easy access, they are available at www.pearsonhighered.com/irc.

CHAPTER 1

The Business of Ethics
Reasoning about Right and Wrong

A book on business ethics has a greater hurdle than most to pass if it is to convince readers of its usefulness. For it is quite legitimate to wonder what a book can teach us about business ethics. One may doubt that books can teach us *anything* about business: Business is, after all, a practical activity that one must practice in order to master. Yet this doubt is one many fields of business study and analysis shrug off easily. Business schools teach courses like strategy, marketing, and accounting: academic subjects that have proved useful—sometimes indispensable—to business practice by offering knowledge, analysis, and techniques that, ideally at least, can help us succeed in commercial life. Is ethics too, like these other subjects, a field of study and analysis of business? If so, what techniques does *it* offer? Should we demand from it, too, that the gauge of its usefulness is how it makes us better at doing business, and if so, better in what ways? In short: What is the point of business ethics?

One fundamental distinction marks business ethics off from other approaches to studying commercial practice. Those other subjects are primarily *descriptive*—they try to *describe* certain aspects of business. (Accounting, for example, aims to capture a company's financial situation.) They are also often *predictive*, asking what is going to happen depending on the choices people make. (Marketing, for example, attempts to identify advertising techniques that will increase sales.) But ethics aims neither to describe the world nor to predict behavior. Ethics asks and aims to answer *normative* questions. Its questions are about how things *ought to be* and how a person *should act*.

Business ethics, then, is the study of what people in business ought to do. But once we put it this way, we must worry if studying ethics is worth our while. For the other business disciplines already tell us how to behave; they are also normative. Law, management theory, or marketing science may variously say that corporations must do X to comply with corporate law, that doing Y will generate the most profits, or that doing Z will boost sales. In describing reality and predicting outcomes in this way, these disciplines at the same time recommend actions X, Y, and Z as things business people ought to do. Moreover, they recommend them on the basis of foundations that can at least claim to be objective, such as the law or hard facts about the market and consumer behavior. The ordinary disciplines of business study would seem to render business ethics superfluous. If they determine what business people ought to do, what questions are left over for ethics to answer?

If this conclusion followed, there would be no point in reading (or writing) this book. But it does not follow. Other business disciplines are indeed also normative, but only in an *instrumental* sense. They examine what we ought to do *in order to* achieve a given goal, and they evaluate actions only as instruments for reaching it. But the goal itself—whether it be obedience to the law, higher profit, or more sales—they take for granted. In contrast, ethics is *intrinsically* and not just instrumentally normative. Ethics asks which goals we *ought* to pursue. For example: *Should* a company seek to maximize profits? If so, should it always aim for profits, and should it aim for only profits and nothing else? What is more, ethics does not stop at evaluating the goals we set for ourselves. It extends its scrutiny to the actions we choose in order to pursue our goals, even when the goals themselves pass moral muster. May we (should we?) choose the actions that achieve our goals most effectively? Or are there considerations beyond effectiveness for choosing some actions and avoiding others? These are not questions the common business disciplines can answer, because those disciplines take them as settled. For business ethics, in contrast, nothing is settled. Business ethics is a radical enquiry in quite a literal sense—it "goes to the roots" of what we ought to do in commercial life.

In response to this view of what ethics is for, one might react in two quite opposite, yet equally natural ways. The first is to exclaim that if *these* are the questions of which ethics treats, then ethics is pointless, for the questions—or rather the answers to them—are trivial. The second is to despair that ethics is pointless, for the questions it asks are unanswerable. We need to put both worries to rest; for the first, a simple example will do.

Those who think ethics is trivial are those who think it obvious what businesses ought to do: They should, *of course*, maximize profit in any way they can without breaking the law. If this were true, there would indeed be nothing left for ethics to do beyond what the study of law, strategy, and other business subjects already tell us. But it is easy to find examples where this is not obviously so. The Internet company Yahoo! launched its Yahoo! China Web site in 1999 as a profit-making move.[1] Since then, the Chinese government has repeatedly ordered the company to pass on personal information, allowing the authorities to identify Yahoo! China users. One was the political dissident Wang Xiaoning, whom Chinese authorities sentenced to ten years in prison in 2002. Should Yahoo! have complied with the Chinese government order, as both profits and law obedience would command? We need not answer that question here, but *if* Yahoo!'s action was indeed right, it was clearly not *obviously* right. In this case, at least, the questions of business ethics are far from trivial.

---

[1] Yahoo!'s press release (http://docs.yahoo.com/docs/pr/release389.html, accessed November 2010) strongly suggests that the company was motivated by profit making and saw this as a profit-maximizing strategy.

Indeed, so far from trivial is this example that it may hurl some readers right into the opposite worry—that there may be no conclusive answers to questions such as whether Yahoo! did the right thing. Although we may have feelings of right and wrong, they may quite reasonably ask, how could we possibly *prove* that some course of action is morally right and another morally wrong? If your feelings disagree with mine, on what grounds can I possibly convince you that I am right? On what grounds could *you* possibly make me change *my* mind? This second reaction is both more justifiable and more troubling than the first. It is skeptical not about whether ethics can ever give anything but trivial answers, but about the more fundamental issue of whether it is possible to find answers to ethical questions at all. If not, then it would be a waste of time to try to reason about such questions, which is what this book aims to do.

We shall devote this chapter, therefore, to the skeptical thought that reasoning about ethical questions cannot bear any fruit. This skepticism comes in several versions. One view, called *amoralism*, sees business as an amoral activity—an activity to which moral considerations simply do not apply. In the context of business, amoralism says that there is no right and wrong in business life, or more precisely, that right and wrong are not categories which apply to business activities. Therefore, reasoning about the rightness or wrongness of business conduct is necessarily misguided.[2] A second view is more complex. It accepts that we make meaningful statements about right and wrong (including in business), but holds that those moral statements are simply a matter of personal taste or subjective preference. They are not something that *reason* can establish as correct or incorrect, any more than we can deduce our tastes for food from reasoning about them. This view—ethical *subjectivism*—leaves little hope that anything useful can result from ethical analysis.

If either amoralism or subjectivism were true, no ambitious enterprise of moral reasoning about business decisions would get off the ground. As we shall see, however, we will find little reason to accept them once we explore what moral reasoning looks like.

A FAMOUS ETHICAL DILEMMA

In 1983, the *Harvard Business Review*, the flagship business journal of the Harvard Business School, published an article that quickly became a classic, although on the face of it, it is not a business case at all. In "The Parable of the Sadhu," Bowen McCoy, a partner of the investment bank Morgan Stanley, recounts an event that happened while he was trekking in the Himalayas during a six-month sabbatical:

> My friend Stephen, the anthropologist, and I were halfway through the 60-day Himalayan part of the trip when we reached the high point, an 18,000-foot pass over a crest that we'd have to traverse . . . Six years earlier I had suffered . . . an acute form of altitude sickness [so] we were

---

[2] There is an important distinction to draw here; it is the distinction between "immoral" and "amoral." To say that business is amoral is not to say that business activities are morally wrong. What amoralism claims is that "right" and "wrong" are meaningless categories when it comes to discussing business (we could also use the word "nonmoral"). "Immoral," on the other hand, means "morally wrong" or *contrary to morality*—so it is a notion that presupposes that moral considerations apply.

understandably concerned . . . If we failed to cross the pass, I feared that the last half of our 'once in a lifetime' trip would be ruined.

To get over the steep part of the climb before the sun melted the steps cut in the ice, we departed at 3:30 A.M. . . . Just after daybreak, while we rested at 15,500 feet, one of the [other climbers] came staggering down toward us with a body slung across his shoulders. He dumped the almost naked, barefoot body of an Indian holy man—a sadhu—at my feet. He had found the pilgrim lying on the ice, shivering and suffering from hypothermia. I cradled the sadhu's head and laid him out on the rocks . . . The sadhu was soon clothed from head to foot. He was not able to walk, but he was very much alive. I looked down the mountain and spotted below the Japanese climbers marching up with a horse.

Without a great deal of thought, I told Stephen and Pasang that I was concerned about withstanding the heights to come and wanted to get over the pass. I took off . . . Stephen arrived at the summit an hour after I did [and] glared at me and said: 'How do you feel about contributing to the death of a fellow man?'[3]

What was this story doing in the *Harvard Business Review*? McCoy calls it a "parable"—a metaphorical story that contains lessons for other situations. The seasoned investment banker sees close parallels between the choice he faced in the mountains and corporate decision-making:

I had literally walked through a classic moral dilemma without fully thinking through the consequences. My excuses for my actions include a high adrenaline flow, a superordinate goal, and a once-in-a-lifetime opportunity—factors in the usual corporate situation, especially when one is under stress.

McCoy's point is that moral dilemmas occur in business, and that business people must prepare themselves to face them. A dilemma is a situation in which you must choose between two actions, but where there are good reasons favoring each action (or good reasons for refraining from both). It becomes a *moral* dilemma when some of those reasons are moral reasons—reasons why one or the other action is the *morally* right or wrong thing to do. Ethics asks, first, what moral reasons there are for acting one way or the other in such situations, and, second, what we have *most* reason to do all things considered. The worry we raised earlier is whether these are questions it is possible to answer.

A most useful first step toward addressing this worry is simply to put it aside and observe how people in practice proceed when they take for granted that it *is* possible. Until McCoy encounters the sadhu, he orients his decision-making around how best to achieve his personal goal of completing the trek, in light of the difficulties of altitude sickness and the melting ice. His decisions, about what route to take for example, are a matter of *instrumental* reasoning. But once the sadhu appears, his need presents a reason for McCoy to make an effort to help him that is entirely non-instrumental. McCoy need

---

[3] Bowen McCoy, "The Parable of the Sadhu," *Harvard Business Review*, 61(5), Sept./Oct. 1983, pp. 103–108.

not and does not evaluate whether helping the sadhu will further his goal (in fact, it will not). He takes for granted that other people matter *for their own sake*, and this makes his consideration of the sadhu's needs a *moral* reason. His dilemma is whether the new moral reason to interrupt the trek outweighs the reasons he has for moving on. McCoy recognizes that what he chooses *matters* morally—he feels the need to justify his choice of moving on rather than interrupting the trek. When Stephen chastises him, he retorts:

> Look, we all cared. We all stopped and gave aid and comfort. Everyone did his bit . . . What more could we do? . . . Here we are . . . at the apex of one of the most powerful experiences of our lives . . . What right does an almost naked pilgrim who chooses the wrong trail have to disrupt our lives? . . . We had our own well-being to worry about . . . Are you really saying that, no matter what the implications, we should, at the drop of a hat, have changed our entire plan?

Stephen is unimpressed: "I wonder . . . what you would have done, Buzz, if the sadhu had been a well-dressed Western woman?"[4]

This exchange is an example of moral reasoning. Against Stephen's criticisms, McCoy offers countervailing reasons why they were right to leave: They did all they could; the sadhu had no "right" to "disrupt their lives"; they had no duty to put their own well-being at risk; the sadhu's need was trivial (just a "drop of a hat"). We recognize these justifications as *moral* reasons, not just by their language, but by their content. McCoy never simply points out that they have nothing to gain from helping the sadhu. Such an answer would miss the point of Stephen's implicit accusation ("How do you feel about contributing to the death of a fellow man?"), for if you act wrongly, the fact that your decision benefits you does not justify your wrongful action. By giving reasons why he did the right thing, McCoy shows that he understands the accusation and the need to refute it. The two friends together engage in reasoned argument to establish what, morally, they *ought to have done*, and McCoy suggests that we should do the same in business.

We seem to have no difficulty understanding McCoy's moral argument with his friend. But that such an argument can be meaningful or fruitful is precisely what is doubted by the skepticism we raised above, and which we must now confront. We start with the amoralist version.

AMORALISM

Suppose someone believes that there is no such thing as right and wrong; that moral concepts are meaningless. Can we rationally convince such a person of the wrongness of an action he proposes to undertake? To answer this question, we have to start by recognizing what is really involved in a truly amoralist view. Bernard Williams has sketched what a consistent amoralist would have to think:

> We might ask first what motivation he does have. He is indifferent to moral considerations, but there are things that he cares about, and he has some real preferences and aims. They might be, presumably, pleasure or power; or

---

[4] Ibid.

they might be something much odder, such as some passion for collecting things. Now these ends in themselves do not exclude some acknowledgement of morality; what do we have to leave out to represent him as paying no such acknowledgement? Presumably such things as his caring about other people's interests, having any inclination to tell the truth or keep promises if it does not suit him to do so, being disposed to reject courses of action on the ground that they are unfair or dishonorable or selfish. These are some of the substantive materials of morality.[5]

Williams does not mean to say that there are such people. Rather, by describing a person who truly does not acknowledge that morality gives him reasons to do certain things and to avoid others, we identify which reasons are in fact generated by the systems of thought that we recognize as moral (as opposed to "amoral," not "immoral"). We identify, that is, the elements of our ordinary thinking about moral matters that a consistent amoralist must renounce. Of these, the most important is that we have moral reasons to care about other people's interests. Now we need to be clear about what makes these *moral* reasons, and the way in which an amoralist does not care about them. An amoralist will sometimes find it useful to do things for others because it benefits him to do so by, for example, prompting others to do him favors in return. He will also have a self-interested reason to pretend that he subscribes to common moral norms, as this affects how others will deal with him—not least in business! Companies find it in their self-interest to treat employees, customers, and suppliers fairly, since a reputation for fairness is a profitable intangible asset. This is why *The Economist* magazine endorses many of the practices that are labeled "corporate social responsibility" when they are good for business. This is clearly not a moral argument; in the same article, the magazine urges business to adopt such practices insofar as they are "good management," not because they are good for others.[6]

What an amoralist does not do—including in his business dealings—is care about other people's interests and needs *for their own sake*. He considers other people's interests only *instrumental* reasons for him to act in certain ways; he does not see their needs and interests as reasons worthy of consideration independently of how they contribute to his own goals. McCoy is clearly no amoralist. He takes for granted that the sadhu's need by itself constitutes a reason for helping him, a reason he must give due consideration even if he ultimately decides to move on. If he were an amoralist, what would his response have been to the dilemma? We can imagine him thinking something like: "I came to climb the mountain, and rescuing the sadhu does not advance that goal. So I have no reason to consider the sadhu's fate; all my reasons point in the direction of hurrying on to the pass." The amoralist version of McCoy, in other words, simply denies the existence of a dilemma. This follows from his denying the existence of moral reasons. Since there are no non-moral reasons for him to help the sadhu, there is no dilemma.

If someone truly believed this, we could not plausibly hope to reason them out of it. But just by spelling out the amoralist's reasoning, we notice how foreign it is to us, and how much it removes from the core experience of being human. If there is nobody

---

[5] Bernard Williams, *Morality: An Introduction to Ethics*, (Cambridge: Cambridge University Press, 1972), ch. 1.

[6] "The union of concerned executives," *The Economist*, 22 January 2005.

"whose sufferings or distress would affect him . . ." says Williams, "it looks as though we have produced a psychopath." This shows how far someone would have to go to consistently dismiss all moral considerations, and how unappealing a position one must take in order to reject moral reasons altogether.

Most people, of course, are not psychopaths, and do not find general amoralism attractive. Moral reasoning may have no grip on the psychopath, but it does on everyone else. Even the most ruthless businessman recognizes that he has *some* moral responsibilities—toward his family, his friends, or perhaps his country. Yet this does not rule out a narrower amoralistic skepticism to applying ethics in *business*. Without rejecting morality across the board, a skeptic could claim that the ocean of morality stops at the shores of business, even if it covers the more personal spheres of life like family and friendship. The business ethicist R. Edward Freeman has defined such a "Separation Thesis" in the following way:

> The discourse of business and the discourse of ethics can be separated so that sentences like, '*x* is a business decision' have no moral content, and [sentences like] '*x* is a moral decision' have no business content.[7]

Of course, hardly anybody explicitly professes the Separation Thesis. Like the hypothetical general amoralist, a business amoralist probably finds it advantageous that others should *think* he believes in moral constraints on what he can do in the pursuit of profits. As a consequence, "talking the talk" is ubiquitous in the corporate arena: "Today corporate social responsibility . . . is the tribute that capitalism everywhere pays to virtue. It would be a challenge to find a recent annual report of any big international company that justifies the firm's existence merely in terms of profit . . . Big firms nowadays are called upon to be good corporate citizens, and they all want to show that they are."[8] But this is entirely compatible with not "walking the walk" of pursuing what one ought, morally, to do; compatible, that is, with an implicit endorsement of the Separation Thesis.

Consider what the Separation Thesis means for a simple act such as promising. In our private lives, we acknowledge two kinds of reasons for keeping our promises. One is that when we make a promise, we put ourselves under a moral obligation to do what we promised. The other is that keeping promises typically advances our interests, because only when people trust us will they do the things we need from them (hence the thought that "honesty is the best policy"). The former is a moral reason, the latter a self-interested instrumental reason for keeping promises. And as everyone (except Williams's psychopath) recognizes, the former may apply even when the latter does not. Sometimes we ought to keep promises even when we would benefit from breaking them.

Businesses also make promises. Several decades ago, U.S. car manufacturers employed many more people than today, and they guaranteed those workers generous pensions. But the costs of these commitments ballooned as automation and competition

---

[7] R. Edward Freeman, "The politics of stakeholder theory: Some future directions," *Business Ethics Quarterly*, 4(4), 1994. Elsewhere Freeman calls it "the Separation Fallacy," but we should use the word "thesis" because whether it is fallacious or not is precisely what is at stake in the discussion here.

[8] *The Economist*, "The good company," 22 January 2005.

shrank workforces while the ranks of pensioners grew. As they were limping toward bankruptcy, many of these companies asked courts to let them cut their pension outlays—which the retired workers complained amounted to breaking their promises. Was there anything wrong about this? Only if there was a moral reason to keep the promise for its own sake, since it clearly did not serve the companies' financial interest to honor it. (We can assume here that any benefit to their reputation would be swamped by the cost of the full liabilities.) But the Separation Thesis denies that there are such moral reasons in business. Unlike in private life, it says, the fact that a company has promised does not constitute an intrinsic reason for doing what it has said it will do. So the car manufacturers should treat this case (and all other cases) simply as a "business decision."

Thus the Separation Thesis, by claiming that moral considerations do not apply to business decisions, seems to regenerate the psychopath of general amoralism, if only within business. *The Corporation*, a popular documentary film, makes precisely this claim—that the business corporation is set up to have all the characteristics of psychopathy in humans. The film means to expose the morally flawed nature of business. If the Separation Thesis is correct, however, there is nothing flawed about corporate psychopathy: Unlike humans in their personal lives, businesses need not consider moral reasons for action. Now in the absence of a proper argument, this distinction seems entirely gratuitous. How can the act of promising create a moral obligation when made in a private setting, and yet *not* constitute a moral reason when done within a business relationship? If morality applies to human life in general, as the Separation Thesis accepts, then what insulates business activities from morality's reach?

Once we admit moral reasons in any area of life, we cannot simply *assert* that the other areas are beyond their reach. Reasons carry a presumption of applying generally unless we establish that they are delimited. To see this, recall Stephen's provocative question to McCoy: "I wonder what you would have done . . . if the sadhu had been a well-dressed Western woman?" Both McCoy and we, the readers, feel the poignancy of the question. But why is it even relevant? After all, it *was* a sadhu they found, not a well-dressed Western woman. We can again imagine an amoral version of McCoy, but this time one who (analogously to the Separation Thesis) accepts moral reasons in some domains of life, but not in others. He might say: "If it were a well-dressed Western woman, that would be an ethical decision, and I would have a duty to interrupt the trek to help. But here, it is a 'trekking decision' and, therefore, there are no moral considerations to take into account." Again, by properly spelling it out we notice how exceedingly bizarre even a limited amoral position is. Stephen's question *is* relevant, but the amoralist misses the point of his remark and the presumption it invokes: that if McCoy would have thought it immoral not to save a Western woman in the same situation, then he must think it equally immoral not to save the sadhu. Stephen's rhetoric is powerful because we (and McCoy) recognize that moral reasons do *not* arbitrarily stop applying.

In the same light, simply asserting the Separation Thesis is unjustified. As a way out of moral reasoning, it comes one step too late, since it itself needs to be backed up by a moral argument. Given the generality of moral reasons, which Stephen's question illustrates, we must justify why they should be suspended when it comes to business decisions. Such a justification must itself take the form of a moral reason—it must argue that *morality itself*, properly understood, permits business not to care about others for their own sake. Such arguments have been made, and we shall consider one in the next chapter. Here, we should simply note that such arguments cannot take business decisions out of the realm of moral reasoning; on the contrary, they place them firmly within it. The amoralistic skepticism toward business ethics is, therefore, unwarranted.

ETHICAL SUBJECTIVISM

Believers in the Separation Thesis do not "walk the walk" in applying moral judgments to business, even though they may "talk the talk." Surprisingly, it also turns out that many walk the walk but do not talk the talk. The business scholars Frederick B. Bird and James A. Waters call this "moral muteness":

> Many managers exhibit a reluctance to describe their actions in moral terms even when they are acting for moral reasons. They talk as if their actions were guided exclusively by organizational interests, practicality, and economic good sense even when in practice they honor morally defined standards codified in law, professional conventions, and social mores. They characteristically defend morally defined objectives such as service to customers, effective cooperation among personnel, and utilization of their own skills and resources in terms of the long-run economic objectives of their organizations . . . Current research based on interviews with managers about how they experience ethical questions in their work reveals that managers seldom discuss with their colleagues the ethical problems they routinely encounter. In a very real sense, 'Morality is a live topic for individual managers but it is close to a non-topic among groups of managers.'[9]

So, even when managers are in fact motivated by moral considerations, they *talk* as if business is an amoral activity. On the face of it, this seems irrational. Why would someone who accepts moral concerns as important in business decisions choose to talk as if that were not the case? If you think moral considerations need to be taken into account in your business decisions, is it not irresponsible to refrain from admitting them and working out with your colleagues how to apply them? Imagine managers who thought privately that profitability was an important consideration in business, but publicly pretended the opposite, and never discussed with each other which course of action would best advance profits. Surely we would think them crazy.

The causes of moral muteness could be institutional; the hierarchies and reward structures in corporations may discourage people from explicitly engaging in moral discussions. We (and the morally motivated manager) may deplore such institutional failings. But they are no ground for moral skepticism. An institutional incapacity for moral deliberation would simply show why businesses fail to engage in a potentially useful activity—a challenge for organizational theory and practice, not a strike against

---

[9] Frederick B. Bird and James A. Waters, "The Moral Muteness of Managers," *California Management Review*, 32(1), 1989.

moral reasoning. More worrying for us is the different idea that moral discussion itself is useless, and that (therefore) business organizations *should* not accommodate it even if they could. According to Bird and Waters, this is a common perception:

> . . .we observe that in general they experience moral talk as dysfunctional. More specifically, managers are concerned that moral talk will threaten organizational harmony, organizational efficiency, and their own reputation for power and effectiveness.[10]

We should proceed carefully here. Even if true, the mere fact that moral discussion has these negative effects would not make it dysfunctional. After all, non-moral discussions—disagreements about strategy, for example—could have similar effects, and yet be necessary to arrive at the best decisions. Similarly, the negative effects of moral reasoning could just be the price worth paying for finding out what we morally ought to do.

But suppose that what we morally ought to do is not something we can find out? Many people hold a view of morality according to which this is impossible. They think that while it makes sense for each person to believe in some moral values (they are not amoralists), each person's moral beliefs are *subjective*, and we cannot say that one set of beliefs is better or more correct than another. This view is *subjectivism*. In everyday discussion, we often hear it expressed as a form of tolerance, in statements like "Who am I to judge?" or "For me *personally*, I believe the right thing to do is . . . but that may not be right for everyone." Behind such statements is often a vague intuition that moral and evaluative judgments can reflect nothing more than one's "personal values" and that *personal* values can have no bearing on what *others* should think. In contrast, to believe that discussing one's moral disagreements or criticizing another's moral beliefs could resolve anything presupposes that someone could be *mistaken* in their moral judgments. By denying that this is possible, subjectivism makes moral discussion look dysfunctional. Since moral disagreement can indeed have a real negative effects—the disharmony, inefficiency, and animosity that "morally mute" managers worry about—it would be idiotic to engage in it for the sake of an impossible benefit. We shall now see, however, that subjectivism—at least some common versions of it—is a deeply problematic view.

According to the simplest version of subjectivism, moral statements just report the preferences of those who utter them. When I say "killing is wrong" I mean something like "I detest killing." On this view, McCoy's rationalizations are not *rationalizations* at all; they simply state in various ways that he liked or approved of continuing the trek more than he did interrupting it to take care of the sadhu. Likewise, Stephen's admonishments report his dislike for what they did. According to simple subjectivism, McCoy and Stephen are "like two persons on a boat, one of whom says that he feels sick while the other says that he, on the other hand, does not."[11] In the same way that these two men are not contradicting each other (that one feels well is no reason for the other to revise his view that he, on the other hand, feels sick), the fact that Stephen does not like what McCoy did does not contradict the fact that McCoy does like it; so, under simple subjectivism the moral claims each makes do not constitute reasons the other must take into

---

[10] Ibid.

[11] Williams, *Morality,* ch. 2.

account. Where amoralism denies the meaningfulness of moral statements, simple subjectivism denies the *interpersonal reach* of those statements' meanings, since they are really just statements about the utterer.

But this is not how Stephen and McCoy themselves interpret what they are saying. They think that their disagreement is meaningful. When McCoy tries to justify to Stephen that they did the right thing, he is not merely stating that he has different feelings from Stephen; he sees himself as contradicting Stephen's claim that they acted wrongly. And when we read their exchange, we interpret what he says in the same way. Regardless of which of the two we agree with, we find McCoy's disagreement with Stephen and their attempts at convincing one another meaningful. Indeed we frequently engage in such moral discussions ourselves. Simple subjectivism, by implying that this activity is absurd, merely succeeds in showing its own absurdity.

A more sophisticated version of subjectivism is *emotivism*, which understands moral expressions not as statements at all, but as interjections with an evaluative flavor. Moral terminology, in other words, is on a par with such words as "Wow!", "Shame on you!", "Bravo!" or "Yuck!" What McCoy really means, in an emotivist interpretation, is something like "Let's not do any more for the sadhu, off we go!" whereas Stephen's criticism means something like "Shame on you for leaving the sadhu behind this way!" Emotivism avoids simple subjectivism's mistake of claiming that McCoy and Stephen's utterances about their actions toward the sadhu are "really" statements about themselves. Therefore, it does not deny that moral disagreements are meaningful. It claims instead that when two people morally disagree, they express different attitudes, much like when two people disagree in their reactions to a dish of food or a work of art. Although they disagree, they do not *contradict* each other in the logical sense, for that requires at least one of them to be mistaken.

Though undeniably subtler than crude subjectivism, emotivism also misses a crucial difference between *moral* attitudes and other evaluative outlooks:

> . . . it fails to account for the undoubted facts that a man may be in a state of moral doubt, which he may resolve—that a man can nonarbitrarily change his mind about a moral matter, not merely in the individual case, but on a general issue and for reasons . . . even if moral attitudes were rarely *determined* by reasons [it] is only if the position to which a man is led by [other] forces [is at the same time also a] position to which reasons are relevant that we can understand it as a moral position at all.[12]

McCoy reveals that he does not conceive of himself in emotivist terms when he engages in moral doubt. He deliberates and second-guesses himself as to whether they did the right thing, thinking something like: "I believe I was justified in leaving the sadhu behind; but perhaps I am mistaken about that and in fact acted wrongly." He worries that he might have "got it wrong"; that is why he is looking for reasons that justify his choice. Such a worry makes no sense if moral beliefs are merely interjections—consider how strange it would be to second-guess your own tastes for food. ("Chocolate ice

---

[12] Ibid.

cream— yum! Pistachio ice cream— yuck! But perhaps I am mistaken about that and in fact: pistachio—yum!") Yet in the moral case, it surely does make sense. When somebody berates you for not eating pistachio ice cream, "I don't like it" is an adequate answer. That will not do, however, as an answer to *moral* condemnation. When somebody confronts you with breaking your promise, answering "I don't want to" simply misses the point of the challenge. To be put forward *as a moral claim*, "I don't want to" needs to be backed up with reasons why your not wanting to justifies your not doing the thing in question. Unlike assertions about taste, it is part of recognizing our own or others' assertions as *moral* assertions that we make them potential subjects of reasoned criticism.

So what we learn from McCoy's internal deliberation (his moral doubt) and his exchange with Stephen—as well as from the moral deliberations and discussions we confront in our own lives—is that moral reasoning at least *sounds* as if it attempts to establish something beyond the existence of our attitudes themselves. It attempts to establish whether those attitudes are *justified*. Morality expresses itself not simply as something we happen to think or choose to believe, but as something we acknowledge that we have the most reason to believe. Subjectivism cannot account for this aspect of how we experience moral thinking.

These remarks do not suffice to show that subjectivism is false. What they do show is that a basic element of how we understand the content of our moral thoughts as we usually experience them—our sense that moral doubt and moral deliberation are not meaningless—is incompatible with subjectivism and its implication that we cannot "find out" anything by engaging in moral deliberation. Many of us will find this a good enough reason to reject it. If we do, we shall then have to believe that our moral beliefs can indeed be challenged "from the outside" and that reasoned criticism can force us to have to justify them.

We may, however, entertain a lingering doubt—as we should do, given that subjectivism cannot be proven wrong, just shown to be implausible. What if subjectivism is correct after all, and our experience of moral deliberation is just an illusion? What if our moral beliefs are superstitions, like beliefs in fairies and witches? Even if this is true, reason still has a role in regulating our purely subjective beliefs. For most of us believe (however subjectively) that our moral opinions should hang together in a consistent way. So I can criticize you if you hold two inconsistent beliefs, subjective or not. Moreover, even if you and I morally disagree in a particular case, we may share some more general and basic moral beliefs (such as "one should not treat people unjustly" or "it is wrong to take unfair advantage of someone"). If so, reasoning can help us determine the logical implications of those shared beliefs in the particular case we initially disagree on. Even if moral reasoning fails to achieve objectivity, it still holds out some hope for intersubjectivity. In either case, the subjectivist form of moral skepticism does not support those pessimists who find moral reasoning dysfunctional.

DOING MORAL REASONING

Ethics identifies moral reasons for or against different courses of action and weighs them against each other. Like other kinds of reasoning, moral reasoning can go from the general to the specific, or from the specific to the general. *Deductive* moral reasoning starts with general moral principles—such as "it is wrong to treat others merely as instruments for your own purposes"—and deduces conclusions from them for specific cases. *Inductive* moral reasoning departs from our convictions in concrete cases, and induces general principles that explain why those convictions are correct. Both modes of reasoning—and this book uses both—support moral claims by rational argument and acknowledge that among moral judgments, some are indeed more justified than others. By finding and favoring the positions justified by the better reasons, we aim to come closer to some moral truths.

Those who encounter formal moral reasoning for the first time may find this to be a tall order. They would be right. Ethics challenges and disturbs. It requires us, when we disagree with someone about the right thing to do, to offer reasons—good reasons—that justify our view over our interlocutor's. It forces us to confront our own views critically. And, sometimes, it shows us that we do not have good reasons for believing what we have always believed. Until we seriously reflect on ethical questions, our intuitions are mostly a product of our upbringing and the attitudes of our peers. That does not make them false. But we cannot know that until we ask ourselves what reason we have to believe them. And realizing that we cannot answer that question—that we have been believing things for no good reason—can be a terrifying discovery. At such times, moral reasoning can seem destructive; it removes the certainty of our pre-reflective moral beliefs, but puts nothing new in their place. Despair of ever finding an answer (which may encourage amoralism: "nothing can be proved; nothing is true") is a real danger of moral reasoning.

It serves us well, therefore, to hold on to some elements of our original moral views, if only tentatively, as we deploy our moral reasoning. Some intuitions are firmer than others, even if we cannot justify them fully. Some general principles seem mostly correct, even if in some cases they entail unacceptable implications. And among the general principles and specific judgments we initially endorse, some fit together better than others. All of these are good candidates for what we can tentatively adopt as part of a more justifiable and complete view. As we go back and forth between principles and judgments, we may notice inconsistencies. We can try to "tweak" our system of beliefs to make it internally consistent, or we can make larger revisions, abandoning some principles and intuitions, modifying others, and adopting new ones. As we gradually expand the subset of our beliefs that is reasonably free of inconsistencies, we may gain a confidence in these beliefs—which taken together mutually support each other—that we could not have in any single belief taken by itself. By gradually increasing the coherence of our moral belief system in this way, we move toward what philosopher John Rawls has termed "reflective equilibrium" in which our individual beliefs are "at rest" with one another and plausible taken as a whole.

Proceeding in this way, we should feel optimistic about the possibility of moving in a constructive direction, for the subject matter of ethics is something that we actually know well. In "The Parable of the Sadhu," we easily understand what both McCoy and Stephen are talking about. This reflects that the stuff of ethics is in large part the stuff of everyday life, where we all encounter small (and sometimes big) moral dilemmas and have to make up our minds. Likewise, we often behold moral dilemmas in the imagination—from the news, through film and literature, or vicariously through friends. In these cases, we usually have immediate hunches about what is right and wrong, and these common-sense intuitions are inputs we can put our moral analysis to work on.

Socrates believed that philosophy just needs to discover and systematize things every human being already knows. While that may be too optimistic, it is encouraging to remember that just by being human, each of us has plenty of raw material to work with in ethics.

This book takes that raw material as it appears when we think about moral dilemmas in business. By looking at a range of difficult business decisions and probing our intuitive moral judgments about them, it refines our inchoate, spontaneous intuitions into more completely formulated world views. Of course, life throws too many things at us for anyone to have a fully worked-out moral system that is always consistent and plausible. But we can aim to get ever closer to reflective equilibrium as we set out on the road of moral reasoning. Hopefully, this book will serve as a good guide down that road.

Summary of the Argument in This Chapter

Business ethics studies the question: *All things considered, how ought we to act when doing business?* This distinguishes it from other approaches to the study of business, which are primarily descriptive and predictive. When other approaches tell us what to do, they are *instrumentally* normative, saying how we should act to achieve some goal. Business ethics is *intrinsically* normative—it asks how we should act, period.

Two views about morality say that this is impossible. One is *business amoralism* or the "Separation Thesis." It says that even if morality applies to the rest of our lives, no moral reasons are relevant for business decisions. But business amoralism is groundless, for as long as actions can be right or wrong in some human activities, we must justify why they cannot be right or wrong in business. Any reason why this should be true would itself be a moral reason that must be analyzed along with reasons for the contrary view, and so business decisions would not be beyond the reach of moral reasoning after all. The other is *subjectivism*, which says that statements about "right" and "wrong" only have subjective

meaning, and can, therefore, never be impersonally reasoned about. But subjectivism fails to account for basic facts about our moral experience—such as meaningful moral disagreements where we try to convince one another, and genuine moral doubt where a person sincerely tries to *find out* what is the right thing to do. If subjectivism were true, these central parts of human self-reflection would be senseless, which is implausible. Even if they were indeed senseless, and most of our moral experiences were an illusion, reason could still play a role in making different subjective beliefs mutually consistent.

We must, therefore, take moral reasoning seriously. We do this by subjecting moral claims to reasoned criticism and see how well they can be justified. We may fall short of a completely coherent and convincing set of moral principles and concrete convictions—we may never reach *reflective equilibrium*. But through the process of moral reasoning, we can assess arguments behind opposite points of view, and establish which view is closer to being true in the sense of having better reasons behind it.

Two Extreme Views
Managing for Shareholders or Stakeholders?

In Chapter 1, we rejected two skeptical views about business ethics: business amoralism—the view that right and wrong have no meaning in business—and moral subjectivism—the view that right and wrong mean nothing more than the "personal values" each individual might hold. The defeated skeptic may now turn to us and retort, with some glee: "So you say there *is* a right thing to do in business, and it is not just whatever feels right to me. All right: What is it then?" Most of us will not have a confident answer ready. So we must accept the skeptic's question as a challenge—a challenge to establish what exactly moral conduct in business requires, and just as importantly, to give good reasons for what we claim.

But we need not concede the rhetorical point. For if the skeptic's question has any sting, it comes from a presupposition we should reject, namely that if there is a right answer to how we ought to behave, then we must know what it is. That presupposition is a fallacy. Whether a question has an answer may well be independent of whether we know, or even whether it is possible to know, what the answer is. This is no less true in ethics than in mathematics or science. (We may not know the value of π. That need not make us doubt that every circle does, in fact, exhibit the same ratio between its circumference and its diameter.) So we can accept the burden of proof for a view of what ethical business requires without embarrassment about the difficulty of formulating or justifying it.

In any case, the main challenge to applied moral reasoning in business is not a lack of answers to what ethical business requires. It is rather the opposite: The business press, popular culture, and academic literature inundate us with views, claims, and theories about how businesses ought to be managed. We shall examine some of them in this book. But the point is not to pick a plausible answer from a menu of choices presented to us. Having an informed view means holding it for good reasons. That is why we can only arrive at a truly informed view at the end of a process of reasoning, which must include disciplined criticism of a range of views—including the one we ultimately settle for. For only by questioning the reasons by which we justify our beliefs can we know whether they are *good* reasons.

In this chapter, we shall examine two famous views that draw quite different conclusions about ethical business conduct. Each has exerted great influence—in opposite directions—on business ethics thinking and on how corporate leaders practice business. That does not make either of them right. Rather, they merit our close attention for the altogether more interesting reason that each fails in instructive ways. To introduce the two views, we may start by reflecting on why ethics should have anything to say about business. The answer is that ethics matters to business for the same reason that it matters in other parts of life: because our decisions, in business or elsewhere, have consequences for other people. What separates business decisions from other decisions is presumably that business decisions essentially deal with questions of economic value—how to transform some resources into other, more valuable ones. Now, decisions that transform and create economic value affect people's lives. That makes them morally significant in many ways, the most obvious being how they determine whom the business activities enrich and whether they may make others worse off in the process. Whom, we must therefore ask, does the manager have moral responsibility *for*? Is there a moral responsibility for society at large—a corporate *social* responsibility—or are managers' moral responsibilities internal to the business enterprise, or even limited to only some of its constituents? Our original question—What ought business people to do?—can be rephrased, then, to ask: For whom should business create value?

The Nobel prize-winning economist Milton Friedman gave one—characteristically provocative—answer to this question. In a capitalist economy, Friedman said:

> there is one and only one social responsibility of business—to use its resources and engage in activities designed to increase its profits so long as it stays within the rules of the game, which is to say, engages in open and free competition, without deception or fraud . . . Few trends could so thoroughly undermine the very foundations of our free society as the acceptance by corporate officials of a social responsibility other than to make as much money for their stockholders as possible.[13]

Views like Friedman's have had tremendous influence in the business world since the 1980s. The legendary CEO of General Electric, Jack Welch, exemplified the managerial focus on increasing "shareholder value" above all else—the predominant normative view in American business for decades after Welch instituted it from the top of GE, one of the world's largest companies. In his own words:

> A company is for its shareholders. They own it. They control it. That's the way it is, and that's the way it should be . . . A company exists to serve the people who elect its board of directors, which, in turn, picks the management that drives the company. It is for its owners.[14]

Of course, being popular among executives does not make a view true. Ought companies really to maximize profits for shareholders when that goes against the interests of the other groups they affect, such as employees, customers, creditors, or the local community?

---

[13] Milton Friedman, *Capitalism and Freedom* (Chicago University Press, 1983), p. 133.

[14] Jack and Suzy Welch, "Whose Company Is It Anyway?" *BusinessWeek*, 14 September 2007.

An alternative rhetoric that has gradually gained attention among business leaders rejects treating shareholders as morally special.[15] It claims that companies should rather create value for *all* "stakeholder groups." This view—really a family of views that go under the rubric of "stakeholder theory"—informs the demands that many activist groups increasingly make on business. If businesses and their managers really bear a moral responsibility not just for their shareholders, as Friedman would have it, but for other groups in society, then it seems to follow that they should show "corporate social responsibility," for example by acting in environmentally sustainable ways or by showing "corporate citizenship."

There are things that ring true in both of these views. That is one reason why the debate between them is an old one. But logic does not allow us the comfort of agreeing with both, since their conclusions contradict each other. To weigh the merits of each of the two views, we need to scrutinize the arguments offered in support for them. We begin with Friedman's.

THE SOCIAL RESPONSIBILITY OF BUSINESS IS TO INCREASE ITS PROFITS

Although Friedman dismisses conventional demands that business must be "socially responsible," he does not deny that managers have moral obligations. Unlike amoralism or subjectivism, his view is deeply moral (in the sense of "moral" that is opposed to "amoral" rather than to "immoral"). Friedman asserts that corporate executives—whether or not they realize this themselves—are under a real moral obligation, which is to manage their corporation exclusively in their shareholders' interests. It would be altogether misguided to caricature Friedman's position as egoistic or interpret it as permitting managers to do whatever they please. He argues for a strict moral duty on managers *not* to do whatever they please and *not* to act for their own benefit. If he is right, it is not only permissible to manage business solely to maximize profits; it is morally required to do so.

This conclusion seems shocking to some. Others think it is obviously correct. In fact, we cannot properly evaluate Friedman's conclusion before we specify in more detail the claim itself and the argument that is thought to support it. First of all, we must note that notwithstanding his exhortation to increase profits, Friedman's position is actually that managers must do *whatever shareholders want*: "a corporate executive is an employee of the owners of the business. . . [His] responsibility is to conduct the business in accordance with their desires."[16] It is quite clear that if shareholders want something else, that something else becomes what managers ought to pursue:

> A group of persons may establish a corporation for an eleemosynary purpose—for example, a hospital or a school. The manager of such a corporation will not have money profit as his objective but the rendering of certain

---

[15] The global financial crisis has put a lot of pressure on the shareholder emphasis. In March 2009, Jack Welch himself told the *Financial Times* that shareholder value maximization was "the dumbest idea in the world" (Francesco Guerrera, "Welch condemns share price focus," *Financial Times*, 12 March 2009). However amusing the irony of Welch's retraction, it of course does not at all help to determine whether his original views were correct. Rather, his change of heart illustrates that for judging the soundness of an argument, who makes it and from which motives is irrelevant.

[16] Milton Friedman, "The Social Responsibility of Business is to Increase Its Profits," *New York Times Magazine*, 13 September 1970.

services. . . the key point is that. . . the manager is the agent of the individuals who own the corporation or establish the eleemosynary institution, and his primary responsibility is to them.[17]

Rather than a "profit-maximization" view, then, we had best call the view that managers ought to do whatever shareholders want the *shareholder primacy view*. Now there are several lines of argument by which one might arrive at such a conclusion; Friedman leaves it open which precise line he is committed to. Indeed, he draws on each of the three main traditions in Western moral philosophy; and, since this book addresses each of these in some detail, it is useful to mention them separately here.

In part, then, Friedman emphasizes that any "corporate responsibility" must refer to the moral responsibilities managers have, not as actual individuals in their actual lives, but *qua* managers, that is, as occupants of a specific social roles. What matters, in this perspective, are not the personal responsibilities and commitments of the individual who happens to be a manager, but the responsibilities conventionally attaching to the role he inhabits (that of manager of a business corporation), which Friedman thinks are to do the owners' bidding.[18] We consider the possibility of a business ethics based on a community's understanding of social roles—an approach that goes back to Aristotle—in Chapters 3 and 4.

A different line of argument refers not to the social role of the manager but to the consequences of profit-maximization and alternative courses of action. Friedman's writings include many claims about what will follow if managers pursue things other than increased profits for their shareholders—in his view, this would hurt, rather than improve, society's well-being. He argues, for example, that if businesses took a "social responsibility" for keeping unemployment low and refrained from firing unproductive workers, technological innovation and productivity growth would grind to a halt, ultimately harming society much more than the unemployment of workers having to shift into a new firm or industry. This thought—that the public good is more securely achieved if businesses ignore it and instead try to concentrate on their own profit—has an estimable pedigree, and we take up its proper place in business ethics in Chapter 6. But note that it is an empirical, not a normative claim. Its moral significance derives from an underlying, unstated, moral principle: namely that the right thing to do is that which will have the best consequences for society's well-being. Theories based on that general premise—*consequentialist* theories—are the focus of Chapters 5 to 7 of this book.

The idea that has pride of place in Friedman's argumentation, however, grounds managers' duty in the rights of owners. This third perspective on ethics is distinct from claims that are fundamentally derived from common understandings of social roles or from the goodness of an act's consequences: It sees an act as morally permissible if it respects the rights of others, and as morally wrong if it violates them. In the case of shareholder primacy, the argument can take different forms depending on what is claimed to be the relevant right of shareholders. Most obviously, shareholders could claim that their *property rights* give the managers a duty to act in their interests. Since the owners have handed their assets to the company for certain purposes—typically making money—and since the managers are hired by the owners (through the board of directors, the

---

[17] Ibid.

[18] In contrast, Friedman locates the responsibility for the well-being of society in the role of public servant.

shareholders' representatives) to pursue those purposes, the managers may not dispose of the money as they see fit, even for noble purposes. For it is not *their* money, and it is morally wrong to use other people's money for purposes, even noble ones, against their will. Engaging in "corporate social responsibility" when it does not increase profits, according to this rights-based argument, is therefore a violation of the owners' property rights, which is immoral in a way that closely resembles theft (unless, of course, the owners agree).

A variant of the rights-based argument for shareholder primacy would say that a manager has *promised* to maximize profits for the owners, since they (or their representatives, the directors) hired him or her on that condition. This gives shareholders the right to have their manager act in the way that they were promised. In this variant of the argument, it would be *fraudulent* (rather than larcenous) of the manager to run the company in ways that did not maximize profits, just like making a false promise to gain control over someone's assets should be characterized as fraud rather than as theft.[19]

Assessing Friedman's shareholder primacy view thoroughly would require pursuing each of these perspectives separately, filling in the gaps he leaves in the development of each so as to build the strongest possible arguments, and determining whether those arguments in fact support the conclusion. We are not in a position to do so until we have at least understood the promises and problems of the three approaches in general, which will take us to the end of this book—by which time we will have seen that there are more convincing accounts of business ethics than Friedman's. What we can do, however, is to ask not whether his arguments justify his conclusion, but whether there is any argument *at all* that could justify it. We can ask, for example, whether the conclusion itself has logical implications that are unacceptable. The philosophical jargon for this is *reductio ad absurdum*, Latin for "reduction to absurdity"—the argumentative technique of showing that a claim is untenable because it logically entails absurd implications. If this were true of the shareholder primacy claim, we would be justified in jettisoning the theory without worrying too much about where Friedman's arguments go wrong.

And on reflection, we can see that the pure shareholder primacy view must be rejected as either absurd or incoherent. For it is certainly a mistake to think that a manager ought to do *whatever* the shareholders desire. When a Mafia boss wants his competitors in the protection racket business to be killed, his agents are under no moral compunction to fulfill his wishes; they would, on the contrary, be wrong to do so. Friedman or proponents of views similar to his clearly do not mean to imply anything else. A plausible shareholder primacy view must respect that *some* moral imperatives take priority over pursuing shareholders' interests. But this lands the theory in very tricky terrain by forcing it to establish what those constraints are. As it tries to do so, the theory threatens to undermine its own primary goal of preventing "social responsibility" from claiming moral priority over business interests.

Friedman himself admits to qualifications on shareholder primacy.[20] He says that managers' "responsibility is to conduct the business in accordance with [shareholders'] desires, which generally will be to make as much money as possible while conforming

---

[19] Such rights-based arguments seem to inspire much of the outrage directed outsize executive compensation. Lavish salaries and bonuses by themselves prompt only muted criticism. It is receiving outlandish amounts of money for actions that at the same time cause losses for shareholders that attract the most public fury.

[20] As did Jack Welch, even before he rejected it wholesale.

to the basic rules of society, both those embodied in law and those embodied in ethical custom."[21] But this is as unhelpful as it is eloquent. What is a manager to do if shareholders do *not* care particularly for "conforming to the basic rules of society"—whether those of the law or those of ethical custom?

The most plausible form of shareholder primacy will surely accept that a company ought not to break the law to make profits for shareholders, even if that is what they want. It will rule out, that is, cases like the Mafia organization we conjured up earlier. So from any plausible shareholder primacy view, respecting the law takes precedence over shareholders' desires. But it seems we cannot say the same about "ethical custom" without undermining the whole point of a shareholder primacy theory. For, if by ethical custom we mean the morality conventionally believed by a majority in society, it could quite conceivably be the case that conventional moral beliefs require companies to be "socially responsible," even against the desires of shareholders. If so, conforming to ethical custom would bind managers to pursuing "social responsibility" to the detriment of shareholder profit, which is surely the opposite of what was intended. Friedman stays clear of this inconsistency: He derides executives who assure us that "that business has a 'social conscience' and takes seriously its responsibilities for providing employment, eliminating discrimination, avoiding pollution and whatever else may be the catchwords of the contemporary crop of reformers."[22] But of course, those catchwords may command wide popularity among the public. Any recognition that some of society's ethical preferences—beyond what society enforces through the law—are morally binding on business threatens the shareholder primacy view with incoherence.

For now, therefore, we shall conclude that a tenable specification of the shareholder primacy view—one that avoids granting an absurd degree of latitude to what managers may do for their shareholders, yet stays true to the motivating principle the shareholder primacy idea aims to express—must say that corporate executives ought to pursue their shareholders' interests with whatever *legal* means are available to them. If shareholders' only desire from their company is as great a return on their investment as possible, then managers are morally obliged to do whatever maximizes profits,[23] including violating commonly held social norms, so long as they do not break the law. Is this the right view? We shall find out by taking it to the field.

MEDICINE FOR THE PEOPLE

Outside the World Health Organization's (WHO) global headquarters in Geneva, Switzerland, stands a statue of a boy and a blind man walking together. The child is helping the man find his way by means of a stick they are both holding on to, child in front, man behind. Until recently, the scene that the statue depicts was a depressingly common sight across many African countries ravaged by the disease river blindness or

---

[21] Friedman, "The Social Responsibility of Business is to Increase Its Profits."

[22] Ibid.

[23] We use "profit maximization" here as shorthand for whatever measure of value shareholders prefer; nothing we have said needs to privilege one measure over another. It could be the share price, or the dividend stream, or some other measure of shareholder financial success. In particular, our arguments are unrelated to the claim (from finance theory) that the share price captures all expected future benefits to shareholders.

onchocerciasis. The disease is caused by a parasitic worm, called *onchocerca volvulus,* which is transmitted by river-breeding black flies when they bite humans. Once inside a human host, the *onchocerca* larvae can grow to become worms more than two feet long. The adult worm spawns millions of tiny larvae called microfilariae, which spread throughout the victim's body, causing itching so intolerable that it can lead people to suicide. When the microfilariae reach the eyes, the victim goes blind. This awful disease afflicted millions of victims as late as the 1980s. In the worst-hit areas of Western Africa, up to a third of adults had lost their sight from river blindness.

The statue of the boy leading the blind man can also be found at the New Jersey headquarters of Merck, Inc., the international pharmaceutical company. In 1978, Merck researchers discovered that a new veterinarian drug compound, ivermectin, was effective against a different species of *onchocerca* parasites in horses. They told Roy Vagelos, head of the research laboratories and later CEO of Merck, that it might be possible to develop ivermectin into a drug against *onchocerciasis* in humans. Any decision to develop a new drug, however, commits a manufacturer to a long and costly research and development process, and no pharmaceutical business takes it lightly. Bringing a new drug from conception to market costs several hundred million dollars, and most projects never succeed. For comparison, Merck earned a net income in 1978 of just over $300 million and paid $130 million in dividends, on revenues of about $2 billion.

What should Merck have done? The company had a real, if uncertain, opportunity to create a product that could relieve enormous suffering in millions of people. Since river blindness afflicts the poorest people in the world, however, there was no prospect of anyone being able to pay enough even to cover the cost of producing the drug— let alone to generate any profit. Merck attempted to convince international organizations and leading governmental agencies for development aid to shoulder the cost, but to no avail. Going ahead with the research and development would, therefore, cause losses, quite conceivably the size of one year's worth of dividends to shareholders.

Few business people have to make decisions as momentous as this. But that is precisely why it is a good case for a theory of business ethics—which, if it is to be of any use at all, must surely offer some guidance for Vagelos's decision. Besides, business people confront similar dilemmas in less extreme form every day. How we think about Merck's very stark choice can teach us how to disentangle what is at stake in lesser problems as well, since it forces us to take a stance on arguments that seem innocuous in more ordinary circumstances.

In the shareholder primacy view, however, the dilemma does not look so stark; indeed, it does not appear to be a dilemma at all, since there is nothing for Vagelos to agonize over. Once the potential drug development's negative effect on profits has been established, the answer is self-evident: It would be wrong to develop the drug. The shareholder primacy theorist must say that Vagelos—who did, in fact, authorize research on ivermectin that led to the drug Mectizan—acted immorally. (Merck subsequently paid for the production and distribution of Mectizan and is still doing so.) He acted immorally by spending money on developing an unprofitable drug for the poor, money which if it had been put to more profitable use would have increased returns to shareholders. Not only that: The shareholder primacy theorist must claim that this answer is *obviously* the right one. There may have been reasons to doubt the profit calculations, but once they were settled, no other considerations could have mattered for what was the right thing to do—not even that the lives and suffering of millions could be relieved by the other choice.

Using the shareholder primacy view to analyze Vagelos's dilemma reveals what is wrong with the theory. It fends off nonprofit considerations by arguing that managers have a particularly important moral bond with shareholders. But to think that this relationship is hermetically sealed off from all other human concerns is surely a superstition. A moral theory can conceivably weigh the concern for the victims of river blindness and ultimately find it wanting against greater imperatives; but a theory that arbitrarily denies to such a concern even the status of a moral reason, to be weighed against others, is not credible.

Those initially drawn to shareholder primacy may resist this conclusion. They tend to argue that, properly understood, the view does give due consideration to the other side of Vagelos's dilemma. They may assert that developing Mectizan would, in fact, be in the shareholders' interest, so that far from violating shareholder primacy theory, Vagelos did exactly what shareholder primacy commands. As an empirical matter, this may, of course, be correct. Merck surely gained good will with the public for its Mectizan donation program, and perhaps that good will, even though purchased at a high price, saved it from greater monetary losses in the future.[24] It is also plausible that a research-driven company like Merck could not afford to demoralize those of its employees who cared about the contribution of their scientific work to human well-being.

But such assumptions obscure our moral reasoning rather than illuminate it. By giving *instrumental* reasons to act in the interests of non-shareholders—by claiming, that is, that acting decently is ultimately best also for profits—they simply deny the existence of a dilemma. And so, rather than refuting the moral case against shareholder primacy theory, they suspend the need for moral argument altogether (for with no ethical dilemma, there is no need for moral argument). But we cannot realistically believe that there are no ethical dilemmas. Thinking that "doing good" is, always and everywhere, the same as "doing well" is not optimism, but naïveté. Moreover, wishfully thinking that there are always instrumental (profit-maximizing) reasons to "do good" simply ignores the source of the agony in a dilemma like Vagelos's: the thought that the river blindness victims' suffering constitutes an *intrinsic* reason to make a corporate decision in their favour, not just a possible instrumental opportunity to pursue shareholders' interests. The hard question that business ethics must pose, therefore, abstracts from the instrumental reasons and asks: "*What if* developing Mectizan must be reasonably expected to cause a loss in profits, all things taken into account—what then would be the right course of action?" In answer to *this* question, shareholder primacy must stand by its unbelievable condemnation of Vagelos's decision as not only morally wrong, but obviously morally wrong.

In all of this, we have assumed that Merck's shareholders want the company to make as much profit as possible. Those who wish to make shareholder primacy palatable in the Merck case might instead challenge this assumption. They may remind us that shareholder primacy requires not profit maximization, but the pursuit of shareholders' desires, whatever they may be—and point out that Merck proclaims its business to be

---

[24] For example, it could be that Merck's good will with the public protected it in the scandal over Vioxx, in which the company stood accused of concealing evidence that its best-selling painkiller increased the risk of heart attacks. The allegations are reported in the *New York Times* ("Despite Warnings, Drug Giant Took Long Path to Vioxx Recall," 14 April 2004).

"preserving and improving human life" and that it "expect[s] profits, but only from work that satisfies customer needs and the quality of life."[25] So, even if developing Mectizan would not maximize shareholder financial return, it was what shareholders wanted Merck to do. This argument can be interpreted in two ways. It can be an empirical assertion—that shareholders do not only care about profits. This may be true, but it is unilluminating for the same reason as before. Certainly, if shareholders wanted Vagelos to act in this way, there is no problem for shareholder primacy theory. But what if they did not? Again, shareholder primacy would have to condemn Vagelos's actions. In any case, it is hard to see how, in the shareholder primacy view, mission statements can be morally important. What matters, surely, is not what managers declare to be the company's goal but what shareholders in fact want.[26]

But speculations about what shareholders actually want also miss the nature of Vagelos's dilemma. His deliberation cannot end with a determination of what shareholders actually want, any more than it can end with a determination of which course of actions will most probably maximize profits. What makes it a dilemma is that the plight of river blindness victims claims the status of an intrinsic moral reason for helping them, independent of what shareholders want. Vagelos must determine not what they want or even how much they want it, but whether the moral reasons to help the sick are weightier than those to give shareholders what they want.

Consider, therefore, a second interpretation of the claims about the mission statement. One may argue that given Merck's public declaration of values, shareholders knew what kind of company they were buying stock in. They knew that this was a company that prided itself on putting profit calculations after considerations of how beneficial a drug would be for society. So they cannot, the argument would go, complain if they receive lower dividends or if the stock price falls because of such choices. Note that this is no longer an empirical claim, but a moral one. This argument does not assert that shareholders do, in fact, accept Vagelos's non-profit-maximizing choice; instead, it claims that Merck was morally permitted to develop Mectizan even against the shareholders' actual desires because they implicitly authorized Merck to do so when they bought the stock, knowing what Merck "stood for."[27] But this is no longer an attempt at squaring shareholder primacy with Vagelos's decision. We have shifted to *curtailing* shareholder primacy, for this argument presupposes a moral reason for managers *not* to act according to shareholders' desires—namely, that the company made it clear how it intended to act before shareholders bought their stock.

This last argument is therefore a *counterargument* to shareholder primacy. Against the latter's assertion that because managers are the agents of shareholders, they must act in shareholders' desires, the present claim presents a reason why managers may, in fact, act differently. Once we contemplate this counterargument, others suggest themselves. One is

---

[25] http://www.merck.com/about/mission.html, accessed 6 November 2008.

[26] If the mission statement misrepresents shareholders' desires, shareholder primacy presumably tells managers to ignore it or change it. (It is useful to ask what moral weight we would grant a mission statement that made it the company's goal to enrich managers as fast and as much as possible.) In any case, most shareholders probably do care only about financial gain, mission statement notwithstanding. Certainly, investors who own Merck stock through their pension funds—often without even realizing it—generally invest with the goal of a pension that is as high as possible.

[27] Even if the shareholders did not in fact realize Merck's plans, the argument may add, they *should* have realized, and it is their responsibility, not Merck's managers', if the company acts contrary to their wishes.

that shareholders are never *forced* to be shareholders. They can sell their stock if they do not like what managers are doing. Since shareholders can always end the principal-agent relationship with their managers, the argument would go, that relationship is not all that significant—certainly not significant enough to override all moral reasons for acting against shareholders' wishes. Another counterargument points out that even in an irreversible principal-agent relationship, principals may not morally make an agent do something on their behalf that principals may not themselves do (recall the Mafia boss). So, if we have reasons to think that *shareholders* may not morally put profits above rescuing the world from river blindness, that provides an argument against shareholder primacy, namely that Vagelos may also not make Merck do so even if shareholders want him to.

In mentioning these counterarguments briefly, we have not shown that they prove shareholder primacy wrong (they do; but it would take a more careful treatment to show it conclusively). Rather, we have shown that attempting to avoid the most unpalatable implications of the theory in a difficult case raises serious normative counterarguments, which a proponent of shareholder primacy must contend with. Friedman's rights-based argument does not do this, which means that shareholder primacy remains, at best, unproven in addition to being implausible. Those are good reasons for not believing its claims.

MANAGING FOR "STAKEHOLDERS"

What, then, should we believe? It is, of course, easier to point out weaknesses in shareholder primacy than it is to propose an alternative theory that fares better. Among the most prominent attempts is a confusing family of theories grouped under the rubric "stakeholder theory" or "stakeholder analysis." This family of views is confusing because it is far from clear that all the different variants of stakeholder theory make the same or even compatible claims. (In some cases, it is not clear what claim they make at all.) But the stakeholder approach is most famously linked with the work of the business theorist R. Edward Freeman, whose opposition to the Separation Thesis we have already noted. His words are no bad starting point:

> . . . scholars and managers alike continue to hold sacred the view that managers bear a special relationship to the stockholders in the firm [who] have certain rights and privileges, which must be granted to them by management . . . [My] purpose . . . is to pose several challenges to this assumption, from within the framework of managerial capitalism [and] revitalize the concept of managerial capitalism by replacing the notion that managers have a duty to stockholders with the concept that managers bear a fiduciary relationship to stakeholders . . . Corporations have stakeholders, that is, groups and individuals who benefit from or are harmed by, and whose rights are violated or respected by, corporate actions . . . The task of management in today's corporation is akin to that of King Solomon. The Stakeholder theory does not give primacy to one stakeholder group over another, though there will surely be times when one group will benefit at the expense of others. In general, however, management must keep relationships among stakeholders in balance.[28]

---

[28] R. Edward Freeman, "A Stakeholder Theory of the Modern Corporation," in Tom Beauchamp and Norman E. Bowie, *Ethical Theory and Business*, 7th ed. (Upper Saddle River, NJ: Pearson Prentice Hall, 2004), pp. 55–64.

Freeman finishes this article with a statement of principles that summarize his theory, one of which is:

> Corporations shall be managed in the interests of its stakeholders, defined as employees, financiers, customers, employees [*sic*], and communities.

This idea, that companies ought to be managed in the interests of all stakeholders, captures the common denominator of stakeholder theories. It is, however, too low a common denominator to be of much help. Many expositions of stakeholder theory are underdefined (in that respect they resemble Milton Friedman's shareholder primacy arguments). To give stakeholder theory content that bears on what business people actually ought to do, we must first, at the very least, identify the "stakeholders." In the text quoted above, Freeman defines them roughly as groups and individuals who are affected by corporate actions. He enumerates employees, "financiers" (shareholders and creditors), customers, suppliers, and local communities. But these are clearly not the only groups that are affected by corporate actions—others include, for example, competitors (who are hurt if the corporation gains market share and they lose it, and vice versa), producers and consumers of complementary or substitute goods (car part manufacturers and auto dealers depend on car producers' success; bus companies are affected by the actions of train operators), and the government (corporations engage in lobbying, and their actions influence the government's tax revenues). Accordingly, Freeman and others have elsewhere expanded the definition of stakeholders to include all "groups that can affect or be affected by the corporation"[29]—a definition that can stretch so far as to include the media and activist groups.

The imperialist nature of the stakeholder concept—its tendency to include an ever wider range of groups within the orbit of "managing for stakeholders"—is part of what is wrong with stakeholder theory. For the more groups count as stakeholders, the less plausible it becomes to claim that managers either can or should run their business in the interest of *all* of them.[30] Even if we set aside the difficulty of identifying who is and who is not a stakeholder, without which the admonition to "manage for stakeholders" is rather unhelpful, there remains the problem of what exactly it means to manage in their interest. For, obviously, different groups have different interests, and sometimes those interests conflict. If we think of stakeholder theory as saying that managers should *maximize* the benefits to all stakeholder groups—much as shareholder primacy says they should maximize the return to shareholders—we are hampered by the inconvenient mathematical truth that it is impossible, in general, to maximize two or more objectives simultaneously. If, alternatively, we think of the theory as saying that managers are the *agents* of all stakeholders[31]—much as shareholder primacy makes managers the agents of the shareholders—we shall quickly find managers stymied by duties that conflict with one another. Shareholder primacy does not suffer from these problems: Even though it is mistaken in claiming that managers' duty is to

---

[29] R. Edward Freeman, Jeffrey S. Harrison, and Andrew C. Wicks. *Managing for Stakeholders: Survival, Reputation, and Success* (New Haven: Yale University Press, 2007), p. 8.

[30] Some business theories have tried to stop the runaway definition of "stakeholders" by distinguishing between more or less "legitimate" stakeholders. I suggest below that such moves are more successful the sooner they leave "stakeholder theory" behind in favor of subtler philosophical arguments.

[31] Freeman, in some of his expositions, suggests this "multi-fiduciary" approach.

maximize profit, there is at least no incoherence in what that duty, if it actually applied, would consist in.[32]

If what is best for shareholders is also what is best for creditors, employees, customers, suppliers and so on, then it is the right thing to do according to stakeholder theory (and for that matter, according to shareholder primacy as well). But it is just as naïve of the stakeholder theorists to expect this to be the general rule as it is for the shareholder primacy theorists struggling to make their view palatable in the Merck case. There are obvious trade-offs between the interests of different stakeholders. For example, there is more to distribute between shareholders and employees if suppliers or customers can be persuaded to accept a less favorable price; committing to a higher dividend rate leaves fewer resources for salary raises or perks; and in the Merck case, Vagelos had to forgo company income to develop Mectizan.[33] To declare in such situations that "management must keep relationships among stakeholders in balance" does not begin to address *how* to balance them.

Some stakeholder analyses are in denial about this:

> Our current way of thinking about business and management simply asks the wrong question. It asks how we should distribute the burdens and benefits among stakeholders. The managing for stakeholders mindset asks how we can create as much value as possible for all of our stakeholders.[34]

> Where stakeholder interests conflict, the executive must find a way to rethink the problems so that these interests can go together, so that even more value can be created for each. . . Managing for stakeholders is about creating as much value as possible for stakeholders, without resorting to tradeoffs.[35]

Whenever possible, it seems obviously desirable to make everyone better off. This thought—a form of the *Pareto principle*—is often taken as a minimal ethical principle that every rational and benevolent person must endorse. When self-interest and the interests of others are all aligned, there is, indeed, little need for ethics. (But we shall investigate the Pareto principle in Chapter 5 and find that even it can be questioned.) Most managers, however, will very quickly exhaust any such opportunities. Where they most need the guidance of moral reasoning is in the remaining situations—where no one can be made better off without acting against someone else's interests; or where everyone can benefit, but there is a choice to be made about each stakeholder group's share of the gain. "Managing for stakeholders rather than just for shareholders" does not say how to make that choice.

Stakeholders may matter morally in two quite different ways, and we will not get very far without distinguishing between them. On the one hand, it may be that managers should act in the interests of stakeholders because doing so is the best way of achieving something *else* that is morally required—such as maximizing profits. That is, it could be that business should be managed in the interests of stakeholders for

---

[32] Even this, though, must become ambiguous if we take shareholder primacy to mean that managers must do whatever shareholders want. Different shareholders may want different things.

[33] There are also tradeoffs to be made *within* each stakeholder group: between different employees; between shareholders who want short-term stock appreciation and those who want long-term dividends; between high-risk, high-reward and low-risk, low-reward strategies.

[34] Freeman *et al.*, *Managing for Stakeholders*, p. 11.

[35] R. Edward Freeman, "Managing for stakeholders," in Tom L. Beauchamp, Norman E. Bowie and Denis Arnold (eds.), *Ethical Theory and Business*, 8th ed. (Upper Saddle River, NJ: Pearson Prentice Hall, 2007), 56–68.

instrumental moral reasons. Alternatively, it could be right to manage in the interest of all stakeholders *for their own sake*—that is, for *intrinsic* moral reasons. Stakeholder theories that make this distinction can treat different kinds of stakeholders differently, which is surely correct. They can say that managers should treat some stakeholders as of intrinsic moral concern—some, perhaps, of greater intrinsic moral concern than others—and some as of instrumental moral concern (according to how their treatment affects the intrinsically important stakeholders). In this interpretation, even the shareholder primacy view is a "stakeholder theory." For it is obvious that maximizing profits sometimes requires treating non-shareholding stakeholders well, insofar as (but only insofar as) their cooperation is necessary to maximize profits for shareholders.

If this, however, is all that a "stakeholder theory" has to say, it has hardly said anything more than that managers ought to do what they ought to do. In other words, it simply says that business is not an amoral activity. That view has the one considerable merit of being true, and it may have been all that some stakeholder theorists have meant to say. It does not, however, teach us much about how business ought to conduct itself. In particular, it does not—as other stakeholder theorists seem to intend—refute the shareholder primacy view, which is already thoroughly moralized.

For stakeholder theory to be an alternative to shareholder primacy, therefore, it must be complemented by further arguments about how management should treat each stakeholder group and how it should trade off their respective interests against each other. It is useful here to recall the different types of arguments Milton Friedman marshals—unsuccessfully—to justify his conclusion that managers' sole duty is to increase profits. One approach—the Aristotelian approach to business ethics—is to explore the norms inherent in managers' social role and ask how they must treat different stakeholders to best fulfill that role. A consequentialist approach instead looks to the consequences of prioritizing stakeholders in different ways and advocates the choices that produce the best outcomes. A third perspective delineates the rights of different stakeholders and derives moral constraints on what managers may do from the need to respect those rights.

We have seen that shareholder primacy is unlikely to emerge looking attractive from such exercises. We may instead expect them to support some form of stakeholder theory. But that by itself is not saying much, given the almost unlimited range of alternative conclusions that could be called stakeholder theory in a broad sense. One "stakeholder theory", based on a utilitarian argument, defends a duty on management to maximize the *total market value* of the firm, counting not only equity capital but all other financial claims including, for example, bonds.[36] Others argue that this misses what truth there is in what Friedman claimed, namely, that shareholders have the right to special treatment (if not absolute priority) because of their property rights. Kenneth Goodpaster, for example, recognizes what he calls the "stakeholder paradox":

> It seems essential, yet in some ways illegitimate, to orient corporate decisions by ethical values that go beyond [instrumental] stakeholder considerations [as they affect the interests of shareholders] to multi-fiduciary [that is, intrinsic] ones.[37]

---

[36] Michael C. Jensen, "Value maximization, stakeholder theory, and the corporate objective function," *Business Ethics Quarterly*, 12(2), 2002, pp. 235–247.

[37] Kenneth Goodpaster, "Business ethics and stakeholder analysis," *Business Ethics Quarterly*, 1(1), 1991, 53–73.

Goodpaster's view, which could justifiably be called a "stakeholder theory," is that we should still see management as having a special duty to pursue the shareholders' interests, but that in acting on the shareholders' behalf, they are constrained by the general moral duties to others that the shareholders would themselves be constrained by. Others again have suggested that managers should treat all the stakeholders as coming together in a "moral community" encompassed by the business activity in question, and act so as to make that community flourish.

There are, then, not one but many ways to specify the moral status of different stakeholders and the management's consequent duties to them. In other words, almost any theory of business ethics is a "stakeholder theory". This should not be surprising. In the essay quoted at the start of this section, Freeman writes:

> 'The stakeholder theory' can be unpacked into a number of stakeholder theories, each of which has a 'normative core,' inextricably linked to the way that corporations should be governed and the way that managers should act . . . I want to insist that the . . . uses of 'stakeholder' are tied together in particular political constructions to yield a number of possible 'stakeholder theories.'

If there is no one definitive stakeholder theory that specifies the moral status of stakeholder groups and the duties of management, all that the stakeholder approach *per se* does is to underline that such a specification is necessary. What this means, in turn, is that all the work—building a normative core, in Freeman's words—remains to be done.

What, then, do we learn from stakeholder theory in the end? The answer seems to be very little, beyond the naïveté of thinking that just because shareholders are owners, corporate managers ought always only to act in their interests. This is, of course, what even a short critical examination of arguments for shareholder primacy sufficed to show. Beyond that, "stakeholder theory" begs the question that began this chapter: For whom should business be managed? Until we fill stakeholder theory with a "normative core," it cannot answer that question; it cannot even rule out shareholder primacy. The rest of this book can be seen as building arguments to justify a normative core. But once we build those arguments, the language of stakeholder "theory" will have nothing further to add; we can develop our moral arguments without it. The normative core, we will find, is the whole theory. It follows that stakeholder theory is best seen not as a theory at all, but rather as the simple acknowledgement that business is a moralized activity. Since that is something we already knew, we do best by simply leaving the term "stakeholder theory" behind.

Summary of the Argument in This Chapter

One of the big controversies in business ethics asks: Who should businesspeople conduct business *for*? The shareholder primacy view and stakeholder theory go to opposite extremes in the answers they give to this question. The shareholder primacy view, most famously argued by Milton Friedman, says that the only moral responsibility a manager has is to do what the shareholders want. There are several ways one may attempt to defend this conclusion. Friedman's main claim is grounded in shareholders' *property rights*: If the corporation and its resources belong to them, it is wrong for the manager to act against their wishes. But no plausible theory can hold that the moral responsibility to shareholders trumps every other possible moral concern. Even shareholder primacy advocates accept that the obligation to obey the law is more important. And in Merck's choice whether to invest funds in a drug against river blindness, the profit-maximizing action is, at least, not *obviously* morally required. Both these intuitions show that there are limits to shareholder primacy. We therefore need a more sophisticated theory to account for those limits—and there is no guarantee that such a theory gives much priority to shareholders.

Stakeholder theory denies any special role for shareholders. It claims, instead, that business ought to be managed in the interests of *all* "stakeholders"—all those groups that can affect or be affected by the activities of a business. But unless it is willing to discriminate among stakeholders, "stakeholder theory" is of little help, since different stakeholders' interests may well conflict. A theory of business ethics must at least differentiate between stakeholders that are of *intrinsic* moral importance and those that are only of *instrumental* moral importance. A theory that does not do this, is of no use; and to one that does, the rhetorical trappings of "stakeholder theory" add little.

Shareholder primacy and the stakeholder approach, in the end, are both guilty of the same fault: going too far, the essential offence of extremisms. Friedman identifies the managerial responsibilities in the manager's relationship with a corporation's owners, as their agent or the handler of their property. His mistake, however, is to take that relationship for the *only* source of moral obligation to the exclusion of all other moral concerns (except the law). Stakeholder theory, in contrast, denies any special moral significance to the manager's role as shareholders' agent—indeed, in refusing to discriminate between different stakeholders' moral status, it ignores the moral specificity of *any* of the relationships that arise out of business interactions. So, whereas Friedman goes wrong by excessively differentiating the moral importance of different stakeholders in the business activity—to the point where only one them matters—stakeholder theory goes wrong by not differentiating enough.

CHAPTER 3

Doing One's Job Well
The Ethics of Social Roles

"I'm just doing my job"—what does this expression mean? Theoretically, one might use it in a purely descriptive sense, in answer to someone inquiring what one is doing. But normally, we understand it as a *justification*. Imagine the middle manager who is ordered to cut jobs. He may not really want to lay off the family father, a long-time employee who will struggle to find new work, but he still chooses to retain the younger, more productive childless worker, who would easily have found something else, reassuring himself that he is just doing his job. Or consider the car manufacturer, criticized for producing fuel-inefficient cars that contribute to global warming, defending itself this way: "We are a car company; we produce the cars our customers want. As long as they want gas-guzzlers, we will make gas-guzzlers for them; if they demand hybrids, we will change our production to meet that demand. Our job is to give our customers the cars they like; we have no business telling customers what they *should* want."

This kind of talk is ubiquitous in business. Its function is to rebut moral criticism by saying that it is not the role of business to address the moral concern raised by the critic. It conducts its rebuttal by arguing that moral reasons are relative to social roles—that what is the morally right behavior for someone in one role may not be the morally right behavior for someone in another role. If this is so, then social roles give rise to role-specific obligations and role-specific permissions. *Role obligations* are those things that someone ought to do in virtue of inhabiting a certain role (which those not in that role are not morally required to do): A lawyer is bound to defend even a monster who from the rest of deserves neither help nor sympathy. *Role permissions* are those actions that it is morally permissible to take for someone who inhabits a certain role (which it would be immoral for people not in that role to do): Police may use force in a wider set of circumstances than ordinary citizens.

The shareholder primacy view that we outlined in the previous chapter failed because it had to claim, implausibly, that the suffering of the river blindness victims did not count as a moral reason for Merck's decision, so that it was *obviously* wrong to fund the development and distribution of Mectizan. But the notion of role-relative moral reasons opens up an argumentative route by which the shareholder primacy theorist can modify his position enough to answer the rebuttal and still argue for his conclusion. He can acknowledge that the suffering of the river blindness victims *is* a moral reason, indeed a very weighty one, but he can also argue that it is not a reason for *business* to act on. Acting on it, he may add, is a responsibility that falls on social roles other than those of businesses or corporate executives—presumably on the roles of public officials, governments and intergovernmental organizations. It is *their* role obligation to address river blindness; it is the role obligation of *managers* to increase their corporations' profits.

Of course role-relative reasons can be found to support the opposite position. A critic of shareholder primacy may, for example, argue that Merck's role as a pharmaceutical company gives it a special role-relative obligation to act in the interests of the sick, even when doing so reduces profits—a role-relative obligation that companies in other industries do not have.[38] This reflects how "it's my job" can be a ground for duties (as with the doctor or police officer who must put other things aside when emergency strikes), just as "it's not my job" can be an exemption from them.

Whether role-relative arguments are convincing is a matter we must investigate in due course. The point here is that they are clearly both intelligible and relevant to business decisions. The actions of managers and employees do not simply "affect" other people; they are carried out within the context of specific social roles and relationships. The relevance of these roles and relationships is taken for granted in everyday arguments about what business ought to do, which makes them an obvious starting point for business ethics. This chapter and the next, then, consider how far we can systematize our intuitions about social roles in moral reasoning about business life. We begin with an example to bring out how strong those intuitions are.

ETHICS AS PLAYING ONE'S ROLE WELL

Consider this story:

Kate's Dilemma

Kate and Lucy both work on Wall Street when the financial crisis hits in 2008. They have been best friends since college. Both were good students, and when they graduated in the early 2000s, they quickly found jobs in the booming financial industry; Lucy with Lehman Brothers, and Kate with another big investment bank. Since they moved to New York City they have shared a glamorous downtown apartment. Both face high pressure and long hours, but they thrive on the excitement, the intense corporate culture, and the good money they earn at their respective banks. Still, they try not to let too many days pass without spending time together to catch up. As best friends do, they share with each other what happens in their private and professional lives, and rely on each other for support and advice. Against the fiercely competitive nature of their work, they find their friendship even more valuable than in their student days.

One late Friday night in September, Kate comes home from work to find Lucy crying in the kitchen. Lucy refuses to tell her what is wrong—it could put Kate in a difficult situation, she says. When Kate insists, Lucy finally relents, but only after Kate promises to keep what she is about to say secret.

(Continued)

---

[38] Such an argument is developed by Thomas Dunfee in his "Do firms with unique competencies for rescuing victims of human catastrophes have special obligations? Corporate responsibility and the AIDS catastrophe in sub-Saharan Africa", *Business Ethics Quarterly*, 16(2), 2006, pp. 185–210.

Lucy then reveals that her boss has told her in confidence that the top management is likely to decide during the weekend that Lehman Brothers will file for bankruptcy. Kate is stunned—it is no secret that Lehman has been under pressure in the markets recently, but everyone has been assuming that some solution will be found and that the government will not let the bank fail. What Lucy's boss has told her is that this has changed—the government seems determined to set an example and not bail out the bank. Nothing is certain—things will be decided this weekend—but Lucy's boss is so pessimistic that he told her, discreetly, to take her personal belongings home from the office and not count on having a job to come back to on Monday.

Staring at the half-open box in which Lucy brought her personal effects back, Kate tries both to console her friend and absorb what this may mean for her own employer. Lehman Brothers, as one of the main traders of over-the-counter derivatives, is a hub in the wheel of finance—virtually all other big banks are exposed to it and stand to lose a lot of money if it cannot meet its commitments. Kate does not fear for herself; she has recently moved to a division of the bank that works for long-standing private clients, where business is reasonably immune to the industry's swings. But her former colleagues in the risk management department will face the worst day of their lives on Monday if Lehman files for bankruptcy. Every additional hour they have to prepare for such an eventuality will help to safeguard the bank's interests to the extent possible—and rescue their own prestige within the firm and any hope of a bonus. Kate could call her colleagues to warn them—but Lucy, already in a frantic state, insists that she must keep her promise and not let anyone know what she has just told her.

Let us set aside any potential legal difficulties by assuming that the law neither requires Kate to pass on the information to her employer nor prohibits her from doing so—and that if she passes it on, no one will know she has obtained it from Lucy. Given these assumptions, what should Kate do? We need not answer this question definitively; the case is instructive not so much for how we ultimately answer it as for what we identify as the most important moral reasons for answering it one way or the other.

Some of these reasons are general ones that make no reference to social relationships. One reason for Kate to keep secret the information Lucy divulged is that she promised to do so. It is a keystone of morality that, in the absence of overriding moral considerations, we should keep our word.[39] There are also reasons in favor of telling that are equally unrelated to social relationships. Many people at Kate's bank and among its clients may suffer heavy losses that could be avoided or reduced if Kate passes on the information immediately. If we can prevent suffering at no cost to ourselves, it is presumably the default position of any plausible moral system that we must do so, unless there are convincing countervailing reasons not to.[40]

These rather obvious remarks illustrate some important points. First, of course, they support the contention that we made in Chapter 1—that we share a fertile common ground of moral intuitions, which provide starting points for ethical deliberation. Second, however, the reasons we have just rehearsed—both of them impartial moral reasons that most people accept when presented with them in the abstract—are inadequate

---

[39] This principle is an example of duty-based or *deontological* reasons, which we shall discuss at length in Chapters 9 and 10.

[40] This principle gives consequence-based reasons for acting one way or another. Whole systems of *consequentialist* theories have been built on such reasons, which we shall examine in detail in Chapters 5–7.

to explain Kate's moral dilemma. For although these reasons spring immediately to mind, they ignore the strongest intuitions triggered by this case. This is easy to see if we modify the scenario in two ways.

Consider this modification first:

Kate's Dilemma with no friendship

Suppose the facts are as in Kate's Dilemma, except Kate and Lucy are not best friends and do not live together. Perhaps they know each other vaguely from college, or perhaps they meet through mutual acquaintances in the banking world. On the Friday night in question, they bump into each other at a bar where bankers often go after work. Lucy, upset that she is probably about to lose her job, has had a little too much to drink when she and Kate, seated next to her at the bar, strike up a casual conversation. Lucy, needing to unburden herself, bursts out: "I've had the worst day ever, you'll never guess what I was just told—but promise me you won't tell anyone else." Kate, expecting nothing important, duly promises. When she hears Lucy's story, she realizes with shock how important this is to her firm and her colleagues. In this modified situation, what ought Kate to do?

Most people will agree that in the modified case, Kate's reasons for telling her colleagues are stronger than before—so much stronger that they may outweigh any initial misgivings against telling. Some who think it wrong of Kate to tell in the original case will say she is morally permitted, and maybe required, to tell if she is not Lucy's friend, as in the modified case. This is a perfectly consistent position to hold: Morality may well dictate different behavior in the two cases. But if we think it does (and even if we do not change our conclusion, but do agree that the reasons for telling become stronger when there is no friendship), then we cannot justify the view that in the original case it is immoral to tell simply because Kate has *promised* not to do so. For in the modified case, too, she has promised, so *that* moral reason is the same in both cases. The only thing that changes is Kate and Lucy's relationship. If that change justifies a difference in our judgment of the two cases, it means that their relationship plays an important part in justifying our judgment in *each* case.

Consider a second modification of the original story:

Kate's Dilemma with no employment relationship

Suppose, as originally, that Kate and Lucy are best friends from college, but when Lucy joined Lehman Brothers, Kate instead started work in a design studio. Although Kate and Lucy are still close friends and share an apartment, they have very different jobs and professional circles. But, some of Kate's other acquaintances from college (not close friends) work for other banks on Wall Street, and she understands that they stand to lose from a Lehman bankruptcy. She could easily look them up and give them the information Lucy has just shared with her, which—as with her colleagues in the original example—could enable them to prepare for the shock. Should she pass on the information?

This modification sways our intuitions in the opposite direction. If we originally judged that Kate ought to pass the information on to her bank—in spite of her promise to Lucy—we shall find the moral reasons for doing so weaker when the affected company is not one she works for. She will seem a priggish busybody if she breaks a promise to her friend out of concern for a bank she is virtually unrelated to. But whatever suffering her telling could have prevented in the original case is neither less severe nor less avoidable in this modification. Again, this is a moral reason that is identical in the two cases. If we think the moral reasons for Kate to tell now become less weighty, therefore, it must be because it matters whether the losses will be suffered by people at *her* company. But this difference cannot be justified with the original impartial principle of preventing avoidable suffering.

In reversals like these, our intuitions point in one direction or the other as we vary the social relationships between the people concerned. The thought experiments we have just carried out suggest that what we intuitively consider most important for what Kate should do is not whether she has made a promise to Lucy or whether she can prevent avoidable suffering. Rather, what matters is that Lucy is *her friend*, and that the people who will suffer if she does not prevent it are her employer and colleagues. The strongest reason against telling, then, is that Kate would be a *bad friend* if she told (but not in the first modification, so there it seems less wrong to tell). The strongest reason for telling, similarly, is that Kate would be a disloyal employee and a *bad colleague* if she did not tell (but not in the second modification, so there it seems less wrong not to tell). More important than the general principle of keeping promises and preventing suffering, it turns out, are the specific imperatives of being a good friend or being a good colleague and employee.

So the most powerful moral reasons in this case are not impartial moral principles but Kate's *social roles*—in this case, the role of friend and the roles of employee and colleague. The argument that presents itself is that when we inhabit a social role, we ought to perform that role well. As someone's friend, *I ought to be a good friend, not a bad one*; if I am someone's colleague, I ought to be a good colleague, not a bad one. And we have a sense of what, concretely, these requirements mean—a good friend is trustworthy; a good colleague is loyal and cooperative. As we contemplate Kate's roles, then, we find that they seem to generate special moral reasons—role-relative obligations and permissions—that do not apply outside those roles.

These intuitions suggest a deeper point with relevance for ethical theory. An adequate theory of ethics—and an adequate theory of business ethics—must have room for this relevance of social roles to our moral thinking. It must, at least, propose an understanding of how our moral responsibilities are connected with and modified by our social roles. Some theories go further: Beyond acknowledging that what we ought to do seems to be tied up with our social roles and practices, they see it as *essentially* tied up with them. They see social roles not just as shorthand *expressions* of our moral obligations and permissions, but as their *foundations*. If this is correct, the most promising undertaking open to us is to use these foundations as the starting point for moral reasoning and derive conclusions for business ethics from them. If we do so, we shall follow in the steps of Aristotle.

GOODNESS, PRACTICES, AND THE VIRTUES

Aristotle's moral philosophy remains the most ambitious effort to build a theory of what we ought to do around an understanding of what, socially speaking, we are. Or, as we might better say, around an understanding of *where* we are socially—that is, of the place we occupy within the web of social interactions and relationships that bind us and other people together in communities. To understand how Aristotle builds his theory, we must understand his concept of *virtue*, through which Aristotelian theory connects our social life with normative claims about how we ought to live and what we ought to do. This is the project of *virtue ethics*.

The word "virtue" is the standard philosophical translation into English of the ancient Greek word *areté*, and it is apt to confuse anyone who comes to Aristotelian ethics for the first time. It means something quite different from the connotation of sexual modesty or chastity that "virtue" has acquired in ordinary language. The virtue in Aristotle's ethics is more literally captured by words such as *excellence* or *perfection* and "virtuous" by a word such as *accomplished*. It is, to put it very simply, a standard of perfection: what makes something good. So we should understand the "virtues" or "excellences" as the characteristics of something that is in a state of accomplishment.

What are the virtues? In Aristotle's words,

> every virtue causes its possessors to be in a good state and to perform their functions well; the virtue of eyes, *e.g.*, makes the eyes and their functioning excellent, because it makes us see well; and similarly, the virtue of a horse makes the horse excellent, and thereby good at galloping, at carrying its rider and at standing steady in the face of the enemy.[41]

Something is in a state of accomplishment, says Aristotle, if it performs its function well. The purpose of an eye is to see, so a good eye is an eye that sees well. Therefore the virtues of eyes are those characteristics of an eye that make it see well—acuity, discrimination, and perspicacity. We can easily apply this thinking to a host of other objects. For example, what is a good knife? Since the purpose of a knife is to cut well and safely, a good or excellent knife is one that cuts well and is easy and safe to handle. So the characteristics that count as virtues in knives are all those conducive to its purpose of cutting well—the most obvious being sharpness, comfort, and "handleability."

These illustrations are banal, but they highlight a point that is not banal at all, namely that the Aristotelian approach of attributing virtues is a natural way for us to think. From the pedestrian examples we can distill a more schematic definition of the virtues:

The virtues of an *X* are what makes it a good/excellent/accomplished *X*.

And what a good *X* is depends on the purpose of an *X*: seeing in the case of eyes, cutting in the case of knives. Aristotelian thinking is *teleological*—after the ancient Greek word *telos*, which means the purpose or end of something—because of the central importance to it of what things are *for*, that is, what their *telos* is. We can extend our formal schema:

The purpose or *telos* of *X* is to *q*; therefore:
A good *X* is an *X* that *q*s well; therefore:
The virtues of *X* are what makes it *q* well.

---

[41] *Nichomachean Ethics*, 1106a.

This account formalizes the way we naturally evaluate a great many things. The Aristotelian way of thinking about the virtues comes easily; it is often immediate to us what the virtues of an X are, provided that we understand what X is. For everyday objects like knives, this is obvious. For specialized objects, we may have to be acquainted with specialized uses; that is, to know what a good fishing rod is, you have to be somewhat experienced with fishing. But if you are, you will be able to evaluate the rod. Indeed, one sign of experience with fishing—one indication of a "virtuous" fisher—is to be able to tell a good fishing rod from a bad one. Being acquainted with an object and the activity it is used for consists in part of knowing the appropriate evaluative standards.

We are able, then, to apply the generic formulas above to a wide range of possible contents of X. But do they work in a wide enough range to be of use to a theory of ethics? For that, the Aristotelian approach must teach by which standards we should judge not just objects, but actions. Knives, eyes and fishing rods do not make choices; people do. Characteristics of excellence or accomplishments—that is, virtues—can only guide us to the right action if they also apply to what people do. For this to be the case, we must think that human beings also have purposes that they can fulfill with greater or lesser degrees of excellence. Do they?

Aristotle certainly thought so. He wrote that "the virtue of a human being will likewise be the state that makes a human being good and makes him perform his function well"[42]. Modern minds, however, find it much harder to accept the notion that human beings have natural "functions" by which we can judge their goodness. But there is at least one perspective from which we can view people and what they do in an Aristotelian light. The language of virtue expresses well how we evaluate people as the occupants of social roles, the virtues then being the characteristics—or rather *character traits*, since we are now talking about people—that make people excel in their roles.

Social roles derive their meaning from the social practices of which they are a part. A social practice is a set of regularized and often ritualized social interactions delimited (sometimes more, sometimes less precisely) by a shared social understanding. That the participants share an understanding of it is a condition for a social practice even to be recognizable as such. This is clear as soon as we examine specific examples. For instance, medicine is a social practice because those who participate in it—doctors, patients, their next of kin, other medical professionals such as nurses, and so on—understand their own and each other's behavior as a set of regularized interactions governed by more or less well-understood social norms. Moreover, they generally expect the other participants to share the same understanding (including the expectation that other participants in turn share it and expect the same, and so on). Indeed, it is a characteristic of a social practice that someone who does not share its common understanding will be seen by other participants in it as *anomalous*—as misinterpreting the actions comprising the practice.

It is because a social practice incorporates specific behaviors and specific expectations about behavior that it generates social roles. It is only once actions and interactions are widely understood as part of a practice, and not just as "naked" acts standing for themselves, that they can be seen as regular features of social life independent of the particular individuals who are at any one time carrying them out. Thus, while it is individual doctors who carry out certain kinds of acts in the practice of medicine—diagnosis,

---

[42] Ibid.

prescription of remedies, assessment of recovery, and so on—those acts have a clear social meaning independent of who the individual doctors happen to be. They are what doctors do *qua* doctors, what any doctor is expected to do. They are, in other words, what the *role* of the doctor involves. Thus, the practice of medicine defines the role of doctor, and similarly the role of patient, and so on.

Two general points emerge from these examples. The first is that to understand a social practice at all we must partake in *shared* understandings. We cannot make much sense of the brute physical acts of measuring a person's pulse, asking questions about his or her body, or writing down names of chemical components on a piece of paper, without describing them as acts defined by the social practice of medicine (diagnosing disease and prescribing treatment), that is, as things certain medical practitioners do. But, that in turn, means we cannot properly describe these actions without importing a reference to what these practitioners are expected to do as participants in the social practice (*e.g.* how are doctors or nurses supposed to act *qua* doctors or nurses) and which function the social practice is expected to play in society (*e.g.* what is the purpose of medicine, which in turn rationalizes the role-specific behavior of doctors and nurses). This leads to the second point, which is that recognizing something as a practice involves more than a mere descriptive recognition. Describing an activity *as* a social practice (and sometimes this is the only way we can meaningfully describe it) implies that *under that description as a social practice* the activity carries with it certain normative standards. By describing a set of actions as practicing medicine, a standard for evaluating them (are they conducive to health?) already presents itself. The simple fact of defining social roles, therefore, endows a social practice with ideas of excellence or accomplishment—virtues—that pertain to them. These ideas express behaviors that the occupants of roles are expected to pursue or refrain from, which may differ from behaviors expected in other roles. The norms may be permissive, as when they allow someone in a given role to do something not otherwise accepted (in the case of role permissions[43]), or restrictive, as when they require the occupant of a role to do things others do not have to do (in the case of role obligations[44]). Social roles, then, come with normative standards "built in." Understanding a social role is impossible without some sense of what it means to fulfill the role well.

Ethics, in this view, is to cultivate and realize as much as possible the virtues relevant to the practices we engage in—to excel at our social roles. The virtue ethicist Robert C. Solomon has written that the "dual translation [by 'virtue' and 'excellence'] by itself makes a striking point. It is not enough to do no wrong. 'Knowingly do no harm' (*Primus non nocere*) is *not* the end of business ethics . . . Virtue is doing one's best, excelling, and not merely 'toeing the line' and 'keeping one's nose clean.'"[45] The virtues, then, are standards or ideals against which we assess the performance of something.

Thus, we may ask: What are the virtues of medical doctors, of medicine? They are, we may answer, the character traits that make someone an accomplished doctor rather than a quack or someone who tries his hand at medicine but is not very good at it.

---

[43] The entertainer or comedian is an example of a role that is permitted to do things others are supposed to refrain from—such as using foul language, for example. The role of the *court fool*, as we know him from Shakespeare's *King Lear*, for example, had the tremendously useful role-relative permission of speaking truth to power.

[44] The archetype is the captain, uniquely expected to go down with his sinking ship.

[45] Robert C. Solomon, "Corporate roles, personal virtues: An Aristotelean approach to business ethics," *Business Ethics Quarterly*, 2(3), 1992, pp. 317–339.

We may point to caring, compassion, a lack of squeamishness, empathy, precision. Similarly, we may ask: What are the soldierly virtues? They are the character traits that makes someone a good soldier. These traits may include such traits as loyalty, courage, obedience, diligence, and perhaps ruthlessness, love of country, and sense of duty. And again: What are the virtues of a lawyer, of lawyering—what makes a good trial lawyer? We may answer intelligence and cleverness, consistency, quick-wittedness, rhetorical ability, conviction, aggressiveness. Finally, to return to Kate's Dilemma, we may identify which virtues distinguish the good friend from the bad one, or the excellent employee, colleague, or banker from the unaccomplished occupant of those roles.

In each case, then, we can without confusion ask the question, "What are the virtues of a doctor/soldier/lawyer?" The question is intelligible, and the answers are informative: They are the characteristics that we think most conducive to excelling as a soldier or doctor or lawyer. That is not to say that the answers are necessarily obvious; it takes reflection to judge what makes, for example, a good artist. Nevertheless, for most social roles we intuitively know what it is to excel at them, and these intuitions we can take as a starting point for ethical deliberation. Of course, people do not share all the same intuitions. We may disagree on what makes a good doctor. Nevertheless, our disagreements will be circumscribed: Not *all* characteristics could plausibly even be candidates for the virtues of doctoring. If somebody thought a good doctor was a deceptive one, or that a good priest was a foul-mouthed one, we would say he or she had misunderstood the nature of medicine or priesthood and those practices' role in society. Conversely, deceptiveness may well be a virtue of the negotiator, and foul-mouthedness a virtue of the entertainer.

To summarize, the claim is that once we understand what a practice such as medicine is, we share enough common ground about what counts as *good* medical practice, to have meaningful discussions about the medical virtues. Although we will not agree on a full specification of what those virtues are, our disagreement will stay within some limited parameters for what the medical virtues could possibly be. And deliberating about them within those limits would bring us along the way of developing an ethics for doctors—a medical ethics. This "deliberation," of course, need not be literally deliberative; indeed, it is usually not. Social practices are formed first of all by being *practiced*, that is, by people participating in them according to certain norms that are more often unquestioned than deliberated upon.[46] They do not shape the practice and its norms any less for being unexamined.

AN ARISTOTELIAN APPROACH TO BUSINESS ETHICS

We may now bring this line of reasoning back to business—for business is also a social practice. Its basic elements are recognizable throughout human history and across cultures that on the surface look quite different. The same socially defined business roles appear everywhere as variations on a theme—the most obvious ones being the roles involved in paid labor (today we would say employer and employee), money lending, and of course market trading, in addition to the various trades and crafts. This is no surprise,

---

[46] As Bernard Williams has pointed out, it is a particular feature of modernity—indeed a social practice of modernity—to question one's own society's social practices in a self-conscious manner.

since any society that operates with even a minimal division of labor must find a way to coordinate the production and exchange of commodities, and it cannot do this completely by political diktat with any efficiency. Therefore, markets for goods and labour have been a fixture of human societies for a very long time. So, too, have social practices for managing transactions within a division of labor—that is to say, for business.

Business being a social practice, the Aristotelian approach of exploring the social norms embedded in it suggests itself as the way to do business ethics. Just as it seems possible to develop a virtue-based medical ethics based on the social meaning of medicine and its roles, so it seems possible to build a business ethics from reflections on social roles in business.[47] Our opening example pushed us to do exactly that—our intuitions in Kate's Dilemma were best understood as probing what is required to be a good friend or to be a good colleague and employee and banker. We naturally see the dilemma through the lens of the virtues relating to friendship and employment relationships.

Can we develop a virtue ethics for business, one that captures more generally and systematically the kinds of intuitions about specific role obligations we encountered in Kate's Dilemma? We must start, presumably, with investigating what virtues pertain to *business* decisions as opposed to other human activities, and ask how someone should act *qua* businessman or businesswoman. Solomon, the virtue ethicist, writes: "Theory in business ethics thus becomes the theory of individuals in (and out) of business roles as well as the role of business and businesses in society."[48] Applying the Aristotelian schema we distilled earlier, we shall say that the business virtues are what enables someone to do business well. The business virtues are character traits and behavioral tendencies that make for excellence in one's role within a company, and that make for the company's excellence within the wider society.

There is obviously no short answer to what these character traits are. Here is Solomon's list, by his own admission incomplete:

> There are a great many virtues that are relevant to business life . . . Just for a start, we have honesty, loyalty, sincerity, courage, reliability, trustworthiness, benevolence, sensitivity, helpfulness, cooperativeness, civility, decency, modesty, openness, cheerfulness, amiability, tolerance, reasonableness, tactfulness, wittiness, gracefulness, liveliness, magnanimity, persistence, prudence, resourcefulness, cool-headedness, warmth and hospitality . . . Then there are those virtues that seem peculiar (though not unique) to business, such as being shrewd and ruthless and 'tough', which may well be vices in other aspects of life.[49]

---

[47] Interestingly, Aristotle himself was hostile to business. While he acknowledged skill and expertise in trading, he distinguished between barter and other exchange needed to satisfy the needs of the household from trading for profit, *i.e.* commerce or business. While accepting that the division of labor in all but the smallest societies means households have to engage in exchange, Aristotle saw the purpose of this activity as naturally limited by what households can usefully consume, since its purpose is "natural self-sufficiency." In contrast, the *telos* of expertise in business for profit is to acquire monetary wealth, which has no natural limit, since the only purpose of possessions beyond what one needs is to use them to acquire even more goods. "The cause of this state," says Aristotle about businessmen, "is that they are serious about living, but not about living well; and since that desire of theirs is without limit, they also desire what is productive of unlimited things." See Aristotle's *Politics*, 1256a–1259a.

[48] Solomon, "Corporate Roles."

[49] Ibid.

This barrage of character traits may give us pause. A cheap accusation against the Aristotelian approach would be that it reduces business ethics to a checklist, and a very long one at that. But that caricature would disserve both virtue theorists and their critics. Virtue theory does have deep problems, as we shall see presently, but its thick description of our moral life is not one of them. Nonetheless it bears the burden of spelling out what this or any other enumeration of business virtues implies for practical action. The paradoxical effect of this long list of laudable behavior is a certain sense of emptiness. If all good things belong to the business virtues, it is difficult to interpret them as anything much more than an overall requirement to "be nice."[50]

But the virtue ethicist has a ready answer to this. First, he will rightly insist that part of the appeal of virtue ethics is that instead of focusing simply on right and wrong, it acknowledges the multiplicity of the virtues. For, clearly, *several* virtues are relevant to excellence in any given role. There are few, if any, human activities where accomplishment is possible without excelling along several dimensions. Solomon is clearly right that business excellence requires loyalty *and* courage *and* persistence *and* many other things. So it is not a liability, but a crucial insight of virtue ethics that the virtues *are* plural—and that part of our job as virtuous people is to cultivate them in a way that balances the demands of each of them. The challenge of the good life—and the ethical life—is *integrity* in a very literal sense: the integration of one's various social roles into a harmonious whole, and the integration of the different virtues relevant to each role into a balance of character.

The need for integration leaves an irreducible role for *judgment* in the virtuous life. Acting virtuously requires not only "having" the virtues, but also cultivating a sense of how to balance them, since in any particular situation they may conflict. We should note the parallel between ethical decision making, as Aristotle conceives of it, and decision making in general—including business decision making. However hard management theories may try, the complexity of business cannot be captured perfectly in an algorithm that can always be consulted to yield the right decision—on the model of the rational utility-maximizing agent that populates neoclassical economics. Successful business people must have sound judgment—which includes an intuitive hunch for good opportunities and an ineffable sense for which strategies best achieve the purpose of the business activity in changing circumstances. Virtue ethics sees ethical decisions as similar. Being good—like being excellent—is the art (rather than the science) of determining the actions that best fulfill the purpose of the practices one is involved in. Just as the virtues are what makes someone excel at his or her role, so how to balance them must itself refer to how that role is best fulfilled—that is, to the role's *telos*.

The *telos* of business gives the virtue ethicist a standard by which to discriminate among Solomon's long list of virtues. Take, for example, loyalty and courage. Often they go together, but sometimes the courageous thing to do is to be disloyal—think of the whistleblowers at Enron. In such cases, should one act on the virtue of courage and blow the whistle, or on the virtue of loyalty and silent? The answer, surely, is that one must judge which virtue is in each case more conducive to the overall accomplishment of one's role.

Even for each individual virtue, there is a need for balancing. The character traits and behaviors that constitute the virtues come in degrees. The strength of a character

---

[50] Or, as Google would presumably say, to "not be evil."

trait that constitutes a virtue, says Aristotle, is rarely extreme: There can usually be too little or too much of a good thing. The opposite of virtue is vice, and a vice can take the form of a virtue's deficiency or its excess. True virtue displays the right character traits in the right amount, hence Aristotle's dictum that "virtue is a mean." Which degree of a character trait best promotes the *telos* of a practice will vary with the practice in question. Thus, courage is a virtue; having too little of it is the vice of cowardice. But having too much is also a vice: that of foolhardiness. Neither cowards nor daredevils make for good business people; the former take too few risks while the latter take too many. But more courage is appropriate in very entrepreneurial fields, where there is no gain without high risk, than in established blue-chip lines business, where the best strategy is more cautious and conservative. Similarly, consider the virtue of loyalty. Not being loyal enough is to display the vice of faithlessness; but one can be loyal to a fault, which is the vice of blind submissiveness. Faithlessness undermines trust and collaboration in a company, but blind submissiveness prevents the feedback of information that can help correct problems before they bring down the firm. Again, business flourishes in neither extreme. The virtue is a mean: What makes for business success is an intermediate degree of strong, but not uncritical loyalty. But the appropriate amount of loyalty in business, where it must not stifle a strong competitive spirit, is lesser than in, say, a military profession, where life and death can depend on it.

The way virtue ethics relies on the *telos* of social roles for identifying moral norms allows it to capture the relevance of *community* for ethical thinking and behavior. These roles are, after all, *social* roles, and the standards with respect to which we measure excellence are socially defined. The community in which we live both defines what counts for us as excellent living (what the virtues are) and gives us the moral training to understand this and, hopefully, be motivated to live accordingly. To the extent that our roles have social purposes, therefore, the good of the community enters virtue-ethical considerations almost by default. The Aristotelian attempt to align individual duty and the common good supports what seems like a fundamental moral intuition, namely that above the many specific social roles we may inhabit, we all share the simple role of being members of a community, and some of the most general virtues are those that will make us good or excellent members of our community. Even though the claims of business life and the claims of the wider community may conflict in specific cases, therefore, there should be no fundamental opposition between them. Aristotelian ethics allows us to say that business activities ought not to be pursued in complete disregard and to the detriment of wider social considerations.

Note also that a business firm is itself a community, which in turn defines roles within it and the virtues that those roles call for. Remember Kate's Dilemma: One of the strongest reasons why she should pass on the information is the loyalty she owes to her colleagues because of her role in the common enterprise she shares with them. Since the community created by a business enterprise may very well extend outside the company's legal boundaries, Aristotelian ethics readily lends itself to justifying stakeholder theory-type conclusions.

All this explains why the social practices we participate in, as a general matter at least, are not just "activities," like a sport we may take up and drop. More typically, they are ways of infusing our life with meaning. Being married, being part of a band or a team, working to attain and then practice certain professional qualifications—the things we do within these roles and practices are not just things we happen to do; they define what we are. In other words, we *identify* with our roles, and the standards that define what it is to play them well are also what it means for *us* to live our lives well.

Indeed, the rights and responsibilities a role assigns to us vis-à-vis the other people implicated in a practice (our spouses or teammates or patients or clients) are undoubtedly a large part of what makes our roles, and the lives we live through them, meaningful and valuable.

It is an appealing aspect of virtue ethics that it justifies the importance of social roles in our moral lives. The moral standards that we internalize and try to live by (or think we should) are deep sources of evaluative feelings, such as pride and shame (in ourselves) or admiration and outrage (vis-à-vis others). And much of the moral evaluation we do in our lives is linked to "excellence"—to doing well the things we do. Since social roles are a fundamental part of our moral lives and the social fabric within which those lives are lived, any acceptable moral theory must be able to account for the special moral demands a role seems to put on us—or explain why it does not.

Virtue ethics recognizes the function that virtues play in our life by seeing them not as external constraints imposed on us from outside—not, that is, as elements of a checklist—but as things that are good for us to live up to, because they help us function well in the communities we are a part of. The "excellences" that are the virtues can be in many senses *enjoyable* and not all terribly serious. "Despite the insistence of many moralists to the contrary," Solomon writes,

> it would seem that the congenial virtues are just as essential to corporate [well-being] as the more moral virtues . . . What is important for a business virtue is its place in a productive, meaningful life in business. And this does not simply mean, 'how does it contribute to the bottom line?' but rather, does it contribute to the social harmony of the organization? Does it manifest the best ideals of the organization? Does it render an employee or manager 'whole' or does it tear a person to pieces, walling off one aspect of a personality from another and leaving one part to apologize or feel ashamed before the other?[51]

So what should Kate do? Using Solomon's approach, it is natural to conclude that a workplace that requires employees to stifle the virtues of friendship is itself immoral. From the perspective of virtue-based role morality, ethics cannot be "checked at the office door."

BUSINESS LIFE AND ITS *TELOS*

Or can it?

The role-based theory we have just explored invites us to see business as a thoroughly socialized practice. In addition, by locating the ethics of business in the social meaning of the practice, it argues that the business virtues are those virtues that help us excel at the social purpose of business. But once we make the critical step of seeing ethics as practice-relative—as *derived* from the social practice, whether business or something else—its links with the greater social good become tenuous. For, if we ground the ethics of a practice in the practice's own internal logic, the content of the ethical theory is at the mercy of the practice's norms. What happens if its internal logic dictates an antisocial behavior?

---

[51] Solomon, "Corporate Roles."

The business theorist Albert Z. Carr has claimed that, far from aiming at a flourishing wider community as Aristotelians would have it, the internal logic or *telos* of business rather resembles that of a competitive game—to be precise, poker:

> We can learn a good deal about the nature of business by comparing it with poker . . . No one expects poker to be played on the ethical principles preached in churches. In poker it is right and proper to bluff a friend out of the rewards of being dealt a good hand. A player feels no more than a slight twinge of sympathy, if that, when . . . he strips a heavy loser . . . of the rest of his chips. It was up to the other fellow to protect himself . . .
>
> Poker's own brand of ethics is different from the ethical ideals of civilized human relationship. The game calls for distrust of the other fellow. It ignores the claim of friendship. Cunning deception and concealment of one's strength and intentions, not kindness and openheartedness, are vital in poker. No one thinks any the worse of poker on that account. And no one should think any the worse of the game of business because its standards of right and wrong differ from the prevailing traditions of morality in our society.[52]

It is easy to recognize Carr's argument as a practice-relative theory of virtue ethics (although he does not express it in these terms). While very different in content, it is similar to Solomon's Aristotelian approach in structure. It sees business as a special social practice, governed by rules derived from the standards built into the practice itself and defined by its *telos*. It is, therefore, a role-relative ethics—how one ought to behave depends on the role one inhabits within the social practice that one participates in. Carr develops a view of what the business person ought to do *qua* business person:

> That most businessmen are not indifferent to ethics in their private lives, everyone will agree. My point is that in their office lives they cease to be private citizens; they become game players who must be guided by a somewhat different set of ethical ideals.[53]

From this line of reasoning, structurally similar to Solomon's, Carr arrives at a diametrically opposite conclusion. His focus is truth-telling and "bluffing" in business. Ought people in business to tell the truth? In a virtue-based theory of business ethics, this question becomes whether honesty is a business virtue—whether being truthful is a requirement for excelling at the business role. Solomon, as we have seen, places honesty first in his list of business virtues. Carr, however, from firmly role-ethical grounds, claims the opposite. Excelling at business, he says, requires the ability to deceive:

> Most executives from time to time are almost compelled, in the interests of their companies or themselves, to practice some form of deception when negotiating with customers, dealers, labor unions, government officials, or even other departments of their companies. By conscious misstatements,

---

[52] Albert Z. Carr, "Is business bluffing ethical?" *Harvard Business Review*, Jan–Feb 1968, p. 145.
[53] Ibid.

concealment of pertinent facts, or exaggerations—in short, by bluffing—they seek to persuade others to agree with them. I think it is fair to say that if the individual executive refuses to bluff from time to time—if he feels obligated to tell the truth, the whole truth, and nothing but the truth—he is ignoring opportunities permitted under the rules and is at a heavy disadvantage in his business dealings.[54]

Note that Carr's claim is entirely teleological. He defends dishonesty as a means to succeeding at one's role. Being a good business person involves, among other things, *bluffing well*. In business as in poker, deceptiveness is a virtue while kindness and open-heartedness are not (although they are undeniably virtues within *other* social practices). And Carr is as concerned as Solomon with the importance of integrity in the sense of keeping the person "whole":

> If he is to reconcile personal integrity and high standards of honesty with the practical requirements of business, he must feel that his bluffs are ethically justified. The justification rests on the fact that business, as practiced by individuals as well as by corporations, has the impersonal character of a game—a game that demands both special strategy and an understanding of its special ethics.[55]

The key to integrity, he says, is to understand that different roles demand different behavior. And, in particular, that the business role requires deceptiveness to be played well.

Aristotelians cannot fault Carr's method of reasoning. It treads familiar virtue-ethical ground in embedding moral norms in social practices and the roles they give rise to. Both Carr and Solomon see business as a special social practice and take the Aristotelian view that the standards are relative to the practice. The ethics that should govern business decisions are described by the business virtues, *i.e.* the behavioral tendencies that make for excellence at the practice of business. It is no good applying to business decisions a general ethics that is valid for everyday social life—those who do, says Carr, "accept serious setbacks to their business careers rather than risk a feeling of moral cowardice." "They merit our respect", he adds, "but as private individuals, not businessmen." Whatever it is they excel at, it is not business.

We should not overplay the difference between Carr and Solomon—both would agree that honesty is usually "the best policy." Where they differ profoundly is in their conception of what it is the best policy *for*—that is, of the *telos* of business practice:

> . . . the better his reputation for integrity, honesty, and decency, the better his chances of victory will be in the long run. But from time to time every businessman, like every poker player, is offered a choice between certain loss or bluffing within the legal rules of the game. If he is not resigned to losing . . . then in such a crisis he will bluff—and bluff hard.[56]

---

[54] Carr, p. 144.

[55] Ibid.

[56] Carr, p. 153.

For Carr, the *telos* of business is the same as the *telos* of poker and other games. It is *to win*. A virtuous business person, therefore, is one who has the character it takes to win. This understanding of business *telos* must inevitably give honesty a rather precarious place among the business virtues. To the question *"How* honest should a business person be?" the answer, on this conception, must be: "As honest as one must be to win—neither more nor less."

Carr's argument takes us far from Solomon's social vision of business and the far more solid position it grants honesty. But we have moved this far without at all leaving behind the teleological, practice-relative framework of virtue ethics. That framework's initial promise has, therefore, produced a disappointment. Our virtue-ethical explorations have not delivered a self-sufficient business ethics, given how precariously their conclusions depend on as yet unjustified claims about the *telos* of business. In the next chapter, we shall see just how big of a problem this is.

Summary of the Argument in This Chapter

Kate's Dilemma illustrates that many moral reasons—and many of the most weighty ones—are role-relative. We intuitively attribute special obligations and permissions to specific social roles, including business roles. A promising place to begin building an ethics for business, therefore, is to systematize our understanding of social roles and the moral norms they generate. This is the Aristotelian approach to ethics.

It starts with the observation that we live much of our life through social practices. A proper understanding of a practice is always in part a *shared* understanding; it is also a *normative* understanding as much as a descriptive one. Social practices, in other words, come with evaluative standards "built in." The Aristotelian approach uses the *purpose* of the practices—their *telos*—to understand the *virtues* that are relevant to it. The virtues are the character traits conducive to excelling in a social role—to realizing the *telos* of the practice it is a part of. *Virtue ethics* is the study and cultivation of one's virtues: ethics as playing one's role well.

So the Aristotelian approach to business ethics—a role ethics or virtue ethics for business—centers around the business virtues. These are, almost by definition, multiple, for there are many character traits conducive to business excellence. The task of the virtuous business person, indeed, is to judge what degree of each character trait is *most* appropriate for excelling in business, and with which mix of virtues business life is most likely to flourish. But that judgment must, in the end, come back to an understanding of what it is to "flourish" or "succeed" at business—and depending on how the *telos* of business activities is specified, the role-ethical approach can reach widely divergent conclusions. A *telos* of a flourishing company community in harmony with wider society leads us to answer the question "Is honesty a business virtue?" very differently from a *telos* of beating the competition. The promise of a virtue ethics of business, therefore, stands and falls on what view of the business *telos* we can justify.

CHAPTER 4

Roles and Conventions
Confronting Cultural Conflicts

Considering the moral significance of social roles in general and of business roles in particular pulled us in two directions. On the one hand, social roles—our positions within established social practices—deeply shape our moral thinking, and an ethical theory that cannot account for what we ought to do (or are permitted not to do) because of the roles we inhabit—as friends, colleagues, employees, *etc.*—seems bound to fail. On the other hand, acknowledging that different "rules of the game" do indeed govern different social practices threatens to obfuscate more than illuminate. Taking seriously the fact that practices and roles come with moral standards built into them turns out to expose above all how difficult it is to establish what those standards are.

In the case of business virtues the trouble is that what it means to be a "good" businessperson depends on what business is for. Although virtue ethics respects our intuitive sense that any professional ethic must be intimately connected with the social practice it claims to govern, its reasoning is only persuasive if we can pin down the *telos* of the profession in a convincing way. If we are free to pick any *telos* we like, virtue ethics tells us little; it certainly does not get us very far in overcoming disagreements about what businesspeople morally ought to do. The success of a virtue-ethical approach to business roles is predicated on the concept of *telos* having a sufficiently nonarbitrary content. The worry is where such nonarbitrary content can be found.

The challenge is that "purpose" cannot be taken in a purely descriptive sense if it is to justify the moral norms that business roles incorporate. Only a normative *telos* can perform this task; that is to say, the purpose must be expressed not as the function business activities as a matter of fact tend to fullfil, but as the function they *should* fullfil. Otherwise, role-ethical analysis would produce such absurdities as that the actions of, say, a Mafioso are justified because they make him a good Mafioso. But the Mafioso's purpose is one that ought not to be pursued. We may in a non-moral sense be impressed by the successful criminal. But though we romanticize the glamorous gentleman thief, his stealing is not justified by the competence with which he carries it out. This reveals a general difficulty. We have seen that just by understanding the content of social roles, we can identify what it means to perform them well. But how can the *internal* logic of roles say anything about whether they ought to be performed at all?

This was not a problem that Aristotle and most premodern thinkers recognized. They considered things and activities to have natural purposes with normative force; that is, the *telos* of anything was a fact of nature. But it is no longer possible for us to think, as Aristotle did, for example that "plants exist for the sake of animals and that the other animals exist for the sake of human beings . . . If, then, nature makes nothing that is incomplete or purposeless, nature must necessarily have made all of these for the sake of human beings."[57] Scientific knowledge of the physical world, and the insights that the social sciences and psychology offer into human nature, undermine any belief in an inherently teleological world. For us, the notion that there are natural purposes must founder under the skepticism we have learned to direct against any idea of a natural moral order.

There might seem to be exceptions. Religious ethics may still admit of natural, in the sense of divine, purposes. But such a notion is inaccessible to those who stand outside of the religion in question, and is therefore unjustifiable to them. (It need not even be rationally justified to the believer, if faith is precisely the renunciation of a need for justification.) Similarly, evolutionary explanations of natural and social behaviors are often expressed in teleological terms; for example, the male peacock has evolved flamboyant tail feathers "in order to" let potential female mates know that it possesses sufficient physiological resources for such an extravagant display. Some evolutionary psychologists claim that humans buy consumer goods (and thus that marketing works) for the same purpose. But this is teleology in a rhetorical sense only. "Purpose" in theories of selection-based evolution, if the term is used at all, simply means the product of evolutionary fitness, that is, success in generating maximally viable fertile offspring. Evolutionary theory itself has nothing to say on whether reproductive fitness is a morally good thing.[58] Thinking that it does is to make the grotesque mistake of social Darwinism.

The only normative *telos* we can make sense of today is subjective—as a purpose that humans *attribute*. If an object has a purpose, it is the purpose that *I* or someone else has for it. The purpose of a knife is indeed to cut but not because this is in the nature of knives. Rather, it is because humans design knives in order to use them for cutting. And it is the purpose of an eye to see only in the sense that seeing is the function for which we make use of our eyes and want our eyes to serve us. In this subjective interpretation, the concept of purpose has a concrete and identifiable meaning that avoids the superstitions of premodern teleology and the renunciation of rational justification that religious thinking can involve. And this is a sense of purpose we can apply human actions as well, since we can legitimately speak of roles or practices as having the purposes their participants attribute to them. The purpose of medicine is to heal insofar as that is what those who participate in the practice of medicine understand its purpose to be.

---

[57] Aristotle, *Politics*, 1256b.

[58] Or even that it is selfishly good for individuals. Fitness may come at a high cost: Growing flamboyant feathers takes energy that could be used for other things.

This is a perfectly understandable interpretation of purpose; indeed, it is the only plausible one. But as a basis for moral theory, it throws up serious difficulties—one practical and one moral. The practical difficulty is the one we have already identified: How exactly do we identify the *telos* of the practice of business specifically, even in this subjective sense? Different groups of people may attribute different purposes to business activities. For shareholders, the purpose of Microsoft may be to pay dividends; for consumers, it may be to sell good software at low prices. Whose attribution of purpose counts?

The moral difficulty is deeper. Can even a subjectively attributed purpose provide a normative *telos*—that is, a purpose justified by moral reasons? For it is obvious that *some* subjective purposes provide no moral reasons for pursuing them. This is often true of a person's *own* purpose for engaging in an activity. The fact that the purpose for which I use a knife is to kill you does not justify my plunging the knife's blade into your back; nor is it any defense for me to say that my purpose was to stab you, and I acted like an excellent knife stabber.

The purpose of a social role or practice is not self-justifying, then, if we define it as participants' *own* motive for participating. This is a mistake Carr occasionally seems to commit, for he refers regularly to the goals business people *themselves* intend to achieve with their business. Like poker players, he says, they enter the game in order to win. But, clearly, if this is what "purpose" means, it is neither here nor there that the "purpose" of business—or more correctly, of businesspeople—is to win. Wanting to win does not morally justify the character traits or actions conducive to winning, whether we think (with Solomon) that those include honesty, or (with Carr) deceptiveness. Whatever morality says, it does not say that wanting something is enough to morally justify what it takes to get it. It follows that it is not enough for the practitioners of a social role to attribute a purpose to it for that purpose to justify the actions they claim the role permits or requires. If the purpose is to serve as a moral justification, it must be derived from something beyond the participants' personal goals. The most plausible candidate is a purpose attributed by *social convention*—by how *society at large* defines social roles and practices and the norms that go with them.

CONVENTIONALISM

An adequate teleological moral theory must establish an interpretation of *telos* that avoids both the superstition of thinking that roles have natural purposes and the egoism of justifying what people do simply by saying that it serves their personal goals. We can meet both requirements, it seems, by looking for social *agreements* about the purpose of a role or practice. We have seen that since a social practice requires a *shared* understanding of what the practice involves, it brings with it a social convention about what its purposes are. For example, part of understanding something as medicine is to understand its purpose as bringing health; and what makes medicine a *social* practice is that most people in society conventionally agree that this is its purpose. Medical ethics derives in large part from this and related social conventions about what medicine (and, derivatively, doctors, nurses, *etc.*) is *for*. A conventionalist view clearly satisfies the need to avoid metaphysics or superstition: *Telos* as social convention simply means purpose as attributed by society. It also satisfies the requirement not to collapse into egoism, since a social convention is not a mere subjective preference. Taking the *telos* of a practice to be its conventionally agreed upon purpose, then, rebuts Carr's claim that the purpose of business (in the morally relevant sense) is to win. For even if he is correct that most businesspeople take part in the "game of business" *for the sake* of winning, presumably society at large sees business as a something rather more than just an arena where business practitioners act out their competition.[59] Many businesspeople should find conventionalism congenial, since it implies that it is not their role to define what their role is. Society must decide what it thinks is acceptable—so one often hears—then business will focus on commercial success within those boundaries.

Indeed, conventionalism sidesteps the subjectivist challenge we confronted in Chapter 1. Recall that subjectivism says that there is no external standard for moral statements, which are merely subjective attitudes. This threatened to leave no place for reasoning in moral thinking. But as we have seen, we can expect that members of a society share an understanding of certain practices and the roles they create (they would hardly be *social* roles otherwise). If so, even subjectivists may find their skepticism addressed by taking as a starting point intersubjective agreements about what norms and purposes social roles comprise, and try to reason from those shared beliefs toward resolving disputes about specific ethical questions.

Can rooting the purpose of business in social convention help us overcome the impasse in the discussion of whether honesty or deceptiveness of the greater business virtue? Carr must claim not just that winning is what businesspeople aim for, but that most people in society at large also see business as a game like poker whose purpose is winning, including by deceptive means. Can such a claim—that there is a *social norm* of treating business like a poker game—be defended? This question, like any other question about what is conventionally believed, can only be answered by empirically establishing what people actually believe. But we can clarify what the moral implications of such a claim would be if it were found to be true. The answer will depend on what we mean by a "social norm."

One thing we could mean by saying that a certain business behavior is a social norm is that it is "normal" in the sense of common and (therefore) expected: It is what everyone expects businesspeople to do. One controversial business practice that is sometimes defended as conventional in this sense is *bribery*. In the 1970s, it was revealed that Lockheed Aircraft Company had bribed Japan's prime minister in order to secure an aircraft order it desperately needed, without which the company could well have gone under. The president of Lockheed, A. Carl Kotchian, later said that he had been certain the bribes would be effective in obtaining the contract. This appears to have convinced him that although the bribes were morally dubious, they were in the end justified:

> Some call it gratuities. Some call them questionable payments. Some call it extortion. Some call it grease. Some call it bribery. I looked at these payments as necessary to sell a product. I never felt I was doing anything wrong. I considered them a commission—it was a standard thing—if you were operating in the Far East, you knew you'd have to pay 2 to 5 per cent on the sales. In the Middle East it's 7 to 15 per cent . . . I was doing it in the best interest of the company, its employees and its shareholders. I think

---

[59] Carr is not refuted, of course, if there is in fact a socially shared understanding that commercial success is the only purpose of business.

> any manager of a large enterprise has a responsibility to look after his employees, and the only thing you can do to keep them working is to sell your product, and that is what I tried to do.[60]

Carr would presumably approve: Kotchian argued that an action that might otherwise appear immoral is made acceptable by the fact that there is a social norm of acting in this way. It is how "the game is played"; it is just what people do and are expected to do. This could well be true: Society at large may as a matter of fact think that bribery is what businesspeople do, and have to do, in order to win. But even if that is true, what does it prove? Society can expect bribery to take place without necessarily accepting or condoning it. In the case of Lockheed, the Japanese public's reaction—the (by then former) prime minister was arrested when he was found out—suggests they did not. If an action is conventional only in the sense of being generally *practiced* and *expected* (this is what we think business people do and what we expect them to do) but not in the sense of being conventionally *approved* (this is what we think they *should* do), how does the fact that the behavior is conventional justify people in engaging in it? The answer is that it does not. If I venture into certain parts of the city after dark, I may expect to be attacked, but I do not consent to being attacked, and my attacker is not acting any less wrongly for the fact that I expected it to happen.

One might say here that although a social norm of *expectation* cannot provide moral justification, a convention could instead be a social norm in the sense of *acceptance*: normal as "correct" rather than "common." That is, we should look not at how businesspeople are expected to behave, but at how (as we often say) they are "supposed" to behave. Having normative (rather than merely descriptive) content is presumably a minimum threshold for a convention to carry any justificatory force. Carr's defense of deceptive business practices, then, must meet a more demanding conventionalist test than he thinks. It is not enough that society shares a conventional belief that businesspeople often deceive; society must share the belief that it is *right* for businesspeople to deceive. Similarly, Kotchian needed at least to demonstrate that the Japanese not only expected bribery in public procurement, but that they accepted it, something the prime minister's subsequent arrest obviously undermines. In contrast, behavior that is conventionally believed to be permissible or required seems on much firmer moral ground.

The strongest way in which a community expresses its conventions on permissions and prohibitions is through *laws*, which are more formalized than nonlegal social norms and usually more strongly enforced. One need not believe the illusion that there is something the law "says" outside of how it is interpreted in order to agree that the content of law is more determinate than the content of nonlegal social conventions embodied in custom or peer pressure. (In part this is because societies also have conventions, institutionalized in its courts, about how to specify what the law says.) For these reasons, it is natural that a conventionalist would take society's laws as the most important conventions that business must respect. That is presumably why a conventionalist like Carr never suggests that businesspeople may break the law, even though his stated argument that they may do whatever is expected and necessary in order to win the game of business applies regardless of whether the practice is legal. Pointing out, reasonably, that

---

[60] A. Carl Kotchian's remarks to Robert Lindsey (Lindsey, "Kotchian Calls Himself the Scapegoat," *The New York Times*, 3 July 1977).

laws are the most fundamental conventions in any society, a conventionalist can avoid Carr's embarrassing implications and affirm that businesspeople must play the game of business according to the conventional rules *provided* those rules do not require them to break the law. It does not follow (although it is often suggested that it does) that business need only make sure they obey the law and are then free to act as they see fit in the pursuit of their own interests. That would only follow—according to conventionalism—if society's nonlegal conventions did not require business to do more than obey the law. That is something a conventionalist wanting to defend conclusions such as Carr's or Kotchian's would have to prove. It is doubtful that they ever could: The lasting debate on corporate social responsibility rather suggests that there is no settled convention on this matter.

But on specific issues, such conventions may exist. When Google decided to open a Chinese Web portal for its search engine—google.cn—the company agreed to censor users' search results according to Chinese law. The reason was that the Chinese government slowed down traffic to Google's international Web site google.com, which Google feared would make it lose market share to local Chinese search engines. To be allowed to operate, Google accepted to scrub google.cn clean of politically sensitive material that its international counterpart google.com would display in searches such as "Falun Gong" or "Tiananmen Square". (In 2010, Google stopped collaborating with the Chinese government, and set google.cn to redirect users to google.com.)

Did Google act wrongly? On conventionalist grounds, it is hard to see why. Not only was what Google did common business practice in China; it was also required by Chinese law, as Google emphasized to defend itself. What Google did not say, but could also have said, was that according to opinion research, a majority of Chinese think it is right of the government to censor the Internet.[61] Returning to our terminology of social roles, we may say that it is conventionally seen to be the government's role to censor—and by extension, it is presumably seen to be the companies' role to help it with this, or at least comply with its orders. Here, then, is a common practice, legally sanctioned and conventionally believed to be right. If conventionalism is correct, Google was doing nothing wrong. And yet, critics thought its behavior unconscionable:

> [Google and others] have caved in to Beijing's outrageous but predictable demands simply for the sake of profits. These captains of industry should have been developing new technologies to bypass the sickening censorship of government and repugnant barriers to the Internet. Instead, they enthusiastically volunteered for the Chinese censorship brigade . . . My message to these companies today is simple. Your abhorrent activities in China are a disgrace. I simply do not understand how your corporate leadership sleeps at night . . . Google [argues that it] must comply with Chinese laws that prohibit online discussions and searching of certain 'sensitive subjects' [and] often cites its adherence to German laws that prohibit neo-Nazi propaganda. This value-free excuse truly sickens me. Germany is a political democracy, and its freely elected leaders prohibited the hate mongering that three generations ago led to Auschwitz. To pretend to argue that this is analogous to the

---

[61] Deborah Fallows, "Most Chinese Say They Approve of Government Internet Control", Pew Internet & American Life Project Report, 26 March, 2008. Available on http://www.pewinternet.org/Reports/2008/Most-Chinese-Say-They-Approve-of-Government-Internet-Control.aspx (accessed November 2010).

> Chinese situation is beneath contempt . . . If tomorrow another repressive government demands that Google block all access to women who want to use e-mail or blogs, will Google comply? What about a Sudanese request to block information on the ongoing genocide in Darfur?"[62]

Do these critics have a point? If we want to say that Google was *not* justified in engaging in censorship, we have stepped beyond what convention itself can tell us. For if that is correct, it must be that the convention itself is mistaken. But can a social convention about right and wrong ever be mistaken? If so, on what ground can this be established? One possible answer is that it cannot be mistaken. That is the answer given by cultural relativism. If a convention cannot be mistaken, then nor can it be criticized. We shall now see whether that answer can be correct.

THE RELATIVIST ERROR

If it was ever rationally possible to ignore the plain fact that conventions about right and wrong vary dramatically over time, across space, and even within a single society at the same time, then affordable travel and instant telecommunication has put an end to that. At least this is true for business that is tied up in global divisions of labor. Even though conventionalism—the thought that what is believed to be right in our society is in fact right—is exceedingly common, it is constantly challenged by the disturbing realization that many conventions are perfectly parochial. The paternalistic traditions of Japanese companies, expected to provide for their employees in all areas of life, are puzzling to Americans who are used to "employment at will"; and Americans' and South Koreans' long hours and short holidays are shocking to Scandinavians. These are business conventions, but the general phenomenon of cultural differences goes much deeper: It covers the most basic elements of any culture, such as how it organizes friendships, social intercourse, and sexual relations.

In the light of such differences, a view has emerged, formulated first by anthropologists and other observers of cultural variation, which is at the same time strikingly similar to conventionalism and its exact denial. It is *moral relativism*, and it says, in its most common version:

Empirical premise: Societies and cultures differ in their conventions, including about right and wrong

Moral premise: Moral right and wrong in a society or culture can only mean what the conventions nurtured by that specific society and culture say

Conclusion: *Therefore*, it is wrong to interfere with the conventions of another society or refuse to obey them when operating in that society

Put more pithily, moral relativism says: When in Rome, do as the Romans do; whatever the local conventions are, they should be obeyed. Relativism's ambivalent relationship to conventionalism resides in the fact that, on the one hand, it sees social conventions as the

---

[62] Statement by Representative Tom Lantos. "The Internet in China: A Tool for Freedom or Repression," hearing before the US House of Representatives Foreign Affairs Committee, 15 February 2006. Transcript available on http://foreignaffairs.house.gov/archives/109/26075.pdf (accessed November 2010).

only valid source of morality, while on the other, it asserts the total relativization of that validity. This would be a mere theoretical problem were it not for the fact that few societies are entirely separated from others. People from one society sometimes have to navigate those of another, and relativism's tension with conventionalism reflects the latter's inability to guide them. For conventionalism—according to which social convention is the final word on matters of right and wrong—cannot address the moral questions that arise when conventions *conflict*. It is clear how moral relativism, which addresses these questions head on, can seem like an enlightened attitude compared to that of parochially clinging to one's native customs.

The problem to which relativism proposes a solution is well known. It marked such confrontations between cultures as Europe's discovery of America, when thinkers grappled with the moral implications of customs shockingly different from their own. Michel de Montaigne in his essay "On Cannibals" related a certain Native American tribe's habit of killing, roasting and eating enemy fighters taken captive in war. The practice was decried as repugnant by many in Europe, but Montaigne pointed out that we are all biased in favor of our own ways. (The same Europeans, for example, were accustomed to putting prisoners on the rack.)

> As, indeed, we have no other level of truth and reason, than the example and idea of the opinions and customs of the place wherein we live: there is always the perfect religion, there the perfect government, there the most exact and accomplished usage of all things.

But what validity do the conventions of our own society have in cultures that call for altogether different conduct? That problem appears in cross-cultural confrontations every day, including in business.

Turn again to Google's decision to collaborate with government censorship of Internet searches in China. However necessary such behavior may be to "win the game," Google would struggle to justify it on conventionalist grounds if it was performed in the United States. The majority of American society, as well as of America's business community, frowns (although far from consistently) on censorship, especially of the government-sponsored kind. But Google needed to choose how to act in a country where the government, with public approval, demanded the action in question. Surely it was entitled to doubt that American conventional beliefs could justify breaking Chinese law in China; especially as there would never be a question (for Americans, at least) of Chinese social mores justifying the violation of American law in the United States.

Consider again the example of corruption. When the British bridge-building company Mabey & Johnson was fined for overseas bribery, the corrupt actions, according to prosecutors, "included paying for the UK funeral expenses of the mother of . . . a Jamaican transport minister, and writing a £500 ($800) check to a Ghana finance ministry official's son while [he was at university]."[63] Aside from the undisputed fact that such payments are illegal under British law, is there anything morally

---

[63] Michael Peel, "Bridge builder fined for bribes," *Financial Times*, 26/27 September 2009. In many other Western countries—except the United States which outlawed them in 1977—bribes to foreign public officials were not only legal, but treated as a tax-deductible expense well into the 1990s.

wrong about them? It would be strange if the details of Jamaican and Ghanaian social mores—for example, whether such small gifts count there as morally unproblematic or even required courtesies—were completely irrelevant to the question of their wrongness. Indeed, it would not be outlandish to think that they are, if anything, *more* relevant to the question of the actions' moral wrongness (though not their legal wrongness) than are other countries' laws, all the more so when the laws in question were only very recently enacted, as was the case here.[64] These and many other examples are apt to make business people doubt that their home values have any normative force once they go abroad. Moral relativism is the formal confirmation of that doubt. It tells us that when local conventions differ from our own, acting as one would in one's own society is at best misguided provincialism, at worst a bigoted display of cultural imperialism.

No doubt, relativism is right to condemn the ways in which powerful societies have too often imposed their standards of right and wrong on weaker groups, inflicting pain and suffering on individuals and uprooting communities from their culture. If all it did was to warn against such errors, it would be well worth a hearing. But moral relativism makes a claim that goes further than this; in fact, it makes two. The first is that there is no valid way of judging one culture's values more correct or more worthy of obedience than any other culture's values. The second is that, *therefore*, one must judge behavior in other societies by those societies' own standards—and that extends to one's own behavior while in those other societies. But this second claim is clearly a *non sequitur*. It attempts to derive a non-relative moral standard (that one ought to tolerate or even obey local values) from the contention that all moral standards are culturally relative. This, of course, is impossible. The moral relativist can only conclude from his premise that if *my own society's standards* tell me to tolerate or accommodate the local values in a different society, then I ought to do so. But this is a far cry from saying that it follows from the moral disagreements between societies that one must tolerate and accommodate the social norms of others. As Bernard Williams points out: "If we are going to say that there are ultimate moral disagreements between societies, we must include, in the matters they can disagree about, their attitudes to other moral outlooks."[65] And, as a matter of fact, few if any cultures include among their conventional moral standards an unqualified tolerance of other societies' social practices, whatever they may be.[66]

---

[64] Ibid.

[65] Williams, *Morality*, Ch. 3, p. 23.

[66] Some might try to avoid relativism's self-contradiction by moving from alleging the *absence* of a point of view from which a society's conventions can be judged to *affirming* as a moral principle the equal moral value of all communal ways of life, whatever they may be. This version of the argument will defend social conventions by pointing to their function in sustaining a community's valuable way of life; we may call it a *functionalist* defense of relativism. Functionalism does not, however, succeed. A minor problem with it is that there may be many conventions the loss or violation of which do not threaten a community's way of life—unless, of course, one trivially defines "way of life" as including all the extant conventions. But more seriously, functionalism just moves the question one step back to ask *why* we should think all ways of life are worth (and equally worth) sustaining. Slavery was functionally necessary for the social life of the antebellum southern United States. The self-contradiction, moreover, reappears when we recognize that many of society's ways of life include not respecting the ways of life of other communities.

In that, surely, they are correct. For the first claim made by relativism—the premise that no society's conventions about right and wrong can be judged superior or
inferior to another—is also dubious. The structure of moral thinking itself—its built-in
impartiality—makes it difficult to limit its conclusions to one society only. (If this brings
to mind the discussion of subjectivism, that is because the same issue is at stake there.)
But even at a more immediate level, relativism must founder on its conclusion that we
can *never* criticize anything that is conventionally practiced in another society, no matter
how horrid. To notice how mistaken this is, it suffices to consider just a few of the foul
practices that have at various times in different societies been sanctioned by near universally accepted social norms, such as slavery or the burning of heretics at the stake.
The fact that many societies have had a social convention of slavery—and associated
understandings of the social roles of both slave and slaveholder—did not make slavery
right in those societies, nor did it give any moral reason to accept the "virtues" that
would be associated with these roles. A "good slave" may well be an obedient and
hard-working slave, but that can never give slaves an intrinsic moral reason to obey and
work hard, no matter how well-advised they may be to do so for the instrumental sake
of their own survival or well-being.

The example of slavery is not an extreme thought experiment of armchair philosophy. At times in history, it has been a question at the forefront of business. The rightly re-
viled Atlantic slave trade is a case in point. A thriving business of capturing and trading
slaves predated the arrival of Europeans to the West African coast. When the Europeans
came, they did, as it were, as the Romans did, and appropriated the local customs with
gusto. (It is hard to see how the moral relativist could object to this—except, perhaps,
that Europeans also exported the practice to the Americas, disrupting pre-existing local
conventions on *that* continent. Concluding that Europeans would have been on morally
safe ground had they only confined their slave trading within African areas where it was
already practiced, however, seems rather to miss the point.) When, in the late nineteenth
century, European chocolate producers were condemned for using cocoa cultivated with
slave labor, the defense that Africans practiced slavery as well failed, as it should, to deflect the attacks. And today, opponents of "sweatshops" who accuse some companies of
exploiting working conditions that resemble slavery need not deny that such conditions
are accepted by people in the poor countries where the factories are located. These arguments reflect how hard it is to believe that *all* conventional business practices are
immune to moral criticism.

As a moral theory, cultural relativism is an error, because its conventionalist premise is wrong. The conventional acceptance of a practice does not suffice to make a practice right. And so just because another culture generally endorses a practice, that does
not mean we need to tolerate it, let alone participate in it. But what, then, shall we do
when another society's conventions differ from ours? What, for example, should a business do when it operates in a country where slavery-like labor conditions or bribery are
widely practiced and where it would not be able to compete successfully without
adopting them? Some will respond that if a company cannot make a profit in a certain
culture unless it engages in practices that are deemed immoral at home, it has no business to be there and should pull out. This is no doubt sometimes true. But if we are still
tempted by conventionalism, on what ground could such a claim be argued? For, if the
belief of many Chinese is that Internet censorship is morally acceptable does not make

it so, then nor does the belief shared by many Westerners that censorship is morally *un*acceptable prove the opposite.

Since we can turn the reasoning with which we defeated relativism back on ourselves in this way, the arguments turn out to apply equally well when there are no cultural clashes. That a majority of us believe something to be right, does not make it right. If it did, the idea of social progress—of overcoming misguided social norms that entrench immorality and injustice—would be unintelligible, for such a notion presupposes that we can say that some social conventions are morally inadequate. A claim that it is morally good to have abolished slavery, for example, would be not only incorrect but nonsensical. This would also mean that any project of social reform to *change* the social conventions in force for the sake of moral advancement would be insane—as would be conservative projects of *protecting* existing norms against moral decay. For the notions of moral advancement and moral decay both presuppose that some moral beliefs are better than others, precisely what relativism denies. But surely attempts at social reform or resistance against it, while variably noble or contemptible, are not illogical. Of the many things one can say about Martin Luther King or Strom Thurmond, that they *made no sense* is not one.

Still, for all of relativism's shortcomings there is something valuable in the impulse that originally inspired it—the sense that cultural differences are owed respect, and that respecting the conventions and practices of another culture requires a more nuanced attitude than applying our own society's beliefs elsewhere without modification. For even though relativism goes astray in concluding from the fact that conventional moral beliefs vary across cultures that no set of beliefs is more correct than another, it does not of course follow that *our* society's beliefs have the greatest claim to truth. The very reasons for doubting the relativist argument, such as its implausible implication that we cannot intelligibly criticize our own social practices, are reasons why we should take seriously its warning against dismissing other practices elsewhere, strange as they may strike us. One implication of this is that Carr's argument fails. Even if the business community, or indeed society at large, thought deception in business was morally acceptable, that would not necessarily make it so.

That it seems obvious that we can envisage *our own* society changing for the better or worse, morally speaking, should in turn reinforce our doubts about a relativist attitude to other cultures. For if we can criticize slavery and corruption—and by extension any other morally questionable practice—in our own culture, why may we not also criticize them in others? Though it was conceived as cosmopolitan tolerance, cultural relativism, if it were true, would justify moral complacency or even complicity in the face of moral wrong committed elsewhere. That it is not true, however, should not be taken as a justification of the bigotry in reaction to which relativism developed. If it is foolish to think that all local customs are worthy of respect simply because they are local, it is just as foolish to believe that they can always be dismissed just because they are not ours. There are indeed good reasons to defer to local customs when operating in societies other than one's own, a practical one being the ease of misinterpreting them until one knows the culture well. The specifics of a social role that may seem irrational—or even immoral—to an outsider could, in fact, play an important function in sustaining a valuable form of social life. And yet such considerations, while crucial, can only be preliminary. Although perhaps we ought to keep our moral judgment in abeyance while striving to understand and interpret local practices in their cultural context, we cannot abdicate that moral judgment. We must, rather, apply it. We must question the purported justification of social practices once we begin to understand them and ask, for example, whether the social conventions that make it the search engines' job to enforce government censorship are themselves ones that ought to be respected. Anything else would be to commit the relativist error.

THE LIMITS OF ROLE-BASED ETHICS

It is time to bring the discussion back to where it started: whether seeing business as a social practice and business positions as social roles provides a foundation from which we can derive the moral responsibilities of business people. Since social roles and the practices that structure them are products of social conventions, they can only play this foundational role in business ethics if conventions have independent moral force. That is what this chapter has thrown into doubt: The fact that everybody acts in a certain way—or even that everybody thinks acting in this way is right—does not make it so. It follows that even when settled social conventions unambiguously specify the norms embedded in social roles, the norms can be contested, because the conventions themselves can be contested. In more concrete terms, we may contest the claim that the fact that Chinese social convention makes it a search engine's role to help the government censor the Internet gives Google a moral reason to engage in such censorship; or we may contest that "our role is to make the cars people want" is a moral justification for the car manufacturer not to care about its cars' impact on global warming.

Realizing that role-relative norms are contestable should not be confused with claiming that they are successfully contested. Whether they are depends in each case on the arguments that can be marshaled for and against the norms in question. But establishing that a certain normative understanding of a role's purpose and built-in norms commands widespread social or even legal backing does not suffice to conclude that the norms also have moral validity. In other words, establishing what a "good X" is supposed to do does not close the moral argument that if one is an X, one ought morally to be a good X. What it does is to *open* the argument, precisely by inviting contestations of that moral validity which may or may not be successfully refuted.

Such contestations of a social role's built-in norms—whether by its occupant or outside critics—can take different forms. Most straightforwardly, one may reject that a particular role and its norms properly apply at all. When Milton Friedman criticized proponents of "corporate social responsibility," he accused them of wrongly attributing the role of a public official to private business corporations. It may well be true that a good public official must act, for example, to keep unemployment low. But since private business practitioners are not public officials, it is simply confused to say that they must be *good* public officials. Demanding that managers should avoid layoffs because unemployment is a bad thing is to evaluate them according to the standards of excellence that apply to public service.

Other roles cannot simply be dismissed. Kate cannot reject the norms of the good employee by denying that "employee" is a role description that applies to her. Nevertheless, without denying that one occupies a certain role, someone may refuse to *identify* with it and, therefore, argue that its norms are not binding. Imagine Kate's Dilemma featuring not Kate but Mary, who unlike Kate does not identify with her work and her firm as a central part of her life. She may say that the role of employee or colleague describes something she does, not something she is. Therefore, she rejects the notion that she must be a "good employee" or a "good colleague" except when she is at work.

Another form of contestation is to reject the norms of a role because one has not consented to it. Bernard Williams points to the archetype of the involuntary role: the drafted soldier. All societies have strong and similar notions about the soldierly virtues—but does someone who is forced to be a soldier have to be a *good* soldier? He might claim he need not, suggests Williams, if he "thought that 'soldier' was a title that applied to him only because it had been forcibly applied to him from the outside; cared nothing for the assessments that go with that title; regarded the hostility of his superiors as a blank external force like the force that had put him into the army; and felt as the only constraint on opting out as much as possible, the fear of punishment."[67] Less dramatically, a similar attitude offers itself to all those forced by poverty or other circumstances of life to do a job that repulses them (prostitution comes to mind). Even if they have *pragmatic* reasons to do their job well (presumably whatever reasons made them take the job in the first place), they need not, at least, think they have a moral duty to excel at it.[68]

Finally, some people may disassociate themselves from their roles—or others may point out that they ought to—because the roles' norms require them to do immoral things. History has no shortage of monstrous crimes that their perpetrators have tried to justify by appealing to what their jobs required. One was Adolf Eichmann, the Nazi military bureaucrat who was responsible for the logistics of transporting European Jews to death camps. At his trial in Jerusalem in 1962, he did not dispute the facts, but defended himself as having followed orders: He was just doing his job. Eichmann's reasoning may aptly be called role-ethics fundamentalism, suggesting as it did that the role of a high-ranking bureaucrat in Hitler's Germany required such strict obedience of state policy that it justified mass murder. Ordinary business activity rarely involves choices like Eichmann's (although business firms were also complicit in the Holocaust); however, such fundamentalism is logically just as unwarranted in less dramatic situations. It is not inconceivable that doing one's job well for an oil company must involve polluting the Ecuadorean Amazon, or that doing one's job well for an Internet search engine entails engaging in censorship in China. But none of this shows that those actions are morally permissible.

We have listed these various ways of contesting the moral force of role-relative norms to show that such contestations are possible. Whether they succeed is a different matter; it is easy to think of examples where they fail. Surely a doctor is not free of the particular demands we conventionally place on medical practitioners (a duty of care, confidentiality, and so on) because he does not "identify" with the profession (perhaps medicine is just something he does because he needs the money). Nor, in a country fighting a defensive and just war, does being unwillingly drafted relieve a soldier of the

---

[67] Bernard Williams, *Morality*, pp. 50–51. This may not be a psychologically restful view to take: "The straightforwardness of this attitude may be bought at the cost of a certain despair, since it naturally goes with a feeling (as in *Catch 22*) that the environment is, just as a matter of brute fact, insane."

[68] Ibid.

duty to be as good a soldier as he can. And even if the capitalist system produces unjust inequalities, that fact cannot at a stroke eliminate every obligation employees have towards the privately owned company that employs them.

Regardless of whether role-relative moral norms can be *successfully* contested, however, there is no doubt that they can be *intelligibly* contested. And that, in turn, means that although "the standards can be . . . logically welded to the [role, the role] is not logically welded to the man; hence the standards are not logically welded to the man."[69] The Aristotelians are right, then, that practices and roles have moral standards built into them—and that sometimes social conventions settle those internal norms definitively—but they are wrong to think that it follows as a matter of logical necessity that the bearers of those roles are morally bound to obey the norms. It is this lack of necessity that the possibility of contestation shows; and this is so even if the contestation is ultimately unsuccessful.

One way of understanding this constant possibility of contestation is to realize that role-relative moral arguments are "strategies of redescription," as the ethicist Arthur Applbaum has labeled them.[70] They draw or alter moral conclusions about a set of facts and behaviors by proposing a certain social description of those facts. Good lawyers, says Applbaum, sometimes try to make a jury or the public believe things that they do not themselves believe, such as that their client is innocent. Are they liars? An argument for saying that they are not is that because they occupy the role of lawyer in the social practice of an adversarial judiciary system, the ordinary description of such an action— lying or at least misleading or deceiving—does not apply; instead, the action should be described in a practice-relative way as, say, vigorous advocacy. A similar strategy of redescription is at work in Kotchian's conventionalist defense of what Lockheed did when it paid money to the Japanese prime minister to win aircraft orders. Did they engage in corruption? The social convention in force in Japan at the time allowed Kotchian to describe Lockheed's actions not as engaging in corruption but as paying a "commission" that was "necessary to sell a product."

Applbaum points out that this strategy of redescription can never settle the moral discussion. This is not because the redescription offered by conventional understandings of social roles is illegitimate, but because it could only settle the matter if it also excluded any *other* description of the actions covered by the practice. But why should one description exclude others? It cannot, if only for the reason that the "brute" facts at least always remain what they are: lawyers trying to make juries think something they themselves believe to be false; Lockheed paying $1.8 million to Japan's prime minister. Even if the proposed practice-relative redescriptions are valid, alternative descriptions remain available to us, such as "lying" for what the lawyers do, or "corrupting a public official" for what Lockheed did. The persistence of the underlying facts and actions, and, therefore, of alternative descriptions of them, keeps open a place from which the conventional understandings can be contested.

This must bring us to a negative assessment of role ethics as a foundation for business ethics. Since the norms built into social roles and practices are ultimately a matter of

---

[69] Ibid.

[70] Arthur Applbaum, *Ethics for Adversaries: The Morality of Roles in Public and Private Life* (Princeton, NJ: Princeton University Press, 1999).

convention, and since we can always contest a convention's moral force, conventionalism cannot in the final analysis justify anything. A plausible moral theory of business, therefore, cannot be based on social roles alone. Admittedly, conventionalist reasoning can provide useful rule-of-thumb guidance to ethical questions. If more businesses tried to do what society conventionally thinks they should do, that would lead to a significant improvement in the ethics of much business decision making. But apart from being intellectually insufficient, conventionalism also falls short from a practical point of view. For conventions are, as a matter of fact, always contested, even within single cultural spheres; this is all the more so for business decisions straddling different societies and cultures. An adequate business ethics for the business world as it really exists, therefore, has no other choice than to address the validity of conventional moral beliefs head on.

This does not make conventional social roles irrelevant; on the contrary, our earlier discussion established that a plausible business ethics must account for the obvious importance of role-relative reasons in our moral thinking. What we still lack, however, and what conventionalism cannot provide, are fundamental principles that justify (or refute) those role-relative reasons. To judge the moral claims of practices and roles as conventionally understood (as well as contestations of those claims), therefore, business ethics must appeal to a criterion that is external to the roles, practices and conventions themselves. Such a criterion will presumably incorporate the kinds of considerations we mentioned as potential grounds for contesting the demands (or licenses) of a role, such as whether the bearers of roles identify with them, consent to them, or are required by them to commit immoral acts. There are undoubtedly other considerations it will also have to take into account. Whatever they are, this means leaving behind virtue ethics' attempt to locate our obligations *fundamentally* in the socially defined roles and relationships we occupy. The normative purpose—the *telos*—of our roles has turned out to be too frail a concept for normative conclusions to rest stably on its shoulders, even when we can determine what it is. How roles and relationships matter must come as the conclusion of an argument, not a premise we take for granted.

The task now is to find acceptable nonconventional first principles that can judge claims about what we ought to do, including the claims made by social roles, relationships, and conventions. There is one seductively obvious candidate for such a first principle. It is *consequentialism*; the idea that regardless of what our social roles (or indeed anything else) conventionally demand from us, morality requires us to do what brings about the best consequences. Once stated, the consequentialist principle may seem incontrovertible: How could it ever be right *not* to produce the best consequences? We now turn to consequentialism's promises—and its problems.

Summary of the Argument in This Chapter

Business ethics must, at least in part, be an ethics of business roles and the responsibilities they put on those who occupy them. What those responsibilities are depends on what we take to be the normative purpose—the *telos*—of business roles and of the social practices in which those roles figure. But, as the difference between Solomon and Carr illustrates, people disagree on which goals constitute the *telos* of business practices. It is, therefore, a task for business ethics to provide principles that can justify which normative understanding of business roles and their purposes is correct.

Since social roles are rooted in social practices, the most immediate such principle is *conventionalism*: the claim that the *telos* of social practices and their roles is just what social convention says it is. In other words, businesspeople ought to act in the way that they are "supposed to" act by society at large (or by a large majority of it). Defined this way, conventionalism admits of several interpretations. Business could be "supposed" to act a certain way in the sense that most people *expect* it to act that way—the interpretation sometimes taken by Carr. But this is a weak foundation for moral justification, for people can expect behavior that they do not morally endorse. At the very least, therefore, conventionalism must take as the starting point how business is "supposed" to act in the sense that a majority of society conventionally believes it *right* to act that way. This interpretation of conventionalism has the merit that it explains why business ought not to break the law. At least in ordinary cases, the law of a well-functioning society captures the most widely shared and strongly believed social conventions about what one should or should not do.

For what it may be worth within a single society where conventions are strong and unambiguous, however, conventionalism offers no guidance when conventions conflict. Clashes between cultures with contradictory social mores recur throughout human history, and modern business is no exception. If social conventions are the foundation of moral validity, as conventionalism assumes, one is naturally led to treat cultural differences with *moral relativism*—the notion that because social conventions differ across societies and there is no ground from which one can judge one society morally superior to another, one ought to respect and act in accordance with the social conventions of the society in which one operates, whatever those may be. But moral relativism is untenable, both on logical and moral grounds. Logically, its conclusion is a *non sequitur*, as it tries to draw from a relativistic premise (that morality is relative to local social mores) a non-relativistic conclusion (that one ought always and everywhere to obey local social mores). Morally, it implausibly confounds tolerance with moral complicity by claiming that we ought to respect local traditions *no matter what they are*, since it admits of no ground from which we can criticize *any* social convention as immoral.

The ultimate failure of relativism—its inability to allow that there could be morally objectionable social conventions—turns out also to condemn conventionalism, because even a single homogenous culture may sustain social conventions that deserve moral criticism: Slavery is the most common example. But this, in turn, means that the socially shared understandings of roles and practices can always be contested on moral grounds. While the conventional understanding of any social role contains a view of its normative purpose and, therefore, of the moral obligations that go with it, those conventional understandings themselves must be justified. The built-in norms of any social role may or may not be morally binding, but whether they are cannot be established just by checking whether the social role and its norms are conventionally accepted. In order to justify or refute claims that social conventions make, we must appeal to moral criteria external to the conventions themselves.

CHAPTER 5

Ethics as Efficiency
Making Everyone Better Off

In 2006, the *New York Times* reported the death of a young man named Joshua Oukrop. Oukrop suffered from a congenital heart weakness, but a heart defibrillator—a device implanted into his heart to stimulate it with electric jolts when necessary—enabled him to live an active life: He was mountain biking when he died. As is standard procedure, the device was returned to the manufacturer, Guidant Corporation, for checks. Guidant told Oukrop's doctors that his defibrillator had failed to deliver the necessary jolt because of a defect in a batch of about 26,000 devices, of which Oukrop's was one. The *Times* revealed that Guidant had already known of the defect from tests of failed devices, although only after the manufacturing process had changed so that no new devices suffered from it. They had, however, chosen not to publicize the defect to the public—not even to those customers who still had a device from the defective batch implanted. At the time of Oukrop's death, this was the case of about 14,000 people with heart disease. (Since defibrillators must be replaced every five or six years, not all of the defective devices were still in use).

The revelation caused a scandal. Oukrop's doctors blamed Guidant for his death, arguing that if they had been told of the defect, they would have had the device replaced. Since the company had at the time been in merger negotiations with another medical device manufacturer, Johnson & Johnson, Guidant was quickly accused of having hushed up the defect—and thereby indirectly causing the death of Oukrop and other patients, according to the critics—in order not to hurt the stock price.

But there were arguments available to Guidant for justifying its decision.[71] First of all, there was no question of Guidant's having broken the law, which only required the company to inform the U.S. Food and Drug Administration of the defect, not the public. But there was also a moral reason not to alert the public. Doing so, Guidant suggested when the scandal broke, would have caused more innocent people to die. The reason

---

[71] The case of Guidant's defibrillators is discussed in much more detail in Martin E. Sandbu, *Dicing with death? A case study of Guidant Corporation*, 2009, available on http://www.martinsandbu.net/guidant.

was that the defect only slightly increased the risk of device failure (by one to two tenths of a percentage point), whereas replacement surgery—the only alternative available to patients who found out their implanted device was from the batch in question—itself carries significant risks of complications, including death. Statistics on these risks show that Guidant could reasonably expect that if a public alert made someone choose to have the device replaced, that person would be more at risk of death than if he kept it implanted.[72] Anyone choosing not to have it replaced, moreover, would presumably be caused unnecessary anxiety for no benefit. A moral justification for Guidant's action, therefore, was that the *consequences of telling the public would be worse* than those of keeping the defect secret. More people would die, and more people would suffer. If one ought morally to minimize deaths and suffering—or more generally, if it is morally good to bring about the outcomes that bring people the most benefit—then surely Guidant did the morally right thing.

Unlike the virtue-ethical reasoning in the previous chapters, this argument makes no reference to any conventional or essential meaning of roles and their responsibilities. All it asks is which action leads to the best consequences. Of course, this could often involve the social meaning of roles and the expectations we have of those who occupy them, simply because how well our lives go is bound up with how our relationships to others work out. Guidant's silence could, for example, be criticized as violating the relationship between heart-disease patients and their doctors by not sufficiently respecting the moral values built into that relationship and into the role of doctor—in particular the doctor's duty to care for the patient's health. But we could reasonably question this criticism. We may query why not telling doctors and patients of the defect should be thought to affect their social relationship *for the worse*. The answer would presumably have to be that it hinders the doctor's ability to fulfill the conventional purpose of her social role; that is, that it makes her a less excellent doctor. But we may then retort that the only *morally relevant* sense in which keeping the defect secret makes the social relationship "worse" is insofar as it makes the *participants* in it—in particular, the patient—worse off. The norms built into the social role of doctor seem to have *instrumental* moral importance insofar as they prevent death and improve health—but how could this possibly justify the greater suffering and more deaths that would follow from "respecting the relationship" by divulging the information? If, alternatively, it is claimed that "disrespecting" the social norms of medical practice is wrong because it *intrinsically* degrades the doctor-patient relationship, then it is surely reasonable to question that the doctor-patient relationship matters morally at all when it does not make people better off.

On this argument, then, roles and relationship matter only in an instrumental sense, and not because of any inherent moral force. Whether to respect or pursue the conventionally understood moral values built into social roles and relationships, Guidant could have said, must depend on whether that leads to better outcomes than the alternative. This is an example of *consequentialist* reasoning. Reducing the moral relevance of respecting social roles and conventions to the consequences of doing so may well be thought a point in consequentialism's favor as against a fundamentally virtue-based

---

[72] Guidant did not quantify the risk. But one can estimate from public information that if all the patients with a potentially defective device implanted had had it replaced immediately, up to fifteen more people would have died than if none of them did. For details, see Sandbu, *Dicing with death?*

analysis of Guidant's dilemma. Such an analysis would quickly run into the difficulty of having to establish what a medical device company's social role is in order to state which virtues it should cultivate. This question has no conventional answer (neither the role of doctor nor the role of a profit-making business seem quite the appropriate standard to hold Guidant up to). Even if one could be found, we have seen that convention cannot underpin morality all by itself. A consequentialist approach, in contrast, cuts through social roles, conventions, and mutual expectations about behavior by reducing them to what (it claims) is the morally relevant thing about them—namely whether or not acting on them has good results.

Consequentialism, then, offers a solution to the problem we identified at the end of the previous chapter—the need for an external criterion to assess the moral claims made on us by conventional social roles. (Indeed, the method of moral analysis it proposes applies more widely than this, since it has something to say even when roles and conventions give no moral guidance at all.) But is consequentialism the *right* solution? To examine whether it is, we must now spell consequentialism out in detail.

CONSEQUENTIALIST ETHICS

There are many forms of consequentialism, but they all share a common moral premise that defines them as consequentialist. That premise asserts that whether an action is right or not depends only the consequences that the action will produce. According to consequentialism, what it *means* for an action to be morally right is that it leads to the best consequences, *i.e.* better consequences than any alternative action available to the person who has to act. (We shall discuss shortly what "good consequences" should be taken to mean; that is where much of consequentialism's justificatory action lies.) We should note here what consequentialism excludes from the category of putative moral reasons as well as what it includes. It says that the goodness of the consequences and *nothing else* is relevant for the rightness of an action. As we shall see later, this is a rejection of a host of considerations that are central to our everyday moral thinking.

We can schematically describe any consequentialist moral theory as follows:

One ought to do X (when choosing between actions X, Y, Z, *etc.*)

if and only if

action X has the best consequences (no worse than any of actions Y, Z, *etc.*)

where how we specify the placeholder "best" determines the exact content of the specific consequentialist theory in question. Now it is an obvious challenge to consequentialism that we often cannot fully predict what the consequences of our different actions might be. We may think—and have good reason to think, given all the evidence available to us—that X has the best consequences, whereas in fact Y does. Guidant may have been wrong about the effects of revealing the defibrillator defect to the public; perhaps informing them would in reality have led to fewer deaths than did secrecy. At times, outcomes may simply be unpredictable; at best we may know, for example, that in all likelihood the consequences will be good, but with a small probability, they will be terrible (think of a well-controlled nuclear power station that carries a tiny risk of meltdown). In such cases, how do we identify the action with the best consequences?

Our inability to predict the future with certainty has led some consequentialist thinkers to distinguish between objective and subjective rightness. Objectively right, they say, is the action that *in fact* has the best consequences. Subjectively right is the action that, *as far as we know*, has the best consequences. What is objectively right has philosophical interest, but what matters for action—for what we ought to do—is subjective rightness. A plausible consequentialism will tell us to do what we believe, with good reason, to be for the best. It would be a perverse consequentialist theory that told us to act contrary to this—unless it was because we knew we had a tendency to make biased predictions. That may of course be true, and important consequentialist thinkers have emphasized that since we easily make mistakes when predicting the consequences of our actions, it is often best—and, therefore, morally right—to follow conventional rules, proved by experience usually to lead to good outcomes.[73] But this is not a retort to consequentialism. It is just a special case of the general consequentialist premise that we should act in the way we have good reason to believe leads to the best outcome: namely the case where acting on conventional moral rules will probably produce better outcomes than acting on a case-specific calculation of consequences.

The problems of uncertainty are considerably more complex than what this brief discussion allows, but simply put, consequentialism just tells us to do the best we can. When we do not know the future consequences of the available actions with certainty, most consequentialists would say we should choose the action that we think has the best *expected* consequences.[74] How hard we should try to predict the consequences is itself a question of which action is best, to which the usual consequentialist formula applies. We may ask: If someone mistakenly believes a certain action has the best consequences and because of this acts in an objectively wrong way, is she in the wrong for not knowing better? The answer, under consequentialism, depends on whether the person *should* have known better, which in turn depends on whether she would have had reason to believe otherwise if she had tried to find out more before acting, and whether she had reason to believe that trying to find out more would lead to sufficiently better knowledge of the outcomes and therefore a better choice.

None of these complications, however, puts in doubt the *moral* premise of consequentialism. While they make it challenging to *realize* what consequentialism tells us to do, these are just empirical difficulties, though they may be formidable. So although uncertainty can sometimes be a great practical problem for consequentialism, it is not a *moral* problem. If consequentialism is true, it may simply be a fact of life that it is hard to find out what the morally right thing to do is. It may also be that human life involves many risks of acting (objectively) wrongly. But ethical inquiry has little to contribute to solving such practical difficulties, which are the domain of empirical disciplines that forecast the consequences of our actions. They play an important role in making ethical decisions in concrete cases, but not in laying down moral principles. We shall, therefore, put these practical worries to one side.

---

[73] But if we *know* that following a conventional rule in a certain case will not lead to the best outcome, it is difficult for a consequentialist to justify not breaking it. We return to this point in Chapter 7.

[74] Even defining "best expected consequences" can be highly complicated, but we need not get into these complications here.

UTILITARIANISM

Until now, we have not specified what we mean by "good consequences." But this clearly matters, for without it, consequentialism is underdefined. We can easily specify consequentialism in ways that make it look ridiculous (had Guidant attempted to cause as *many* deaths as possible, it would obviously have acted wrongly). A plausible consequentialist theory, then, must define good consequences as something that can itself be justified as morally valuable. The most influential attempt to do so is *utilitarianism*, the view historically fathered by Jeremy Bentham, and developed by David Hume, Adam Smith, and John Stuart Mill. The classic definition of utilitarianism is that the best consequences are those that bring about the most happiness for as many people as possible: "the greatest happiness for the greatest number." On its own, however, the maxim of pursuing the greatest happiness for the greatest number is still not a fully defined guide to action. Suppose, for example, that we can make a few people very happy while leaving most people miserable, or make everyone just a bit happy. Then it is not clear what it means to pursue the greatest happiness for the greatest number. (Mathematically speaking, we cannot maximize more than one thing at a time.) Since utilitarianism's beginnings two centuries ago, however, ever more refinements (in particular under the influence of economic science) have turned the theory into a sophisticated guide to action, to the point of underpinning the standard technical tools for modern policy evaluation: welfare economics and cost-benefit analysis.

Modern utilitarianism is defined by three key features. First, as we have already said, utilitarianism is a form of consequentialism: It says that consequences are all that matter morally. What distinguishes utilitarianism from other forms of consequentialism is *which* consequences it takes to be the best, and why. The second defining element gives part of that specification: Utilitarianism sees the goodness of consequences consisting in the *well-being* (the classical utilitarians' "happiness") that individuals enjoy in it. In fact, *all* that matters for how morally good a state of affairs is, according to utilitarians, is how well off individuals are in it. This component view is called *welfarism*.[75] Putting the first two characteristics together, *welfarist consequentialism* (or welfare-consequentialism) is the view that we ought to choose our actions with a view to how they affect human happiness or well-being—and only that.[76]

Welfarism may seem obvious; but it is easy to think of things other than well-being that, on the face of it, seem like morally valuable aspects of outcomes. One is, simply, *lives*: Many will say that avoiding deaths is morally valuable even if the lives saved are not happy ones. Other candidates for morally valuable consequences are certain ideals of self-realization that need not involve well-being in any plain sense (we may imagine an artist who decides he must sacrifice his happiness to his art). The point is that since welfarism does not logically follow from consequentialism, one can be a consequentialist without being automatically committed to welfarism. Therefore welfarist consequentialism, and *a fortiori* utilitarianism, must be justified against possible alternatives.

---

[75] Welfarism should not be confused with *hedonism*, the view that all that matters morally is pleasure. While pleasure is not morally irrelevant, human well-being is a much broader concept than pleasure, and a much more plausible candidate for the moral standard by which consequences should be assessed.

[76] Welfarism without consequentialism would be the view that only people's well-being matters for how good consequences are, but that the goodness of consequences is not all that matters for moral choice.

Welfarism, the view that well-being or happiness is all that matters, immediately points to the third defining element of utilitarianism by raising the question: *whose* well-being or happiness? In addition: *How much* should each person's well-being count? How should different people's happiness be weighed against each other? These are questions about how we should aggregate the well-being of multiple individuals. Utilitarianism answers that *everyone's* well-being matters, and that it matters *equally*. "The most happiness" should be taken to mean the largest *sum* of each individual's level of well-being added together. Seen as a recipe for making choices, then, utilitarianism tells us to consider how the actions available to us will affect the well-being of each person, add up the losses and gains in well-being to everyone affected, and choose the action that brings about the greatest total net gain. Take the choice facing a company between using profits to raise salaries for the workers or to pay dividends to the shareholders. The two actions clearly affect the two groups' well-being differently. Utilitarianism says that the company should resolve the salary-dividend trade-off by finding the division that maximizes the sum total of individual well-being of both workers and shareholders. We may call this *additive aggregation* of individual welfare.

This completes our formal specification of utilitarianism. It is defined as *welfarist consequentialism with additive aggregation*. It is a form of consequentialism since it only looks to the consequences of actions to determine which one we ought to choose. It is welfarist because it evaluates those consequences only by people's levels of well-being. And it aggregates those individual levels into one overarching measure of "social well-being" by adding up every individual's happiness level.

As the most influential form of consequentialism, utilitarianism merits our greatest attention, but it is important to distinguish it from consequentialism *simpliciter*. Our dissection of utilitarianism makes it clear that we can develop many other consequentialist theories. Later in this chapter, we consider a form of welfarist consequentialism that does not use additive aggregation; and, as we have already pointed out, a theory could take into account more than just well-being when judging the goodness of consequences (and so not be welfarist). These technical preliminaries matter not just for taxonomical purposes. They also have substantive moral implications. When we consider moral objections to utilitarianism in later chapters, we shall see that some of these apply to consequentialism as a whole, whereas others only pose difficulties for utilitarianism and have no force against non-utilitarian forms of consequentialism. To understand how far each objection reaches, we must, therefore, take care to distinguish between utilitarianism in particular and consequentialism in general.

We used Guidant's justification for keeping the defibrillator's defect secret as an example of the consequentialist approach. Is it also an example of utilitarianism? Without implying that Guidant meant to make a utilitarian argument, it is easy enough to present it as one. Indeed, that might have been the most persuasive way for Guidant to defend itself against Oukrup's doctors. Let us accept the doctors' claim that had they known of the defect, they would have performed replacement surgery on Oukrup, who might then have survived. Guidant could have responded that this would have come at the cost of *other* people dying in surgery complications instead (and suffering from the anxiety of worrying about a device malfunction if they did not choose replacement surgery)—and that the total amount of suffering would have been greater. This defense would have allowed Guidant to express full sympathy for Oukrup and even to acknowledge its role in his death, all the while arguing that it had done the right thing.

Such a response would have brought Guidant very close to utilitarianism. It would have presupposed that the consequences one morally ought to aim for are those with the smallest amount of overall suffering—which is close to arguing for maximizing well-being.[77] Even those who hesitate to adopt full-fledged utilitarianism, and prefer to justify Guidant's action simply by saying that one ought to minimize deaths, commit themselves to additive aggregation by implying that it is the total sum of lives saved that matters morally.

This elaboration of how a principled utilitarian would analyze Guidant's case shows one of the theory's most appealing assets: its promise of actually giving an answer. So long as the facts can be established and the possible consequences estimated, utilitarianism gives a firm moral conclusion—and if that is impossible, it is the fault of how the world is, not the fault of the moral theory. We can appreciate the same conclusiveness of utilitarian reasoning when applying it to the other examples we have encountered:

- In the Merck case, the choice was between maximizing profits and developing ivermectin at the cost of lower expected dividends for shareholders. The amount of well-being brought to a victim cured of river blindness is clearly much greater than the well-being shareholders enjoy from higher dividends—even *much* higher dividends. Moreover, the number of sufferers from the disease is on the same order of magnitude (millions) as the likely number of Merck shareholders (at least when savers in mutual funds are taken into account). Although a proper estimation would be needed, this suggests that the total well-being to be had from developing ivermectin is considerably larger than the alternative, and that utilitarianism therefore would tell Merck to develop the drug.
- In the Parable of the Sadhu, the well-being that the sadhu derives from being saved is obviously very large—and presumably larger than the extra well-being the already well-to-do mountaineers can get from reaching the mountain pass rather than canceling their hike. If so, other things being equal, utilitarianism morally obliges them to go to great efforts to save the sadhu's life.
- What about Albert Carr's argument? When business bluffing is a zero-sum game—the bluffer's gain is exactly equal to the loss of the person bluffed—utilitarianism would seem neutral. But very probably, bluffing in general reduces trust and increases suspicion, which means it could make it more difficult to conclude deals that would be mutually beneficial. This would cause an overall loss of well-being. And it is easy to think of specific examples of bluffing where the gain in well-being to the bluffer is smaller than the loss in well-being to the victims, such as Carr's examples of dishonest advertising. So on a first analysis, utilitarianism would seem to deem deception in business wrong in most cases (but as the next chapter shows, things are more complicated than that).
- Finally, in Kate's Dilemma, the consequences of telling seem much better those of not telling. Her friend's dwindling chance of keeping her job will not be much affected by Kate's telling her colleagues, whereas those colleagues in contrast stand to lose a lot—money, prestige, and employment—if they are not told immediately.

---

[77] Close, but not identical. One might think that we have a moral duty to prevent suffering, but not to increase the well-being of those not suffering. This view has been called *negative utilitarianism*.

Other things being equal, that makes it right to tell according to utilitarianism, since telling results in a larger total sum of well-being (specifically, a smaller loss of well-being) than not telling. The only negative effect telling could have would be Lucy's disappointment in Kate's choice to break her promise.[78] This is unlikely to match the much more serious impact on Kate's colleagues. It simply means that Kate should tell her colleagues, but she should also make sure, if possible, that Lucy does not find out about it.

These short analyses may not agree with your immediate intuitions about the right thing to do in each case. Two things could cause the disagreement. One is that you doubt the empirical assumptions set out above—about which consequences would actually result from the actions. Such a doubt is compatible with a utilitarian moral premise: It would just be a claim that utilitarianism in fact concludes differently in the cases above once causes and effects are correctly understood. A more interesting possibility is that you are disturbed by the moral premise—that is, the utilitarian argument itself. Many find that *even when* the consequences are as assumed above, they cannot endorse the conclusions that then inexorably follow from the utilitarian principle. Those, for instance, who think it is wrong in itself to break a promise regardless of the consequences will resist the conclusion that Kate should tell her colleagues what she has learned from Lucy.

As we shall explore later, there are powerful intuitions that tell against utilitarianism as a moral theory. But even those who resist the utilitarian premise should recognize utilitarianism's appealing features:

- It does not base morality on the shaky ground of social conventions or for that matter of religious belief, both of which we have seen to be labile and question-begging to those who do not already agree with them. Instead, it builds a moral theory on a simple premise that seems very difficult to reject, namely that morality must always reflect an impartial preference for more, rather than less, human well-being. Much of utilitarianism's early appeal came from the fact that it offered a fundamental principle that referred to empirical reality and yet seemed universally valid, since all humans desire well-being. It is not coincidental that utilitarianism caught on in Great Britain in the nineteenth century, when many intellectuals were losing their faith.
- The "principle of utility" seems benevolent and plausible—indeed irrefutable. How could one disagree that the point of morality is to make people better off? If human welfare cannot be the basis of morality, what can? In addition to these humanistic considerations, the utilitarian principle appeals because it promotes *efficiency*—it advocates actions that maximize human welfare within the limits of the possible. It does not allow opportunities for increasing well-being or relieving suffering to go to waste. Utilitarianism offers a rationality that improves on arbitrary superstitions found in other theories.
- Finally, utilitarianism offers a *unified* theory that promises an answer to all ethical problems in principle, if not in practice. A correct answer always exists, even if it can be hard to establish with certainty. Utilitarianism's strong empirical component affords it the power of social science, as modern welfare economics shows.

---

[78] It is possible that Kate herself may also feel unhappy about breaking her promise—but note that on utilitarian grounds, she has no reason to feel remorse since she would not be doing anything wrong.

Since the moral principle is so straightforward, the only thing left for the utilitarian to do is to determine what the consequences of our actions will be. That is no small task, but ultimately just a matter of prediction and calculation. The more profound questions of moral principle have, according to utilitarians, been solved.

"EFFICIENCY" AND THE PARETO CRITERION

Consider the third defining feature of utilitarianism: It treats individual happiness or well-being as something that can be added up across individuals. Utilitarianism demands that we act "efficiently" in a specific sense: that we not let any potential aggregate happiness go to waste. Efficiency, as we pointed out, is an appealing feature of the theory. But does it make sense to demand efficiency in this sense? Utilitarianism is only logically coherent if individual well-being is the sort of thing that can be *interpersonally compared* in a way that allows it to be added up across people. It presupposes that we can say, in principle at least, that an action increases some people's well-being *more than* it reduces someone else's well-being (or vice versa); this is what it *means* in utilitarianism that the action is morally good. Sometimes, this seems unobjectionable enough—for example, we think that the development of ivermectin would increase the well-being of victims of river blindness more than it would reduce the well-being of shareholders left with lower dividends. But is it always possible?

In Kate's Dilemma, there is something odd about saying that the change in her colleagues' well-being resulting from Lehman's bankruptcy can be lumped together with the effects on Lucy's happiness from being betrayed or not by her friend. It sounds odd because it ignores any *qualitative* differences between the kind of well-being that can be had from a job and the kind that is involved in friendships. But utilitarianism must assume that these can be measured in comparable quantitative units, otherwise the positive effects of an action on the well-being of some cannot *outweigh* the negative effect on others—which is what additive aggregation does.[79] That is not the only problem with additive aggregation. Even in the unlikely case that individual well-being can be convincingly shown to be interpersonally comparable in the right way in all instances—so that it does not pose a *logical* problem for utilitarianism—there remains the further question of whether we *ought to* trade off different individuals' levels of well-being as utilitarianism would have us do: a possible *moral* problem. Additive aggregation is disturbing in the way it allows, indeed requires, sacrificing individuals for the greater good. If we can benefit some people by making others suffer, utilitarianism says we should do so as long as the beneficiaries gain more than the sufferers suffer—regardless of *how much* they suffer, and even if the sufferers have done nothing wrong.

Many find this aspect of utilitarianism unconscionable. In later chapters, we shall analyze the objection in depth. Here, we should let it prompt us to consider alternatives to the utilitarian way of aggregating well-being. Remember that utilitarianism is just

---

[79] Not all utilitarians agree. John Stuart Mill, one of the theory's most eloquent defenders, distinguished between "higher" and "lower" pleasures in *Utilitarianism*. The intellectual pleasures, Mill suggested, are worth more than the physical ones—"it is better to be Socrates unsatisfied than a fool satisfied; better to be a man unsatisfied than a pig satisfied"—because those acquainted with both types of pleasures will prefer the former. Mill's argument on this topic, however, ultimately fails to convince.

one member of a family of theories—the family of all consequentialist theories at the widest level, but more narrowly, the family of all welfarist consequentialisms. These have in common that they are consequentialist (only consequences matter) and welfarist (only human well-being matters), but differ in how they compare individual levels of well-being. The easily understandable discomfort many feel about additive aggregation explains why alternatives have been explored. One such alternative, which remains welfare consequentialist but eschews additive aggregation, is the *Pareto criterion*, which says that:

> A state of affairs X is better than another state of affairs Y
> > if and only if
> nobody is worse off (has less well-being) in X than in Y, and at least one person is better off (has more well-being) in X than in Y.

This "better"-ness is called *Pareto superiority* or *Pareto dominance*. In the definition above, X is Pareto-superior (or Pareto-dominant) to Y, and Y is Pareto-inferior to (or Pareto-dominated by) X. In contrast, the utilitarian criterion says that a state of affairs X is better in utilitarian terms[80] than a state of affairs Y if and only if the *sum* of individual well-beings in X is greater than that in Y.[81] The practical importance of these definitions is that they determine what, concretely, welfarist consequentialism tells us to do, depending on which criterion we use.

Whereas utilitarianism commands actions that (most) increase the total sum of well-being—even if some people are made much worse off in the process—the Pareto criterion only commands actions that make *everyone* better off (or that make some people better off without making anyone worse off). If an action takes us from one state of affairs to another state of affairs that is Pareto-superior to the first—that is, it makes some people better off without making anyone worse off—such a move is called a *Pareto improvement*. (The opposite move is called a *Pareto worsening*.) Only actions that are Pareto improvements need be morally compulsory under a Pareto-based consequentialism.

It is clear that the Pareto criterion also encapsulates a notion of efficiency, albeit a different one from that of utilitarianism. Utilitarianism demands efficiency in this sense: It is not satisfied with outcomes where there is less total well-being in society than there could be. The Pareto criterion, however, only condemns outcomes in which *every* single individual could be made better off (or no worse off). This sense of efficiency—which is often used in economic analysis—can be defined formally:

> A state of affairs *Pareto-efficient*
> > if and only if
> there is no other available state of affairs that is Pareto-superior to it.

---

[80] An ugly but useful locution is "utilitarianly better."

[81] There could be many other criteria, each of which would generate a different form of welfarist consequentialism. For example, some may that a state of affairs is better than another if the individual levels of well-being are more *equal*.

Conversely, a state of affairs is Pareto-*inefficient* if there *is* a state of affairs (or more than one) that is Pareto-superior to it. These three formulations of the Pareto criterion—Pareto superiority, Pareto improvement, and Pareto efficiency—all describe the same idea. Their relationship to each other, and to the utilitarian criterion, is best shown graphically:

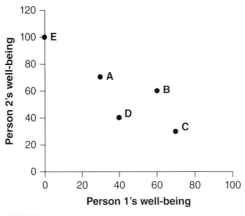

FIGURE 1

In Figure 1, each point illustrates a possible state of affairs in a world where only two people are affected by changes between these states. The axes measure the amount of well-being each person has in a state of affairs. In state A, person 1 has 30 units of happiness or well-being and person 2 has 70; in state C, the amounts are reversed; in state B both have 60 and in state D both have 40; and finally in state E person 2 has 100 and person 1 no well-being at all. It is plain to see that points A, B, C and E are all Pareto-efficient, since there are no states that are Pareto-superior to them—or put differently, no Pareto improvement is possible from any of them. Point D, in contrast, is Pareto-inefficient, because there *is* a state of affairs that Pareto-dominates it, namely B. Since D is Pareto-inferior to B, by definition D cannot be Pareto-efficient. This also means that an action that takes us from D to B is a Pareto improvement.

Between the four Pareto-efficient points, however, neither is Pareto-superior or inferior to another (this follows from the definition of Pareto efficiency, and is also clear from Figure 1). Note that even though D is Pareto-inefficient, it is *not* Pareto-inferior to A, C, or E (only to B); nor, of course, are they Pareto-superior to it. This general possibility is sometimes misunderstood. It is not enough to know that one state is Pareto-inefficient while the other is Pareto-efficient to conclude that the second is Pareto-superior—and therefore morally better, if the Pareto criterion is adopted—to the first. One may be neither superior nor inferior to the other: The two states may not be *Pareto-comparable*. The definition of Pareto superiority implies that two states are Pareto-noncomparable whenever some individuals are better off in the first than in the second, but others are better off in the second than in the first. Utilitarianism, in contrast, can in principle compare all possible states of affairs by ranking them according to the sum total of well-being they contain. Each point of Figure 1 is associated with the sum of well-beings to the two individuals. In state B, both get 60 for a total of 120, which is utilitarianly superior to A, C, and E, where the individual well-beings add up to 100. Worst from a utilitarian perspective is outcome D which yields a total of only 80 well-being units. This highlights the different notions of efficiency implicit in the two theories. While the Pareto criterion can only say that D is inefficient, utilitarianism says that anything but B is suboptimal.

It should be clear why the Pareto criterion is a tempting alternative to utilitarianism: It avoids sacrificing some people for the greater good of others by being silent on whether a change that hurts anyone at all is an improvement or not. A move that counts as an improvement in utilitarian terms may make some people worse off (as it does in the move from D to E, in which person 2 gains 60 but person 1 loses 40), and this, many would think, could be a morally significant objection to it. In a Pareto improvement, nobody is made worse off, so that objection does not apply. The Pareto criterion only says that the state of affairs improves when it lifts *everybody*'s well-being (or does not lower anyone's) and that it worsens when everybody's well-being goes down (or stays the same). When the Pareto criterion is expressed as a comparison between two states (superiority or improvement), therefore, it is a logically stricter requirement than the utilitarian criterion—more has to be true in order for it to be satisfied. It follows that showing an action to be a *utilitarian* improvement (such as a move from D to any of the other four points) is a less conclusive moral argument for it than establishing that it is a *Pareto* improvement (such as the move from D to B)—since the conditions for the former are less demanding than those for the latter (indeed, the latter entails the former). This makes the Pareto criterion more palatable to the intuition that utilitarianism offends—that it matters morally when some individuals have to pay the price for an "overall" improvement by becoming worse off. Some take this as far as thinking that there can be *no* persuasive objection to the Pareto criterion; after all, if an action benefits everyone (or at least makes no one worse off), what could be wrong with it?

On the other hand, as a component of a consequentialist moral theory, the Pareto criterion is much less helpful than additive aggregation, precisely because it recoils from making so many comparisons. To be Pareto-efficient, a state merely has to not be Pareto-dominated by anything else (A, B, C and E). In contrast, utilitarianism only counts a state of affairs as *the best* if there is no other achievable combination of individuals' well-being that would add up to more (only B is utilitarianly optimal in Figure 1). So (in contrast with the notions of superiority or improvement) Pareto efficiency is a logically *weaker* requirement than utilitarian efficiency or optimality. Indeed, utilitarian optimality entails Pareto efficiency (a utilitarianly optimal state of affairs is necessarily Pareto-efficient), but not the other way around. The Pareto criterion says nothing about what we ought to do if we must choose between Pareto-efficient states, of which there are typically a lot, making Pareto-based welfare consequentialism dramatically incomplete. It only helps us with the easy cases—those where we can benefit someone without hurting anyone else. But few moral dilemmas involve Pareto improvements; they will typically require choices between several Pareto-efficient outcomes (they would hardly be dilemmas otherwise). In those cases, utilitarianism provides guidance while the Pareto criterion is silent. And in cases where the Pareto criterion can advise us, its advice is weak; for the only thing a Pareto-efficient state has to commend it is that a form of waste has been eliminated (it is not possible to make anyone better off without making someone worse off). This could still leave extreme suffering in place (consider point E, which is Pareto-efficient), and if this suffering is morally objectionable that is not something the Pareto criterion can ever register.

ACT- AND RULE-CONSEQUENTIALISM

So far we have applied consequentialism to each individual action, asking whether it is the one (among all the available alternatives) that produces the most well-being: "What will happen if I do this now, and will that outcome be better than the consequences of other actions I could take?" Some consequentialist thinkers have suggested that assessing the consequences of each action individually is a mistake. The relevant moral question, they argue, is not "What will happen if I do this now?" but "What would happen if people *in general* or *usually* acted in this way when they found themselves in such circumstances?" This is still a consequentialist theory—it says that only consequences matter morally. But what makes an action right in this view is not whether its *own* consequences are the best possible, but whether it belongs to a general pattern of behavior which, when widely or universally adopted, has better consequences than alternative patterns of behavior. It is a form of consequentialism that formalizes the basic moral intuition parents instill in their children with the question: "What if everyone did that?"

This type of consequentialism is often called *rule-consequentialism* because it locates moral value in the moral consequences of following a "rule" of behavior—as opposed to *act-consequentialism*, the form we have analyzed until now, which situates moral value in the consequences of the specific act. This distinction—between the consequences of a single act and the consequences of a rule being generally followed—can be applied to every specification of consequentialism. So a rival to what we have called utilitarianism (which we could more precisely call act-utilitarianism) is *rule-utilitarianism*. Rule-utilitarianism says that we should act in such a way that, if everyone acted that way when faced with the same circumstances, more happiness (additively aggregated) would be enjoyed than if everyone generally chose one of the other available actions when facing the same circumstances.

Rule-utilitarianism will in some situations give very different answers from act-utilitarianism. Guidant's choice, we saw, allowed an (act-)utilitarian defense: The act of keeping the defect secret could reasonably be believed to lead to more well-being (less suffering) than the act of divulging it. But a rule-utilitarian may object by asking what the consequences would be if medical device companies routinely withheld information about defects in their products. Even if companies only did this in instances where they honestly thought secrecy would bring about the most well-being, a general practice of withholding potential information about defects would make the public distrust products even when they were not defective. This, in turn, could plausibly lead to fewer patients choosing to use a device at all, which would cause more deaths. For this reason, the overall consequences of the *regular practice* of keeping defects secret may well be more suffering than if information was always published. If so, rule-utilitarianism would consider this behavior morally wrong, even if in any specific instance divulging the information causes more suffering than keeping it secret, all else being equal. All else being equal is what rule-consequentialism does not assume. Instead it tells me to evaluate an action by the consequences that would follow if others (including myself on other occasions where I face similar circumstances) were to act the same way I envisage doing.

This must not be confused with a claim that my action *causes* others to act in the same way. Such a claim is not generally true—not because my action *cannot* cause similar actions in others (people copy each others' actions all the time, for good reasons or bad), but because they need not logically do so—and therefore cannot be taken as a premise to support the rule-consequentialist conclusion. An argument that said Guidant should have divulged the information because not doing so would lead other companies not to divulge their information (and the consequences of such a pattern of behavior would be bad) would be hostage to the very plausible possibility that Guidant's action did *not* cause others to do the same (it was, after all, meant to be a secret). This putative argument could only say that Guidant should publicize the information *if* not doing so would cause other companies not to do so either. Not only is that a less than forceful conclusion; it is also no different from many forms of act-consequentialism. Act-utilitarianism, for example, considers all effects on well-being, so it obviously also takes into account the possibility that others will copy Guidant and the consequences of a "chain effect" for the well-being of those affected by them.

Instead, rule-utilitarianism asks for the *hypothetical* consequences of an act becoming a universal practice, without assuming that it in fact will become one. The statement "if everyone did as Guidant did, more/less total well-being would come about" does not imply "everyone will do as Guidant did; as a result, more/less total well-being will come about." Even if Guidant's action has *no* effect on whether other companies do the same (which is not to deny that it might), rule-consequentialism says that what matters morally for whether Guidant was morally right or wrong is whether the consequences would be best if, hypothetically, other companies all acted in the same way.

Giving relevance to hypothetical rather than actual consequences is difficult to justify within a consequentialist framework. An action does not, after all, actually result in its hypothetical consequences. Some argue the difficulties cannot be overcome, and that rule-consequentialism is therefore untenable. We shall consider this problem in Chapter 7, where we address objections to utilitarianism and consequentialism generally. Here it is worth noting that if rule-consequentialism can be sustained, it offers an alternative foundation to role-relative ethics. We concluded in previous chapters that a theory of the virtues defended on conventionalist or relativist grounds is a flimsy justification of moral obligations and permissions derived from the internal logic of social roles and practices. Whether or not bribery is ever justified, for example, the fact that it is commonly practiced within a society does not by itself make it right. But rule-consequentialism provides an external criterion for judging the moral value of a widely adopted practice; namely, whether it produces better consequences than would any other widely adopted alternative practice. It provides, therefore, an answer to our question of what can morally justify a practice and its built-in notion of normative purpose, since convention cannot. In the case of Lockheed in Japan, the rule-consequentialist would compare the consequences of a widespread pattern of bribery with a social practice banning bribes. This would quite probably lead to the conclusion that Lockheed acted immorally.

If we can defend rule-consequentialism, we may be able to rescue the appeal to role morality in business (and other) ethics. Rule-utilitarianism, to take the most common form of rule-consequentialism, can be applied to the various role- and practice-relative obligations and permissions we considered in the previous two chapters. Our problem was that some roles involve social roles that seem morally unacceptable—and we cannot, on pain of circularity, distinguish roles, practices and conventions that are morally valid from those that are not by reference to other roles, practices and conventions. Rule-utilitarianism offers a way out of the circle by asking whether the practice in question—such as deceptive business practices—is one that, when universally adopted, produces a larger sum of well-being than could be had if some other practice were adopted instead. Albert Carr's conventionalist argument that business people may morally engage in deception because that is a social norm in business can be put to this rule-utilitarian test. Do people in a society where deception is commonly expected in business enjoy more well-being overall than they would in a society in which the social norm in business is for businesspeople to be honest? The "rules of business" that we ought to follow, says the rule-utilitarian, are those that bring the most well-being into the world if business people follow them, whether or not they are the way business is conventionally practiced. It seems highly unlikely that Carr's sweeping justification of deceptive business behavior could be sustained as the outcome of such an analysis.

In addition to analyzing consequentialism's general structure, we have dwelt at some length on its utilitarian specification as well as on its weaker welfare-consequentialist relative based on the Pareto criterion. Much more justificatory work has to be done to pick any one specification—without which the theory does not provide much practical guidance—and we have yet to seriously examine the many objections to consequentialism in general and utilitarianism in particular. Even so, it is plain that consequentialism provides a powerful method of moral analysis by narrowing down the kinds of considerations that are taken to have moral relevance and by definitively clarifying how, according to the theory, those considerations matter.

Summary of the Argument in This Chapter

The "purpose" built into conventional social practices—and the various normative implications, such as role obligations or permission, that flow from it—is not a sufficient foundation from which moral judgments could be defended, because it itself needs justification that convention cannot provide. The theory of *consequentialism* offers a promising external criterion against which conventions themselves can be assessed. At the most general level, consequentialism says that an action is morally right or wrong depending on how morally good its consequences are. Thus consequentialism is deeply committed to empiricism—to facts about the world. Even when consequences cannot be known with certainty, plausible consequentialist theories tell us to act so as to bring about the consequences we can *reasonably expect* to be the best.

What determines the precise commands of any consequentialist theory is how it defines the *goodness of consequences*. Its most influential form is *utilitarianism*, which says that the goodness of consequences amounts

to the quantity of well-being they bring to individuals, and that they are morally better the bigger is the sum total of well-being added up across individuals. In technical terms, utilitarianism is *welfarist consequentialism* with *additive aggregation*. Although, as we shall see, the objections to utilitarianism are formidable, it is a theory that holds great promise. It offers a determined method for establishing what is right; it eschews appeals to supernatural or religious authority; and it rests on a basic principle of benevolence which says that morality is about increasing human well-being. It also has a strong claim to rationality in the sense of *efficiency*; that is, it condemns letting any opportunities for human well-being go to waste.

Its definition of efficiency, however, has also been used against it, because it allows (indeed it requires) sacrificing one person's well-being if it contributes to a greater gain for others. Locating this controversial implication in the additive aggregation element of utilitarianism shows that we can rescue its other elements—consequentialism and welfarism—from the objection. An alternative welfarist consequentialism is based on the *Pareto principle* which ranks a state of affairs as morally superior to another only if *all* individuals enjoy more or as much well-being in the first as in the second. The Pareto principle also captures an intuitive value of efficiency—albeit a less demanding one that only requires that no opportunity for making *everyone* better off (or no one worse off) be wasted. This weaker claim allows Pareto-based consequentialism to sidestep the objection that utilitarianism sacrifices the one for the many. But it also weakens the reach of Pareto consequentialism's conclusions, since this theory cannot compare one outcome with another in which some individuals have more well-being than in the first but others have less.

In their act-consequentialist form, these theories evaluate each act by the goodness of its consequences. In their rule-consequentialist form, they judge each act by its conformity with rules of behavior which, in turn, are judged by the consequences of their general adoption. Rule-consequentialism, therefore, offers a way to bring role morality back into the justification of behavior. By asking whether a conventional social practice produces better outcomes than alternative social conventions would do, rule-consequentialism gives an answer to the question of which conventional social norms are morally justified. But whether in the act- or rule-consequentialist form, both utilitarianism and Pareto-based welfarist consequentialism offer possible foundations for a consequentialist business ethics similar to those at the heart of normative economics and cost-benefit analysis.

CHAPTER 6

Is Greed Good?
Advancing Society through Selfish Action

In the movie *Wall Street*, Michael Douglas gives an Oscar-winning performance as Gordon Gekko, a ruthless financier who buys inefficient companies, restructures them—often by firing workers—and strips the increased value from the company for great profit. In a famous scene, Gekko gives a rousing speech to the shareholders of the company Teldar Paper that persuades them to vote for his restructuring plan:

> In the last seven deals that I've been involved with, there were 2.5 million stockholders who have made a pretax profit of 12 billion dollars. [Applause from shareholders.] Thank you. I am not a destroyer of companies. I am a liberator of them!
>
> The point, ladies and gentlemen, is that greed—for lack of a better word—is good. Greed is right. Greed works. Greed clarifies, cuts through, and captures the essence of the evolutionary spirit. Greed, in all of its forms— greed for life, for money, for love, knowledge—has marked the upward surge of mankind. And greed—you mark my words—will not only save Teldar Paper, but that other malfunctioning corporation called the USA.

Wall Street is a morality tale, told from the perspective of Gekko's young apprentice Bud. Bud admires Gekko's success and soon begins to emulate his unscrupulous business practices—searching out inside information, and selling off the assets of failing companies at a profit, even as the employees lose their jobs. As in all morality tales, the villain gets his comeuppance: When Gekko tries to take apart Bluestar Airlines, where Bud's father has worked his entire life, Bud changes his ways and collaborates with a police sting operation that puts Gekko in jail.

But what if Gekko is right? His speech, though a caricature, expresses in extreme form a certain argument for why companies and their managers should single-mindedly increase shareholder value, no matter if it hurts other stakeholders such the workers at Bluestar. By claiming that "greed is good," Gekko attempts to forestall moral criticism. For if greed is indeed good; if greed "works"; if greed marks "the upward surge of mankind"—then how could there be anything immoral about corporate raids that hurt nonshareholder stakeholders so long as they increase profits?

This argument influences a great many discussions of how businesses ought to behave. When activists berate companies for putting "profits before people," a common response is that the actions result in greater social benefits. Profit maximization, it is said, creates economic progress through what the economist Joseph Schumpeter called "creative destruction" as it unsparingly replaces inefficient practices by better ones. We have here an argument against "doing good" whenever it comes at the cost of not "doing well"—it says that you in fact do the most good when you do well for yourself.

In a 2005 survey on Corporate Social Responsibility (CSR), *The Economist* magazine wrote:

> Companies today are exhorted to be 'socially responsible'. . . It will no longer do for a company to go quietly about its business, telling no lies and breaking no laws, selling things that people want, and making money. That is so passé. Today, all companies, but especially big ones, are enjoined from every side to worry less about profits and be socially responsible instead. . .
>
> The one thing that all the nostrums of CSR have in common is that they are based on a faulty—and dangerously faulty—analysis of the capitalist system they are intended to redeem . . . Simply put, advocates of CSR work from the premise that unadorned capitalism fails to serve the public interest. The search for profit, they argue, may be a regrettable necessity in the modern world, a sad fact of life if there is to be any private enterprise. But the problem is that the profits of private enterprise go exclusively to shareholders. What about the public good? Only if corporations recognize their obligations to society—to "stakeholders" other than the owners of the business—will that broader social interest be advanced. Often, governments can force such obligations on companies, through taxes and regulation. But that does not fully discharge the enlightened company's debt to society. For that, one requires CSR.
>
> This is wrong. The goal of a well-run company may be to make profits for its shareholders, but merely in doing that—provided it faces competition in its markets, behaves honestly and obeys the law—the company, without even trying, is doing good works. Its employees willingly work for the company in exchange for wages; the transaction makes them better off. Its customers willingly pay for the company's products; the transaction makes them better off also. All the while, for strictly selfish reasons, well-run companies will strive for friendly long-term relations with employees, suppliers and customers. There is no need for selfless sacrifice when it comes to stakeholders. It goes with the territory.
>
> Thus, the selfish pursuit of profit serves a social purpose. And this is putting it mildly. The standard of living people in the West enjoy today is due to little else but the selfish pursuit of profit. It is a point that Adam Smith emphasized in *The Wealth of Nations*: 'It is not from the benevolence of the butcher, the brewer, or the baker, that we expect our dinner, but from their

regard to their own interest.' This is not the fatal defect of capitalism, as CSR-advocates appear to believe; it is the very reason capitalism works.[82]

Put simply, the argument is this: When everyone aims for their own self-interested advantage, the combination of all their actions put together creates the best outcomes *for society* and not just for themselves. Therefore, companies may—indeed they should—focus only on maximizing profits or shareholder value. From the previous chapter, you will recognize this as a consequentialist argument, since it justifies the action in question (the self-interested pursuit of profits) by its consequences (the public good).

Notice how this argument differs from Milton Friedman's, even though it asserts the same conclusions. As we saw in Chapter 2, Friedman bases his conclusions primarily on the property rights of the shareholders and the proper role of government (though he does not underplay the alleged ill effects of corporate social responsibility). The consequentialist argument, on the other hand, makes no reference to these. It is because it is good for society that businesses ought to maximize profits, not because of some special rights that shareholders have.[83]

Like all consequentialist arguments, this one contains an empirical premise and a moral premise. We can write down the argument in stylized form as:

> **Moral premise (consequentialism):** We ought to choose the actions that produce the best effects for society.
> **Empirical premise:** Aiming exclusively at maximizing profits produces the best effects.
> **Conclusion:** Therefore, business people ought to aim exclusively at maximizing profits.

This is a powerful argument. It is clearly *valid*—if the premises are correct, then the conclusion necessarily follows. If it is also *sound* (*i.e.* if the premises are in fact true), it undermines all the criticism leveled against business leaders and corporations for not being kind, generous, or humane—in short, for not being "socially responsible." If we want to make such criticisms, we must show where this argument goes wrong. As it happens, it goes wrong in quite a few places, but in order to see where and why, we must carefully reconstruct the argument in detail.

AS IF BY AN INVISIBLE HAND

When capitalist society started to grow into its industrial form in the eighteenth century, it burst apart many of the pre-existing strictures on the economy. The creation of wealth quickly shifted into activities beyond the reach of royally sanctioned monopolies and traditional craft guilds, which in earlier historical phases had regulated who might

---

[82] *The Economist*, "The good company—Capitalism and ethics" (leader article), 22 January 2005.

[83] By now, we should recognize it as a strength that an argument makes no special claims for shareholders, since it would then have to justify why shareholders are special. The consequentialist argument values benefits to shareholders only instrumentally—as the most effective way to benefit society at large.

practice a trade and which prices they could charge. People worried that an economic system guided just by personal self-interest, without anything to regulate conduct for the public good, would both undermine virtue at the individual level and lead to chaos in the aggregate. The idea that uncoordinated self-interested action could advance the common interests of society was widely seen as paradoxical. Among those who explained the paradox was Adam Smith, the father of economic science and a professor at the University of Glasgow. Many people—including *The Economist*—attribute to Smith the argument we see in extreme form in Gordon Gekko's speech, though Smith never argued anything as simplistic as the thesis that "greed is good."[84] Of course, it does not matter for us whether Smith advanced the argument, but whether it holds water. To understand it well, however, it helps to examine what Adam Smith did in fact say.

Adam Smith's *An Enquiry into the Nature and Causes of the Wealth of Nations*, one of the greatest works written in economics, starts by pointing out how every person's "desire to better his own condition" (what we would call pursuing one's self-interest) gives us a natural "propensity to truck, barter, and exchange one thing for another." This sets the sense in which we must understand Smith's famous sentence:

> It is not from the benevolence of the butcher, the brewer, or the baker, that we expect our dinner, but from their regard to their own interest.[85]

Individuals who seek to promote their self-interest will choose to enter into economic transactions that benefit them. But to entice others into doing business with you, you must offer something that also advances *their* self-interest—not because you necessarily care about them, but to ensure that they will give you what you want. This means—to use the concept we developed in the previous chapter—that in a free market people need no other motivation to enter into *Pareto-improving* transactions than simply wanting to do well for themselves. To maximize their own advantage, they must exploit every available Pareto improvement, which brings them, by definition, to a Pareto-efficient situation.[86]

Unrestrained profit maximization leads to social benefits, then, in the sense of Pareto-efficient outcomes (at least under certain conditions, which we shall examine shortly). But we can say more. Profit-maximizing firms and individuals choose not just any Pareto-improving exchange, but the one that brings them the highest profits. They strive to buy their goods at the lowest price and sell their products or labor to the highest bidder. As a result, they allocate their resources and efforts to the most productive uses, and they distribute the goods and services that those resources produce to where they are in the highest demand—*i.e.* to those willing to pay the most for them. Therefore, if we measure the economic value of a product by the amount someone will pay for it, then when profit maximizers sell products to the highest bidders, they unintentionally bring it about that the products and services produced by society have the

---

[84] Smith was a professor of moral philosophy. In addition to his masterpiece on economics mentioned in the text, he wrote *A Theory of Moral Sentiments*, an important work on ethics and moral psychology.

[85] Adam Smith, *Wealth of Nations*, Book I, Chapter II.

[86] Recall that a situation is Pareto-efficient if no Pareto improvement from it is possible.

greatest economic value they possibly could. In short, they maximize social wealth. Smith describes it as follows:

> Every individual is continually exerting himself to find out the most advantageous employment for whatever capital he can command. It is his own advantage, indeed, and not that of the society, which he has in view. But the study of his own advantage, naturally, or rather necessarily leads him to prefer that employment which is most advantageous to the society . . . by directing that industry in such a manner as its produce may be of the greatest value, he intends only his own gain, and he is in this, as in many other cases, *led by an invisible hand to promote an end which was no part of his intention.* Nor is it always the worse for society that it was no part of it. By pursuing his own interest he frequently promotes that of the society more effectually than when he really intends to promote it.[87]

Modern economics has developed this insight in great detail and in much mathematical complexity, but the main point is simple. People will freely enter into arrangements that are to everyone's advantage (in the sense that they ensure Pareto efficiency and maximize society's wealth) without any direction or command from above, *or even any ethical motivation.* Self-interest alone can achieve this result, since the "invisible hand" of the market snatches morally desirable consequences from the jaws of self-interested behavior.

If consequentialism is true, it does not matter morally whether people *intend* the good consequences of their actions. As long as those consequences actually materialize (or are the most likely to materialize, when they cannot be predicted with certainty), they make the actions that caused them right. Arguing that companies ought only to aim for profits on the basis of Adam Smith's insights, therefore, appeals to actions' *unintended but foreseeable consequences* as a justification. Let us call this the *invisible hand argument for profit maximization.* Does the invisible hand argument actually deliver the moral conclusions that Gordon Gekko and *The Economist* expect? That depends, of course, on whether the invisible hand can actually do the moral work required of it. As we are about to see, it often does not.

WHY THE EMPIRICAL PREMISE IS OFTEN FALSE

From Adam Smith until today, economic science has not only shown how the individual pursuit of happiness can lead to socially good outcomes; it has also identified the conditions that must be fulfilled for that result to follow. These conditions are very demanding indeed, and this gives us good reason to doubt the invisible hand argument's empirical premise in many circumstances.

Externalities

In 1996, a group of Ecuadorean and Peruvian citizens, many of them indigenous people from the Amazon, sued the oil company Texaco for polluting the rain forest and the rivers in those countries. They brought the case to a U.S. court since they feared Ecuador's under-resourced and corruption-ridden judicial system would not grant the

---

[87] Smith, *Wealth of Nations*, Book I, Chapter II, italics added.

remedies that they sought. The U.S. judge, however, dismissed the case on grounds of *forum non conveniens*—Texaco had not committed any of the alleged acts inside the United States, so the judge ruled that U.S. courts did not have jurisdiction. As a result, Texaco's actions were likely never to be ruled illegal either in the United States or in the countries where they took place.[88] The judicial decisions, of course, make no difference to whatever actual harm Texaco's pollution had caused. During the two decades of Texaco's oil extraction in the Ecuadorean Amazon:

> Large tracts of forest were clear-cut to make way for [roads and pipelines . . .] Indian lands . . . were taken and bulldozed, often without compensation . . . the primary pipeline alone has spilled more than 16.8 million gallons of oil into the Amazon . . . production pits dump approximately 4.3 million gallons of toxic production wastes and treatment chemicals into the forest's rivers, streams, and groundwater each day . . . Significant portions of these spills have been carried downriver into neighboring Peru . . . Rivers and lakes were contaminated by oil and petroleum; heavy metals such as arsenic, cadmium, cyanide, lead, and mercury; poisonous industrial solvents . . . and other highly toxic chemicals. Health officials and community leaders report adults and children with deformities, skin rashes, abscesses, headaches, dysentery, infections, respiratory ailments, and disproportionately high rates of cancer.[89]

Did Texaco act immorally? Its actions were not ruled illegal by any court, and they presumably maximized the company's profits. (Just cleaning the production pits would have cost an estimated $600 million.) U.S. consumers who bought the oil also benefited from the transaction. Were we just to look at the producer and the consumer, like the basic invisible hand argument does, this would look like a Pareto improvement. But the victims of the pollution are obviously worse off than before, so in this case profit maximization did not lead to a Pareto improvement overall.

Pollution is the classic example of what economists call "externalities." Externalities are the effects of a production process on the well-being of "external" parties who did not agree to the transaction (the victims of Texaco's pollution, for instance).[90] In settings with externalities, the invisible hand of the market does not secure a Pareto-efficient result. If the parties deciding the transactions pursue their own self-interest only, they will ignore the well-being of the external parties, so a producer's action to maximize profits may make other parties worse off.[91] What is more, if the

---

[88] At the time of writing, a case is still languishing in Ecuadorean courts.

[89] These allegations are drawn from Denis G. Arnold's case study "Texaco in the Ecuadorean Amazon." Chevron, which has since taken over Texaco, denies responsibility for the damage.

[90] Externalities cause problems in consumption as well as production, but since businesses are more typically seen as producers than as consumers, we focus on production here. A consumption externality would be the effect that a consumption activity has on those not involved in the transaction that makes the consumption possible (that is, neither the consumer nor the seller). A typical example is CO_2-emissions from car driving.

[91] There could also be *positive* externalities—effects that improve the well-being of third parties. A typical example is national defense. A national army defends all citizens equally, regardless of whether they pay for it or not (this makes it a *public good* in the terminology of economics). Self-interested individuals have no incentive to pay their share voluntarily. In a market where everyone maximizes their individual self-interest, therefore, national defense would be underprovided, which is Pareto-inefficient since all would be better off with national defense financed by compulsory taxation. This resembles the coordination problems discussed later in the chapter.

outcome of free exchange is not Pareto-efficient, it will also not maximize society's wealth measured by willingness to pay.

Information Problems

Even if a transaction between you and me affects only the two of us and no external parties, each needs to know *how* it affects us to make sure we are making the decision that actually benefits us. But we can rarely know for sure whether we are getting a good deal for ourselves. We can rarely obtain *complete* information about the product we are about to purchase or the job we are about to accept, and buyers and sellers often have different information. Therefore, even self-interested people sometimes enter transactions that are bad for them because they wrongly think they will benefit; or they turn down transactions that would be mutually beneficial, because they do not know this for sure.

The economist George Akerlof analyzed such situations in a famous article[92] on markets for "lemons" (low-quality used cars). If a used car buyer cannot distinguish between lemons and "peaches" (high-quality used cars), he will take into account the risk that the car could turn out to be a lemon—and only accept a price below what he would pay if he knew for sure that the car was a peach. But sellers of peaches, who know how good their cars are, will not want to sell at such a low price. They would rather pull out of the market. Then only lemons would be sold, even though there would be buyers who would buy peaches at a price that sellers would accept—if they could only be sure that it was a peach they had bought.

The problem is not, of course, confined to used cars. A big problem in the 2008–2009 global financial crisis was lack of confidence in banks because of their holdings of "toxic" assets backed by U.S. subprime mortgages, whose worth no one knew for sure. Before the crisis, billions of dollars had been wagered on assets that were so complex and based on such flimsy (and sometimes false) information that their riskiness completely disappeared from view—an example of how flawed information can encourage Pareto-nonimproving transactions—until it suddenly brought the entire world economy to its knees. Once the impenetrability of mortgage-backed securities became clear, the private market for securitized loans collapsed completely, just as Akerlof's model predicts.

Lack of information, therefore, makes Pareto-efficiency less likely. This in itself invalidates the empirical premise of the invisible hand argument. Moreover, it points to an important *economic* role of ethics. In situations like the used-car market or the securitized loan market, trade can be inhibited because the buyer cannot observe the quality of the product *and cannot trust the seller to be truthful about it*. Otherwise, the buyer could simply ask the seller how good the car is or whether the mortgage borrowers have reliable incomes. But if the seller is acting purely out of self-interest, he cannot be trusted when he talks up the car or the financial asset. This illustrates a general point: distrust weakens the invisible hand's ability to advance the public good. The more people generally act on moral motivations and not merely in their self-interest, the easier it will be to sustain a background of trust and the Pareto-improving trades it facilitates.

---

[92] George A. Akerlof, "The Market for 'Lemons': Quality Uncertainty and the Market Mechanism," *Quarterly Journal of Economics*, 84(3), 1970, pp. 488–500.

Cooperation and Commitment Problems

Some argue that firms cannot possibly survive if they do not focus only on profits. If this is true—if Gekko is right—the moral discussion may seem pointless, since after all, nobody can be morally required to do the impossible. In response, the economist Robert Frank has shown that not only can firms survive even if they have other goals beyond profits, but that, in fact, such firms may do better than purely profit-maximizing firms, even in terms of profitability.

To understand this paradox, Frank draws on two famous models from game theory. In a *Prisoner's Dilemma* two bank robbers have been caught with guns on the street, but no witnesses can identify them. If prosecutors cannot make them confess, they will send both to jail for three years for criminal gun possession, rather than the stricter fifteen-year-sentence for armed robbery. As the prisoners sit isolated in separate holding cells, the investigator offers each of them the following deal: Whoever gives testimony against the other will have his sentence reduced by three years. This means that if one prisoner accepts the deal and the other does not, the one who talks will walk free while the other will get fifteen years. If neither talks, they will both go to jail for three years, while if they both talk, they will both get twelve years. They have to make their decisions simultaneously without being able to communicate with or knowing what the other is going to do. The payoff matrix could look like this (with player 1's payoffs first):

		Prisoner 2	
		Don't talk	Talk
Prisoner 1	Don't talk	(−3, −3)	(−15, 0)
	Talk	(0, −15)	(−12, −12)

You may recognize this as a model of negative externalities—talking adds twelve years to the other prisoner's term while reducing one's own by three. A prisoner looking at his situation in purely selfish terms will see that he does better from collaborating with the prosecution than he does from staying silent, whatever the other robber does. This gives each robber a reason to testify against the other. What complicates the "game" is the strategic interdependence of the two players' decisions. They must choose between a "cooperative" action (staying silent) and a "noncooperative" action (talking), and each player does better in self-interested terms by not cooperating with each other, no matter what the other does. But if both parties cooperate with each other, they are both better off than if they both fail to cooperate. They jointly benefit, that is, if they can overcome the externalities they impose on each other and coordinate on the cooperative action (staying silent). But why would a purely self-interested player cooperate, since it is *always* selfishly better not to—at least if the encounter happens only once?[93]

Players with ethical motivations, beyond self-interest, will do better. Suppose, improbably, that the two robbers believe in utilitarianism and think it wrong to hurt other people's well-being significantly for the sake of a small gain to themselves (ignore how

---

[93] In a repeated encounter, players may gradually come to a tacit or explicit understanding to cooperate with each other, and it would better for each to abide by this understanding, since the other party will surely respond to noncooperation by not cooperating in turn.

they justify the robbery itself on utilitarian grounds). They would both play "Don't talk" and end up with $(-3, -3)$, better than two players who aim to maximize their individual self-interest—*even* in purely selfish terms! If economic transactions take the form of one-shot Prisoners' Dilemmas, a population of altruists achieves more well-being for all than a population of selfish maximizers, in contradiction to the empirical premise of the invisible hand argument.

Frank's second illustration points to *commitment problems*, where it benefits everyone that one player commits to a certain action in the future, but once the time comes, that player will gain most from breaking the commitment. Imagine a hostage-taker who gets cold feet and wants to release his hostage rather than kill her. But he would rather kill her than be caught by the police. The hostage, of course, prefers to go free, but most of all she wants to go free *and* see her hostage-taker in jail. This can be formalized as follows (with the hostage-taker's payoff first):

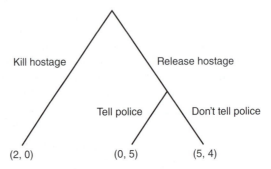

Suppose both the hostage-taker and his hostage always pursue their self-interest. Then if the hostage is freed, she will tell the police where the hostage-taker is. Predicting this, the best option for the hostage-taker given the hostage's future action is to kill her. But both would prefer the outcome where the hostage goes free and does not tell the police. Surely she should promise not to tell the police—and if her promise is *credible*, he will let her go. But making a promise and keeping it are two different things. In this situation, she will not in the end want to *keep* the promise she wants to make. If the hostage-taker knows this, he will not believe her promise, for someone who acts only out of self-interest cannot credibly commit to an action that is not in her self-interest when she has to carry it out. Ethical motivation offers a solution to this commitment problem. Imagine a hostage who does not always aim for her self-interest, and whose strong sense of honor makes her think she ought to keep her word even when she would benefit from breaking it. If the hostage-taker sees this, then she can credibly promise ("my word of honor") not to reveal his whereabouts, and he would then prefer to let her go. Like in a Prisoner's Dilemma, both parties benefit *in selfish terms* when pure self-interest is not their sole motivation.

These are theoretical arguments, but real examples of such situations arise in business all the time. Consider a possible solution that readily presents itself to the "market for lemons" problem: The seller of a peach can offer the buyer a money-back guarantee. Since it is in fact a good car, the seller will not have to make good on the guarantee, and the buyer knows that a seller with a lemon would not offer it. Therefore, he would willingly offer a price high enough to satisfy the seller and realize the Pareto-improving exchange. But notice that this is a commitment problem, for it requires the seller to commit to giving the money back in the future should the buyer wish so. But if the seller is purely self-interested, he will not want to make good on the guarantee should it ever come to that—so he cannot credibly commit.

Frank gives other examples of coordination and commitment problems in business:

- Commitment problems with employees occur in the context of production that cannot be monitored (where there is an incentive to shirk), compensation by piece rates (where the firm has an incentive to reduce the rates as productivity increases), career lock-in (where employees' firm-specific skills make it difficult to get other jobs), rising wage profiles (where employers have an incentive to replace older workers by younger), and other implicit, but legally unenforceable agreements.

- Commitment problems with customers occur when the consumers know less about the product than vendors. Typical examples are used cars and medical services. A customer or patient who suspects that a salesman or provider is just pursuing his self-interest might refrain from engaging in transactions that would benefit both.

- Commitment problems with other firms occur, for example, for subcontractors who incur costs to tailor their business to a particular client (who can then threaten to stop buying in an attempt to negotiate lower prices), in the case of asymmetric information (such as in markets for lemons), or in the sharing of confidential information.

In such strategic interactions, people whose motivations go beyond self-interest have a way of overcoming the inefficiencies that can result from abstaining from transactions. Paradoxically, they may therefore do better—even in selfish terms—than self-interested people. In these kinds of situations, therefore, we have reason to doubt the empirical premise of the invisible hand argument, which says that selfishly motivated actions produce the best outcomes.

We should note a subtlety here. The reasoning we have just pursued does not say that business should restrain profit maximization because such restraint in the end maximizes profits, as in the adage that "honesty is the best policy." The point is that there are situations where *having self-interest as your motive* will frustrate your ability to realize your own interests. Put the other way around, there are situations where you benefit the most if your benefit is not what motivates you. Recall the hostage-taking case. Promising can only solve the commitment problem if the hostage-taker believes that the hostage is motivated to keep her promise once she has to make good on it. How can he be reassured? He will be reassured if he believes that she wants to keep the promise *for its own sake*, that is, even if it were to go *against* her self-interest.[94] He will be reassured, in other words, if he believes she has a *moral* motivation to keep her promise. So it is in her self-interest to make the hostage-taker believe that she is motivated by other things than self-interest (such as keeping promises for their own sake). Now, she will probably find this much easier if she does in fact have moral motivations, for human beings are surprisingly good at recognizing one another's motives. As we

---

[94] Alternatively, external institutions can sometimes do the job (for example, legal punishments for not fulfilling contracts) as can reputational considerations (breaking a promise may make people distrust you in the future, to your detriment). But even if they improve matters, they will rarely be sufficient to produce the socially *best* outcome. We discuss this next.

quickly notice when we think about people we encounter in our own lives, we usually have a good sense of who is trustworthy and who is selfish. Scientific experiments confirm that people are capable of recognizing the motivations even of strangers—for example, they are very good at predicting who will cooperate in one-shot Prisoner's Dilemmas.[95] There is all reason to believe that the same is true in business encounters.

We can see now how all this applies to business. A morally motivated company is one that sometimes restrains profit maximization because it thinks that is the right thing to do, not just because it hopes that "doing the right thing" will ultimately bring the lost profit back (it may hope for this and it may come true, but this is not the only reason why it acts in this way). In Prisoner's Dilemmas and commitment problems, firms that have genuinely moral motivations in addition to the profit motive are more likely (because of the transparency of motivation) to succeed, even in terms of profits, than firms which aim only for profits. A company's values can bring it greater returns—if it holds the values for their own sake and not for the greater returns they may bring.

In these situations, then, it is not true that if all companies focus just on maximizing their profits, the socially best outcome in terms of Pareto efficiency or social wealth (nor, indeed, in terms of company wealth) will result.

The Role of Government

We have identified a number of situations in which the invisible hand may get it wrong, including externalities, incomplete information, and cooperation and commitment problems. We could list more. Now, for each of these failures, the proponents of the invisible hand argument may make two counterclaims, one empirical and one moral. The empirical counter is that governments can mitigate each of the situations that create problems for the invisible hand. This is true. Governments can address externalities through taxes, subsidies and regulations that give companies incentives to "internalize" the externalities. They can remedy the information problem by requiring certain forms of disclosure or by securing information themselves, for example through performance tests of products. And as we mentioned earlier, the government substitutes for honesty and honor as sources of trust with contract law and the judicial system. If you know that your counterparty will be fined or thrown in jail if he double-crosses you, you can "trust"—in an amoral sense—that he will keep up his end of the bargain as long as it is backed by a legal contract (unless it is more costly for him to do so than to take or try to avoid the legal punishment). The moral counterclaim is that not only *can* the government address these problems, it *ought* to do so; addressing them, we may say, is its role. ("Role" here must, of course, be understood in the moral sense that we discussed in Chapter 3.) Since we focus on the duties of business, we shall not go too deeply into the question of what governments ought to do, but our discussion of role obligations suggests that one duty of government is to create the institutions conducive to economic efficiency and prosperity. For the purposes of this discussion, we shall take this as given.

But both counterclaims are beside the point insofar as we are discussing what *businesses* as opposed to governments ought to do. Recall our reasoning so far. The

---

[95] Robert H. Frank, T. Gilovich, and D. Regan, "The Evolution of One-Shot Cooperation," *Ethology and Sociobiology* 14 (July 1993), 247–56.

invisible hand argument justifies unrestrained profit maximization on the grounds that profit maximization has unintended, but reliable, consequences that are good for society. What we have shown is that in many cases, these consequences do not reliably follow; indeed they are likely not to follow. The obvious consequentialist conclusion is that companies should *not* maximize profit in such cases. Claims such as "it's the government's job" or "we don't make the laws" attempt to forestall that conclusion. But such attempts must fail, for three reasons.

The first is simple: It may be the government's job to address market failures, but sometimes it does not do its job or does not do it well. When both the market fails and the government fails to correct it, unrestrained profit maximization is not good for society. It was the Ecuadorean government's job to make Texaco internalize the cost of its pollution. But that did not make Texaco's spills any less harmful once they happened. Whether the consequentialism of the invisible hand argument justifies unrestrained profit maximization does not depend on what the government *should* do—only on what the government does in fact do. There may be moral reasons why companies need not prevent the harmful effects of profit maximization even when the government fails to do so—but it cannot be that it is better for society that they do not.

Second, suppose the government does regulate optimally. Regulation requires resources for analysis, decision making, and enforcement, all of which cost money. This means that optimal regulation will never be complete regulation. In some instances where profit-maximizing behavior does not lead to Pareto-efficient or wealth-maximizing outcomes, the cost of the regulation needed to change this would outweigh the gains. In those instances, the invisible hand argument fails to justify profit maximization without concern for the social costs. Furthermore, even when the government does use costly regulation to correct the social outcomes of profit-maximizing behavior, that is itself a negative consequence of such behavior. For example, we said that contracts can create trust among purely self-interested people. But contracts require a system of enforcement to have the right motivational force. This costs money—paid through taxes (to pay for courts, police, and prison) or directly (lawyers' fees). When people are motivated by moral reasons as well as self-interest, however, this cost may be lower since the government does not need to provide as much enforcement. So the existence of widespread ethical motivations to fulfill one's commitments—and the trust that this sustains—in fact improves social outcomes relative to a world where only the threat of legal sanction motivates people to comply.

The third reason is that how business behaves itself affects government policy. Some actions that companies can take—lobbying is the most obvious—directly influence how the government interferes with their pursuit of profits. Sometimes, those actions make government policy less effective in correcting market failures; indeed, that is precisely their point. It is evident that *these* actions of business, however profit-maximizing they may be, cannot be justified by the invisible hand argument if they themselves undermine the link between individual self-interest and the public good.

WHY THE MORAL PREMISE IS FALSE

We have discussed many circumstances where the empirical premise of the invisible hand argument fails. But in many other circumstances it holds. A proponent of the invisible hand argument can, therefore, concede everything we have said so far, and still maintain that when the empirical premise *does* hold, it is right for business to aim sole-ly at maximizing profits. To know whether the premise holds in any particular industry or market, we would need a thorough empirical investigation that we cannot pursue here. (But a proponent of the invisible hand argument would have to do so, since he as-serts the empirical premise as true.) Instead, we turn our attention to the *moral* premise, for if the moral premise is implausible, then the invisible hand argument fails even in the circumstances most favorable to the empirical premise.

Let us for a moment set aside our doubts about the empirical conditions, and as-sume it to be a fact that individual profit maximization leads to socially beneficial con-sequences. How impressive is this fact, morally speaking? That depends crucially on what exactly we pack into the term "socially beneficial consequences." Proponents of the invisible hand argument frequently leave this unclear, but we can most plausibly in-terpret "best for society" in one of three ways—as Pareto efficiency, as maximum social wealth, or as the utilitarian optimum.[96] Of these criteria, the easiest to satisfy is Pareto efficiency, so we begin our analysis with that.[97]

In general, many possible Pareto-efficient outcomes exist. Here are two: I own all the wealth in the world, and everyone else is miserable; or *you* own all the wealth in the world, and everyone else is miserable. Both are Pareto-efficient because no one can be made better off without making someone else worse off (me, in the first case; you, in the second case). But so what? There does not seem to be much *morally good* about either of these situations. Is the fact that any change will somewhat hurt the one who has every-thing any reason for leaving everyone else miserable? The appeal of the Pareto criterion flows from the idea that a Pareto-*inefficient* situation is morally defective. Since *everyone's* well-being could be improved (or at least not reduced), Pareto inefficiency is *wasteful*, and to waste potential well-being for no reason rightly feels ethically unsatisfactory or even sadistic. But the fact that every Pareto-*inefficient* situation is morally unsatisfactory does not make every Pareto-*efficient* situation morally satisfactory. Indeed, some Pareto-inefficient situations may be morally superior to some Pareto-efficient ones. Recall the environmental damage that Texaco's operations caused in Ecuador. Once the damage is done, there may be no way of making the victims better off without making Texaco worse off. Now imagine that the judge had forced Texaco to clean up the damage. That exact decision may well have turned out Pareto-*in*efficient (both Texaco and the plaintiffs may have preferred a different form of punishment, such as monetary compensation in-stead of environmental restitution). But even a Pareto-inefficient decision against Texaco could conceivably have been morally preferable to the Pareto-efficient *status quo*.

The point here is that the Pareto criterion does not take us very far, even if a Pareto improvement is a good thing in most circumstances. No matter if the single-minded pursuit of self-interest produces a Pareto-efficient outcome, we could reach a *different* outcome by acting differently, and this other outcome (Pareto-efficient or not) could

---

[96] Virtually all uses of the invisible hand argument outside of the philosophical literature refer to one of these three consequentialist criteria. Still, one could consider different criteria than these, as we remarked in the previous chapter. An alternative consequentialist defense of profit maximization could, perhaps, fare better against the reflections presented here.

[97] Recall that a utilitarian optimum is necessarily Pareto-efficient, but not every Pareto-efficient state is a util-itarian optimum. The same is true if we substitute "social wealth maximization" for "utilitarian optimum," at least if we ignore noneconomic contributions to well-being.

well be morally superior to the one we reach through our self-interested actions. Morally speaking, therefore, the Pareto criterion simply does not do much to justify unrestrained profit maximization. Nor does the social wealth criterion. Profit maximization may be instrumental to generating the largest possible amount of wealth in society; whether this is a morally attractive outcome, however, surely depends on how that wealth benefits people. But neither the Pareto criterion nor the wealth maximization criterion pay any attention to the *distributive* consequences of economic transactions, to the question, that is, of who should get how much of the surplus that is generated. Most of us, however, think that distributive effects are morally highly important. (Chapter 11 discusses distributive justice at length.)

Now if, instead, we could show that the pursuit of self-interest leads not just to a Pareto-efficient or social wealth-maximizing outcome, but to a utilitarian optimum, we would have a much more powerful argument.[98] Utilitarianism does care about who gets what: In the utilitarian optimum, goods and resources are allocated to where they generate the most well-being. But the utilitarian optimum is exceedingly unlikely to be achieved if all market participants look only to their self-interest, for the following reason. Profit maximizers sell their goods and services to those willing to pay the most for them. Their actions maximize *willingness to pay* in society. They only maximize overall *well-being*, however, if willingness to pay and well-being track each other systematically—in other words, if those who pay more for a product also *enjoy* it more that those who offer less. But this is quite unrealistic in a society with economic inequality. Compare how much two different individuals are willing to pay for a loaf of bread: One is Bill Gates, the other is a homeless man. Bill Gates would be willing to pay much more for the loaf of bread than the homeless person. But this in no way indicates that the loaf would do more for Bill Gates's well-being than it would for the homeless person's. When some people are richer than others, the money they will pay for something reflects not only or even mainly the well-being they expect to get from it, but also what they are able to pay. After all, nobody can effectively be willing to pay more for what they want than they can afford. Therefore, economic demand is an unreliable measure of well-being when wealth is highly unequally distributed.[99]

This brings us to the following observation about the invisible hand argument. It is only sound if *both* premises are true, which in turn depends on the exact consequentialist criterion we choose. If by "good consequences" we mean a Pareto-efficient or wealth-maximizing outcome, then the empirical premise is more likely to hold than if

---

[98] There are many criticisms of the utilitarian criterion as well. We address them in the next chapter.

[99] Here are two complications. One may counter that Bill Gates is so rich because he contributed something to society that increased overall well-being enormously. Therefore (so the argument would go) the loaf does contribute more to overall well-being when it goes to him, if we count it as having "bought" a part of Gates's creativity. But this argument does not work, because it assumes that Bill Gates's money does in fact reflect the well-being his work has generated in society. That is precisely what is in dispute here, so the "counterargument" is circular. Another complication is the converse of the situation considered in the main text—where self-interested behavior maximizes social wealth and precisely for this reason falls short of a utilitarian optimum. We have already said that the conditions for the pursuit of self-interest to maximize social wealth frequently fail. When they do, can we hope that purely self-interested behavior will produce the utilitarian optimum *instead*? The answer is no. When the invisible hand fails, it will probably not even produce a Pareto-efficient outcome, let alone a utilitarian one. By odd coincidences, such outcomes could occasionally result, but not as a systematic tendency that could justify systematic profit maximization.

we mean a utilitarian optimum. But Pareto efficiency or wealth maximization are underwhelming moral criteria, for the reasons listed earlier. Utilitarianism, on the other hand, is a much more plausible moral criterion; but under that criterion, the empirical premise most probably does not hold. So not only are both premises dubious on their own merits even under the most generous interpretations, but the interpretation that makes the moral premise more plausible makes the empirical premise less likely to hold, and vice-versa.

We finish with one more reason to reject the moral premise, which is that if it is true, the invisible hand argument proves too much. For consider the premise again: Business should act in ways that produce the best consequences for society. This consequentialist justification of maximizing profits comes at the price of condemning actions that do *not* maximize profits. It is an essential part of the consequentialist view that rightness simply means having the best consequences, and any action with less-than-the-best-possible consequences is immoral (*how* immoral depends on how far the consequences fall short of the optimal ones). But this is presumably much more than the advocates of profit maximization bargained for. As moral philosopher Waheed Hussain has pointed out, it entails that even if shareholders *wanted* their company to sacrifice profits to other goals, it would be *wrong* to do so. Milton Friedman, as we recall, never goes that far; in basing his argument for profit maximization on property rights, he allows that companies ought to do whatever the owners want (typically to maximize profits, but not necessarily). The consequentialist argument offers no such latitude. If companies should maximize profits because that leads to the consequences morality requires us to pursue, then it must be wrong of us not to maximize profits, whether or not we want to. It must be wrong, for example, for a nonprofit corporation such as the Metropolitan Museum of Art not to maximize profits. Most advocates of the invisible hand argument do not believe this; but their argument, if the empirical premise holds, logically commits them to it.[100]

Since it does not generally hold, they may be spared from that bizarre conclusion—which would morally condemn nonprofit corporations and *pro bono* work except when companies do them just for profit's sake. Instead, consequentialists must accept the following conclusion, stated in a conditional form: If unrestrained profit maximization does *not* lead to the best outcomes for society, then business ought morally to act in other ways, namely in the ways that do lead to the best outcomes, whatever they may be, and even if this comes at a great cost to profit. The consequentialist argument entails, for example, that when Texaco planned its operations in Ecuador, it had a moral duty not to maximize profit—which in this case would not produce the best outcome for society—but rather advance the well-being of everyone affected by the project. This could have meant not drilling for oil at all, or to do so in a way that was much more protective of the environment and the local population than the government required—and much less profitable.

We end up, therefore, with the original argument rather turned on its head. What looked like an argument for profit maximization instead turns out in many cases to be an argument for "corporate social responsibility" even when social responsibility

---

[100] Waheed Hussain develops this argument in his "Profit Maximization and the Boundary Problem" (unpublished manuscript, University of Pennsylvania/Wharton School, Philadelphia, PA), from which the example of the Metropolitan Museum of Art is also borrowed.

means lower profits. This may come as a relief to supporters of CSR, but it is clearly not what the proponents of the invisible hand argument intended. And it is, in any case, not a sound argument for CSR if, as we argued above, the moral premise is false.

Our reasoning in this chapter does not mean that companies do wrong in maximizing profit, even to the exclusion of every other motive. We have simply demonstrated how implausible the *premises* of the invisible hand argument are (and how implausible it is that both premises should be true simultaneously). We cannot say that its *conclusion* is incorrect, only that it is unproven. What we have shown is that, if companies are indeed justified in aiming to maximize profits in all legal ways, it cannot always be because of the good consequences for society.

Summary of the Argument in This Chapter

The *invisible hand argument* is the most common justification for profit maximization in popular culture and policy debate. The invisible hand argument says that because profit maximization by firms produces the best outcome for society, it is morally right, and perhaps even morally required, of business to focus only on increasing its own profit. Like all consequentialist arguments, the premises of the invisible hand argument can be separated into two different assertions. The *empirical* premise states that when all economic actors pursue their self-interest, the combination of their actions produces the overall best possible outcome. The *moral* premise—consequentialism—states that one ought morally to pursue the action that has the best overall consequences.

The invisible hand argument fails as an argument for single-minded profit maximization because neither the empirical premise nor the moral one is tenable. The empirical premise is only true under very strict conditions, which may hold exceptionally but not generally. When they do not hold—in situations of market failure or strategic interaction—the invisible hand argument turns into an argument *against* maximizing profits, in favor of whatever action produces the best overall consequences.

The government may intervene to solve market failures, but when it does not or will not, consequentialism calls for acting in non-selfish ways—or it would, if the moral premise were true.

But the moral premise will not be true, at least not on the three specifications we have considered of the consequentialist criterion. If the "overall best outcome" means any Pareto-efficient outcome, the moral premise is unacceptable, for it seems that Pareto-efficient situations can be morally deficient if they involve extreme suffering by some which can be remedied by making someone who is very well off a little worse off. The stronger criterion of social wealth maximization is also unpersuasive, since it ignores how maximizing social wealth affects human well-being. In contrast, the utilitarian criterion, which directly evaluates outcomes by how much human well-being they generate, is a more promising moral premise. But even in its utilitarian specification, the invisible hand argument falls short. One the one hand, if by "the overall best outcome" we mean the utilitarian optimum, generalized profit maximization is highly unlikely to achieve it. On the other hand, even if it did, the utilitarian criterion also suffers from grave problems, to which we now turn.

CHAPTER 7

Consequentialist Complications
Sacrificing One for the Many

It is easy to be seduced by the analytical power and elegance of consequentialism in general and of utilitarianism in particular. But as we concluded in the previous chapter, their ability to justify self-interested profit maximization by its tendency to lead to the most efficient outcomes hinges on the truth of that questionable empirical premise. If it is false, then welfare-consequentialist apologies for profit maximization may turn into their opposites, namely justifications of profit-reducing "corporate social responsibility"—provided, that is, that consequentialism's *moral* premise is true and that we ought indeed to act in such ways as to achieve the best consequences. It is now time to ask whether that moral premise, in its various incarnations, is indeed true.

Consequentialist arguments are generally *deductive*: They start from the most abstract moral premise—morality requires us to bring about good outcomes—to logically derive concrete conclusions in specific cases. Most counterarguments to consequentialist ethics, in contrast, begin *inductively*. They identify situations where the consequentialist logic produces conclusions that contradict our most fundamental and seemingly indisputable intuitive moral judgments. Such cases—and what we must conclude from them about the prospect of a satisfactory consequentialist theory of business ethics—are the subject of this chapter.

A TROLLEY PROBLEM AND A HOSPITAL CASE: TWO DIFFICULTIES FOR UTILITARIANISM

Here is a classic thought experiment in moral philosophy. A runaway trolley is hurtling down a railway track on which five people are trapped who will be killed by the trolley unless you push a lever that redirects the trolley down a sidetrack. But on the sidetrack one other person is trapped, and if you redirect the trolley, it will kill him instead. What should you do? If you share the moral intuitions of most people, you will answer one of two things. Either you think you ought to push the lever, causing the one person to die to rescue the five. Or you think, at the very least, that you are morally permitted to push the lever, although you may not have an obligation to do so. Very few think it is morally *wrong* to push the lever and redirect the trolley. And on both utilitarian and broader consequentialist reasoning, it is easy to justify these intuitions: Saving five lives is better than saving one—or seen from a more sinister perspective, causing one person's death is better than letting five people die.

But now consider this: Many otherwise healthy people have critical organ failure and would live good lives for many years if they could have an organ transplant. Most often, however, there are not enough organs donated for all who need them. Now, suppose you know that there are five people on a certain hospital's organ transplant ward, each one needing a different organ. They are all in a critical state and will not survive long, but if they can have a transplant within a few hours, they will all recover and, as far as we can predict, go on to live long and happy lives. If you kill a healthy person and harvest his organs, this will save the five others who would otherwise die. Most people would think this action horrific. But why may you not do it? Why, in fact, do you not have a *duty* to do it, if five lives are better than one as the Trolley Problem suggested, and as the utilitarian accounting for Trolley Problem intuitions would explicitly endorse? Conversely, if it is wrong to kill someone for his organs, how could it be right (or permissible) to divert the trolley in the Trolley Problem if the choices are substantially the same in the two cases as far as their consequences go?

These examples may strike one as fanciful. But the exaggerated moral stakes with which they confront us help clarify what is significant in analogous, if less momentous, moral dilemmas that occur in everyday life—including in business. By identifying what it is about these two thought experiments that utilitarian moral reasoning struggles to make sense of, we can learn something about utilitarianism's adequacy in less drastic situations. The cases expose two problems with the utilitarian approach. The first relates to the disturbing fact that an action leading to the most overall well-being may make some people worse off—sometimes *much* worse off. In such cases, utilitarianism permits— in fact, it requires—sacrificing those people for the sake of the greater good.[101] The issue here is not so much whether, in doing so, utilitarianism is correct or mistaken (although the answer to that clearly matters enormously). The problem is that utilitarianism is quite happy to sacrifice one for the many *without further justification*. From the utilitarian (or any consequentialist) point of view, the greater good is all the justification that we need, because it is all the justification that can be had. But this entirely misses what troubles us so much about the Hospital Case. Explaining exactly what is wrong about sacrificing the involuntary organ donor requires reasoning which we will develop over the next few chapters, but we can at least begin by noting that however the answer is elaborated, it must involve a claim that killing a person for his organs is to *treat him unfairly*— even though it results in a greater good. It fails to treat that person as someone whose individuality is a matter of moral importance, and whose interests and well-being have a claim to respect that is separate from the interests of other people or from some aggregated "social well-being." In particular, utilitarianism has no room for the notion that we must be able to defend the way we treat him not merely in the abstract, but in a way that justifies his treatment *to him*. Nor does it comprehend the notion that this cannot be

---

[101] Dostoyevsky's *Crime and Punishment* is, in part, a literary exploration of utilitarianism taken to such extremes.

done by blithely viewing his well-being in a way he cannot: that is to say, as perfectly substitutable with the well-being of someone else, so that any well-being enjoyed by him is dispensable if more can be enjoyed by others.

Second, utilitarianism cannot, it seems, make sense of the moral *difference* we perceive between the Hospital Case and the Trolley Problem. Few would question that the killing in the Hospital Case is wrong, but it seems much easier to doubt whether this logically commits us to the position that pulling the lever in the Trolley Problem is also wrong. If we accept utilitarianism, of course, we shall be forced to conclude the same in the two cases; but whether it should be accepted is precisely what is in question. It is at least conceivable that morality permits or even requires sacrificing the one for the five in the Trolley Problem but not in the Hospital Case. It seems possible to think that the unwilling organ donor in the latter case is treated unfairly even if the single victim in the former is not. Whether or not it is correct, this position is hardly *obviously* mistaken with no reasons counting in its favor. That, however, is what utilitarianism entails, since the consequences are equivalent across the two thought experiments. (If we are not convinced that they are equivalent, we can always tailor the cases to make them so). So utilitarianism runs up against *two* plausible intuitions: the first, that it is wrong to sacrifice one for the many in the Hospital Case; the second, that the Hospital Case and the Trolley Problem are not morally equivalent. Unless it can refute both of these intuitions, utilitarianism is in trouble.

FAIRNESS AND WELFARIST CONSEQUENTIALISM

Utilitarians can resist this argument in one of two ways: by showing that utilitarianism is not incompatible with these intuitions; or by arguing that it is the intuitions that are unfounded, not the theory. Both argumentative routes have been attempted. Before pursuing them, however, we should identify exactly which part of the theoretical architecture of utilitarianism is vulnerable to the concerns raised by the Trolley Problem and the Hospital Case. The taxonomy we outlined in Chapter Five suggests asking if another form of welfare consequentialism fares better than utilitarianism. In particular, does the Pareto criterion?

That may at first glance seem to be the case. Since Pareto-based welfarism only commands Pareto improvements and only condemns Pareto worsenings, it does not say that we must sacrifice the healthy patient for the sake of the five patients needing organ transplants. It therefore escapes the accusation that it is too cavalier in sacrificing one for the many. But as we mentioned in Chapter 5, this "solution" comes at a high cost. If the Pareto principle is more innocuous than utilitarianism, it is because it says so much less. Although it does not, like utilitarianism, tell us to kill the healthy patient, it also does not tell us not to. Since the alternatives in the Hospital Case are not Pareto-comparable, the Pareto principle says *nothing* about what ought to be done. As for the other intuition—that morality may call for different actions in the two cases—the Pareto principle can only accommodate it with a fudge, by saying that in both cases morality does not call for anything at all. While this allows for different choices in the two cases, it also permits the same choice in both. But the intuition we need either to rationalize or refute is that morality *requires* different actions in the two cases (pulling the lever but not killing for organs). The Pareto principle avoids the charge of unfairness only by being silent on the intuitive difference between the two cases.

And on closer scrutiny, the charge of unfairness catches up with Paretianism as well. The Pareto criterion does not, it is true, condone "transfers" of well-being from one person to another as utilitarianism does. The Pareto principle does not unfairly sacrifice one for the many, because it does not sacrifice anyone for anything at all. For that very reason it is fundamentally conservative: It never requires any change in the distribution of well-being across people. A situation of extreme inequality is Pareto-efficient if the most wretched cannot be made better off at no cost to those best off. If a Pareto-efficient distribution of well-being were all that mattered from the point of view of ethics, there would be no point in questioning whether extreme inequality is fair. But such questioning seems very much to have a point. The same applies to questions about how the *gains* from a Pareto-improving change are shared. It intuitively seems to matter whether all the gains in well-being from a Pareto-improving transaction accrue to those who are already the best off. But this is something on which the Pareto principle is silent.

These are not merely theoretical problems. Most exchanges in well-functioning markets are about achieving Pareto improvements, so whether or not the Pareto criterion avoids unfairness is central to its adequacy as a guide to ethical business conduct. Consider this example:

> [The] Plasma International Company, headquartered in Tampa, Florida, purchased blood in underdeveloped countries for as little as 90 cents a pint and resold the blood to hospitals in the United States and South America. A recent disaster in Nicaragua produced scores of injured persons and the need for fresh blood. Plasma International had 10,000 pints of blood flown to Nicaragua from West Africa and charged hospitals $150 per pint, netting the firm nearly 1.5 million dollars . . . a group of irate citizens, led by prominent civic leaders, demanded that the City of Tampa, and the State of Florida, revoke Plasma International's licenses to practice business. Others [called for] legislation designed to halt the sale of blood for profit. The spokesperson was reported as saying: 'What kind of people are these-selling life and death? These men prey on the needs of dying people, buying blood from poor, ignorant Africans for 90 cents worth of beads and junk, and selling it to injured people for $150 a pint . . .' [The founder of the company responded:] 'I just don't understand it. We run a business just like any other business; we pay taxes and we try to make an honest profit' . . . [A medical] consulting team, after extensive testing, and a worldwide search, [had] recommended that the blood profiles and donor characteristics of several rural West African tribes made them ideal prospective donors. After extensive negotiations with the State Department and the government of the [West African country], the company was able to sign an agreement with several of the tribal chieftains.[102]

---

[102] T. W. Zimmerer and P. L. Preston, "Plasma International," in Robert D. Hay, Edmund R. Gray, and James E. Gates (eds.), *Business and Society: Cases and Text* (Cincinnati: Thomson South-Western, 1976); reprinted in Thomas Donaldson and Patricia Werhane, *Ethical Issues in Business: A Philosophical Approach, 6th ed.* (Upper Saddle River, NJ: Pearson Prentice Hall, 2008), pp. 156–7.

Quite clearly, Plasma's business is both profitable and Pareto-improving. The African donors presumably find the deal advantageous, as do the injured Nicaraguans who are happy to pay for the blood. But equally clearly, the founder's response to the critics is unsatisfactory, regardless of whether the practice can ultimately be justified. The claim he must address is that Plasma is, as one says, "profiteering," which presumably means that even though Plasma's transactions are Pareto-improving, the company takes an *unfair share* of the gains they generate. It disproportionately and unjustifiably enriches itself, critics may say, by unfairly taking advantage of both the suppliers' and the customers' situation to pay the donors too little (less than what morality requires, even though they accept the price) and charging the customers too much (more than what morality allows, even though the customers are clearly willing to pay the price). To establish whether Plasma is profiteering in this sense, we need a substantive theory of fairness claims—what the moral value of fairness is and what fairness demands—which we shall turn to in Chapter 11. The important point here is the failure of welfare consequentialism, even in its Pareto form, even to recognize the challenge. Since the moral premise of efficiency maximization does not self-evidently fend off unfairness concerns, the two main welfare-consequentialist theories we have examined—Paretianism and utilitarianism—remain vulnerable to criticism.

Consequentialists' simplest response to the fairness objection is to reach beyond utilitarianism and Paretianism while, so to speak, keeping it within the family and ask whether there is another welfarist consequentialism that escapes the problem. One could attempt to make the theory accommodate fairness by choosing an appropriately fairness-sensitive way of judging distributions of well-being—for example, an aggregation principle saying that the best consequences are those which make for the most *equal* distribution of individual well-being (or some more complicated formula) rather than the greatest sum. But there are reasons to think that this would be a fruitless effort, and that the reservations thrown up by our moral intuitions undermine welfarist consequentialism at a deeper level than what these superficial redefinitions of "social well-being" address.

We may first note that every welfarist alternative will struggle with the comparison between the Trolley Problem and the Hospital Case. Since those two cases are constructed to feature identical choices as far as distributions of well-being are concerned, whichever outcome the welfarist specification under consideration considers "optimal" cannot give different answers in the two cases. If it is wrong to harness the organs, then it is wrong to pull the lever; and vice versa. The reason that welfarism produces this conclusion is that it treats all sources of well-being as morally equivalent. However it chooses to evaluate the amounts of well-being different individuals enjoy—by their sum, their Pareto efficiency, their equality, or some other aggregation criterion—every welfare consequentialist theory must, by definition, say that nothing else matters morally. In particular, it rules out from moral relevance the way the well-being comes about, for if well-being is the only thing that has moral value, then there is nothing left that can morally distinguish between two ways of obtaining an identical amount and distribution of well-being.

But this beggars belief. If I am a psychopath and I torture you because I enjoy it, I am acting wrongly, and not just because my gain in well-being from torturing you is outweighed (according to whatever criterion we use for comparing the changes to our respective well-being levels) by your loss of well-being from being a victim of my torture. If this were the reason why my torture is wrong, it would open up the ghastly possibility that I would be justified in torturing you if only I enjoyed it *enough*.

If anything, the opposite is true: The fact that my well-being arises from an act of sadistic torture disqualifies it from carrying any moral weight *at all* in justifying what I do to you. "It makes me happy" is simply not a morally relevant concern in such a case. In the same vein, the well-being to be had from profiting from certain lines of business may be thought morally questionable (profits from prostitution and drug dealing come to mind—and since about 2007, aggressively peddled subprime mortgages). Recall the example of Texaco, which allegedly profited handsomely from operations in Ecuador that poisoned the environment for the local residents. A welfarist would ask whether Texaco's benefit outweighed the suffering of the locals. But that seems to miss the important point that *if* the pollution was morally wrong, then it is hardly made less wrong by the fact that the polluter profited from it. Any wrongness there may be seems independent of Texaco's gain; indeed, if it acted wrongly, that would be a reason for judging whatever well-being it derived morally tainted. Since there can be such things as *ill-gotten gains*, well-being cannot be the only currency of moral value. To evaluate whether and how someone's well-being should count in the consequentialist calculus, one has to appeal to *other* moral principles than well-being itself.

This last line of reasoning leads us to conclude that welfarism can be *too permissive* because it treats all gains in well-being equally as "moral positives," including some that intuitively have little moral force or should even count negatively. Because it does not differentiate between different ways of generating well-being—in particular, whether the actions that generate well-being treat others fairly or unfairly—welfarism cannot accommodate our intuition that this matters.

NEGATIVE RESPONSIBILITY: DOING VERSUS ALLOWING

Since the challenges to utilitarianism cannot be easily avoided by withdrawing to other welfarist theories, the question becomes how much one can rescue by retracting from welfarism altogether and settling for a commitment to consequentialism in its most general form. Such a strategy would offer some definition of "good" outcomes that does not refer merely to distributions of well-being, while remaining wedded to the notion that morality is ultimately reducible to choosing the actions with the best consequences. But notice that this move will only deflect the objections we raised earlier if they can all be described as saying that utilitarianism (and welfarism generally) *misidentifies* which outcomes are best—which would entail that the problem can be solved by specifying them better. But some critics intend these examples to persuade us of something else, namely that an action could bring about better consequences and still be wrong.

Those objecting to Plasma International's business, for example, may admit that the Pareto-improving outcome—where the donors get money, Plasma gets profits and the recipients get blood—is better than the *status quo ante*. But they could still think that *despite* producing a better outcome, the action is morally blameworthy. Those who think, like Waheed Hussain, that it is absurd to claim that nonprofit organizations must maximize profit when the conditions for the invisible hand argument are satisfied, need not deny that profit maximization might produce the best outcomes (though they probably would deny this); all they *logically* need to deny is that the good consequences of profit maximization create a duty to pursue it. Such views, if they can be defended, threaten not just some specific consequentialist theory but consequentialism as such.

For what they reject is the fundamental premise that our moral obligation is always to do what leads to the best (expected) outcome. They hold, in other words, that there are situations where an act leads to the best outcome, yet is the *wrong* thing to do; or where an act leads to a suboptimal outcome, yet is the *right* thing to do. For that to be possible, of course, there must be other criteria than an action's consequences for whether it is right or wrong.

What could those criteria be? In two famous thought experiments, Bernard Williams suggests what consequentialism might be missing:

1. George, who has just taken his Ph.D. in chemistry, finds it extremely difficult to get a job. He is not very robust in health, which cuts down the number of jobs he might be able to do satisfactorily . . . An older chemist . . . says that he can get George a decently paid job in a certain laboratory, which pursues research into chemical and biological warfare. George says he cannot accept this, since he is opposed to chemical and biological warfare. The older man replies that he is not too keen on it himself . . . but after all George's refusal is not going to make the job or the laboratory go away [and] he happens to know that if George refuses the job, it will certainly go to a contemporary of George's who is not inhibited by any such scruples and is likely if appointed to push along the research with greater zeal than George would. Indeed, it is not merely concern for George and his family, but . . . some alarm about this other man's excess of zeal, which has led the older man to offer to use his influence to get George the job.

2. Jim finds himself in the central square of a small South American town. Tied up against the wall are . . . twenty Indians . . . in front of them several armed men in uniform. A heavy man in a sweat-stained khaki shirt turns out to be the captain in charge and, after a good deal of questioning of Jim which establishes that he got there by accident while on a botanical expedition, explains that the Indians are a random group of the inhabitants who, after recent [antigovernment protests] are just about to be killed to remind [others] of the advantages of not protesting.

   However, since Jim is an [honored] visitor from another land, the captain is happy to offer him a guest's privilege of killing one of the Indians himself. If Jim accepts, then as a special mark of the occasion, the other Indians will be let off. Of course, if Jim refuses, then there is no special occasion . . . [It is clear to Jim that] any attempt at [overpowering the soldiers] will mean that all the Indians will be killed, and himself. The . . . villagers understand the situation, and are obviously begging him to accept.[103]

It is clear what utilitarianism would have to advocate in both situations: George should take the job, and Jim should kill one unfortunate Indian. Now there is nothing very specifically utilitarian about this. *Any* consequentialism[104] would have to agree with

---

[103] Bernard Williams, "A critique of utilitarianism," in J. J. C. Smart and Bernard Williams, *Utilitarianism: for and against* (Cambridge, UK: Cambridge University Press, 1973), pp. 97–98.

[104] At least any act-consequentialism. Below, we consider whether rule-utilitarianism escapes these objections.

these conclusions—as long as we (reasonably) think that the outcome where George grudgingly takes the job is overall better than the outcome where his zealous rival puts all his energy into advancing CBW technology, and as long as we (even more reasonably) think that the outcome where Jim shoots one Indian and the rest go free is overall better than the one where the captain kills all twenty. What is more, these answers to the dilemmas follow *straightforwardly*; indeed, if consequentialism is true, they are hardly dilemmas at all. And yet they *are* dilemmas: Our deep-seated moral intuitions pull in both directions. Some of these intuitions, then, cannot be consequentialist—and if they are valid, consequentialism is at best incomplete, and, at worst, an error.

Williams's examples may seem far-fetched, but they isolate what is morally relevant in decisions that are much more common, although less stark. The first case probes whether one ought to engage in conduct one finds morally problematic in order to forestall conduct by someone else that would be even more morally problematic. This is analogous to Google's dilemma when it had to comply with censorship to open the locally based google.cn search engine (see Chapter 4). The second case asks whether it is right to directly cause harm to someone when not doing so would lead to more harm being afflicted on more people but by other causal forces. That captures Guidant's predicament (see Chapter 5). So these thought experiments, artificial though they appear, are analogues of real business dilemmas. What we conclude about Williams's cases will logically also apply to Google's and Guidant's decisions and others like them.

Our intuitive reactions to the two cases recognize the possibility—indeed the plausibility—that there are reasons for declining the job in Case 1 or refusing to shoot the one Indian in Case 2 (and we can recognize this even if we think, all things considered, that taking the job or firing the shot are the right things to do). Given how the cases are set up, consequentialism denies this possibility. So what our intuitions bring to the fore is that consequentialism ignores an idea that is central to our moral thinking. That idea is the following: *I am particularly responsible for *my* action, and there is a moral difference between the things that I *do* and the things that are done by others as a result of what I do*—even if these things have the same overall consequences. Since consequences are all that matter in consequentialism, it cannot capture this difference. Yet it seems fundamental that the fact that an action is *my* action generates special reasons for *me*. In the case of George and the CBW laboratory, must it not make a difference to *George's* reasons for acting one way or another whether it is he or someone else who will have helped develop such weapons? Similarly, in the case of Jim and the Indians, should it not matter for *Jim's* choice that the blood will—if he so chooses—be on his hands?

One thing we may want a moral theory to do is to distinguish the special responsibility we sense that we have for our own actions and the things they directly cause, from our responsibility for the more remote consequences of what we do or refrain from doing, including in particular what other people do as a result of our doing or refraining. Consequentialism cannot do this, because it "essentially involves the notion of *negative responsibility*: that if I am ever responsible for anything, then I must be just as much responsible for things that I allow or fail to prevent, as I am for things that I myself, in the more everyday restricted sense, bring about."[105] Negative responsibility, Williams points

---

[105] Ibid, p. 95.

out, must deny the special moral relationship between *us* and the actions and consequences that are reasonably called *ours* (in the sense that the zealous research George's rival would perform could not be called *George's* action or that the captain's killing of the twenty Indians would not be *Jim's* killing of them).

We said earlier that welfarism was in a sense too permissive, because it counts well-being as morally valuable no matter where it comes from. We could have added that in another sense, welfarism is too *demanding*, because it puts us equally in charge of the well-being of every other person.[106] But this problem, we can now see, extends to consequentialism in its most general form. Negative responsibility holds us to account not just for how our actions affect others, but for the actions of others, if these are causally linked to us, however remotely. But then the question must arise of what limits there are to our responsibility for others—if there are any at all. For it is hard to imagine choices that neither affect the well-being of others nor influence their actions. It is always open to us, whenever we do something to improve our own well-being, to choose to improve someone else's well-being instead.[107] And whenever we can influence the well-being of others, we can also alter their self-interested reasons for acting in one way or another. If consequentialism is true, we are at least potentially morally responsible for *everything*.

Business decisions do not escape consequentialism's implication of runaway responsibility. For example, we saw in Chapter 6 that utilitarianism demotes the various motives people have for entering business—including but not limited to the profit motive—to so many instruments for maximizing social well-being. But the world is so full of suffering that, by any plausible criterion for aggregating the interests of different individuals, maximizing social well-being will almost always require directing a company's resources toward those who suffer rather than to reaping profits from the business. This, as Milton Friedman has pointed out, turns business into a public office rather than the pursuit of a private purpose. But if consequentialism is true, that is just as it should be, for private purposes have no special claim except insofar as fulfilling them makes the overall outcome better.

So negative responsibility makes morality encompass the totality of people's lives. This is why consequentialism does not leave room for what Waheed Hussain terms a *personal sphere* within which we may pursue whatever private purpose we please without needing to justify it as maximally conducive to the common good. Among other things, this leads to the absurd conclusions that we have already noted: that it is immoral to conduct business for a profit whenever forgoing the profit leads to better consequences, or that it is morally wrong to conduct *non*profit business whenever profit maximization makes the outcome better. This totalizing tendency does not make for a more enlightened morality; rather, it is a mark of ethical impoverishment.

---

[106] We ignore here the egoistic version of welfarist consequentialism, according to which a person ought to maximize his or her own well-being only.

[107] This is, for example, the near-permanent situation in which almost all middle-class citizens of Western countries live: Most things they buy gives them much less well-being than the same money could produce if it was spent, say, on vaccines for sub-Saharan Africa. Some utilitarians have concluded that people in the Western world have a moral obligation to give most of what they earn to charity (see Chapter 11).

DIRECTED OBLIGATIONS

As Williams has argued, one manifestation of that impoverishment is that consequentialism cannot make sense of the moral value of *integrity*, of taking special responsibility for the actions that are *ours* and for how they relate to each other over time. We often experience that what we have done in the past matters intrinsically for what we ought to do now, in a way that is independent of the consequences of our present actions. Thus in Kate's Dilemma, the fact that Kate has made a promise is important in its own right, before the results of keeping or breaking it are considered. Promising creates, we can say, a backward-looking moral reason. It is a reason, moreover, for a *directed* obligation: It is owed only by the promisor, and only to the promisee. Promising is a way for us to *put* ourselves under a special obligation that is owed by us only, to someone specific, not just to whomever it would best benefit or to "society".

Consequentialism, looking only ahead to consequences, denies backward-looking reasons any intrinsic importance for our moral deliberation. It can only say that we ought to keep a promise if the consequences of doing so are better than the consequences of breaking it. But that is not what we think we are committing ourselves to when we promise. If only consequences mattered for whether we should keep a promise or not, then the act of promising can never by itself alter what we ought to do (except, trivially, if the act of promising changes the consequences of our later actions). A consequentialist morality robs us of an ability our ordinary moral thinking strongly suggests we have, namely the ability to *create* obligations for ourselves, as it were out of nothing.

Other examples of backward-looking moral reasons we ordinarily accept as valid are the duty to compensate people one has wronged and the duty to remain loyal to those with whom one embarks on a project. Most people believe that there are times when reasons such as these must enter moral deliberation quite separately from the consequences of the actions under consideration. As with promising, these backward-looking reasons are hard to fit into a consequentialist framework. And yet if ordinary moral intuition is right that such reasons have force for how we ought to behave, then that clearly matters for business ethics. For such considerations also arise in business decisions, which almost always are part of collective ventures that play out over time. If so, consequentialism leaves a lot to be desired as a theory of business ethics.

The problem consequentialism has with backward-looking reasons, moreover, is not simply the difficulty it has with rationalizing that our past actions can bind us in moral relationships where we owe special obligations to specific people. It must more broadly deny that there are such moral relationships at all: Consequentialism has no room for special obligations to family, friends, compatriots or colleagues that arise from the simple fact that we are in these relationships with them. The most that consequentialism can do is tell us to prioritize the people we are close to whenever that is the best way to bring about the best overall outcomes. This is, of course, often the case, if only because we have more impact on the well-being of those close to us. But consequentialism must ultimately see such personal bonds as of only instrumental moral relevance. If it *seems* that we have special obligations to those close to us, the consequentialist must claim, that is because this is how we best discharge our *actual* duty of bringing about the best outcome, which remains defined in impartial terms. My family, friends and colleagues—and, indeed, myself—have no privileged place in the determination of what is best *overall*. Negative responsibility implies that the moral burden of what happens in the entire world rests, in the last instance, on my moral shoulders.

Making us responsible for everyone's fate in this way is sometimes presented as a selling point of utilitarianism and its cousins. On reflection, however, such impartiality must strike us as unbearable. It dismisses the stronger sympathies we have for those close to us than for complete strangers as having no intrinsic moral validity. If that were correct, then there would be no truly directed obligations: All our duties would be general. We would be mistaken in our sense that we have intrinsically greater moral responsibility for our own parents than for others' or that a stranger's well-being counts less than our own child's well-being for what we ought to do. Similarly, it would be a mistake to think that the well-being of Lockheed's employees is intrinsically of greater moral importance to its CEO than the well-being of other people. Morality can make us responsible for everyone's well-being equally in this way only at the cost of ignoring (even violating) some of the deepest and most salient relationships in our personal and professional lives. This is hard to believe.

Consequentialism's blindness to integrity and directed obligations not only underrates our relationships with others; it is also an impoverished view of our moral relationship to ourselves. If he were a strict utilitarian, Jim would not worry about being the one pulling the trigger. Nor would a utilitarian George see a problem in being the one moving CBW research forward. In both cases, the alternative is that someone else does something much worse. But there is something odd, to say the least, in treating oneself as no more than one causal link among many others and as just one of many constituents of moral or immoral outcomes. These strict-consequentialist versions of Jim and George strike us as overly selfless men—literally, men without selves. This is not just a point about how morality tells us to decide; it is also a point about which decisions it says something about at all. In addition to taking a strangely impartial perspective on moral obligations, consequentialism enforces this perspective on all individual choices. Because of negative responsibility, every choice becomes a moral decision, and one to be determined from the impartial standpoint of what is best overall. That means personal preferences—including life projects such as pursuing one's ambitions in the arts or in the professions—come to look like indulgences. Its overarching impartiality makes consequentialism dismiss the desire to pursue *one's own* path, whether it is paved with whims, ambitions, or life projects, and whether one's object is profits or something more esoteric like climbing Mount Everest or writing the Great American Novel. At the very least, it relegates every individual desire to the position of just one want among all others with an equally good intrinsic claim to being satisfied, all to be weighed against each other only in terms of their contribution to the overall goodness of the outcome.

What is the problem, the consequentialist may at this point be straining to ask. Consequentialism, by endorsing negative responsibility, may narrow down to nothing the personal sphere of our life within which we can focus on what we want and on what we care about rather than on what we owe to the world as a whole. That, the consequentialist could claim, is precisely what is attractive about the theory: It does not allow personal preferences to rationalize a neglect of other people's needs. If the theory reaches every one of our decisions and thereby demands more from us in a way that makes for better outcomes, what is wrong with this?

At the level of personal morality, the answer is that this rules out most of what seems important in life. The ongoing relationships and projects we pursue—from rearing a family to achieving greatness in the public eye—are the kinds of things that give life meaning. Since such choices—and commitments to follow them through over time—are to a large extent what makes us who we are and not someone else, a morality that treats them as mere indulgences rather than as considerations generating some of the most significant reasons for how we ought to act, seems misguided.

Moreover, it is particularly awkward for a theory of *business* ethics not to recognize a sphere within which we may act on the ambitions we choose to pursue and not by what would most benefit humanity. As we have already pointed out, if actions are immoral unless they bring about the best achievable outcome for society, engaging in business in pursuit of a self-centered goal such as profits is inherently suspect. Just as in the case of individual choices, utilitarianism never stops demanding that we sacrifice ourselves for those who are worse off than we, so in the case of business decisions, consequentialism seems not to allow a business simply to look to what is good for the business rather than what is good for society. But that demands both too much and too little. Too much, because it makes business always and everywhere responsible for how things are in the world. Too little, because by failing to explain when business is responsible for the world at large and when it is not, it says nothing about which particular groups of people business has particular responsibilities for.

CONSEQUENTIALIST RETORTS

We have traced out an inductive argument by surveying a number of real and imagined examples where a consequentialist approach leads to conclusions that seem intuitively objectionable. All in all, consequentialism seems to go too far—implying obligations it is hard to believe that we have—and at the same time not far enough—not accounting for obligations that we do seem to have. And, too often, it leads to counterintuitive conclusions, such as in the Hospital Case.

There are several lines of argument that a consequentialist might resort to in order to rebut the objections. A common first retort is to deny that the consequentialism being defended really entails the kinds of uncomfortable conclusions we have derived. In practice, a consequentialist may say, respecting fairness and acting with integrity will always produce better consequences than the alternative, so the theory will favor such conduct. But this answer will not do. At best, the consequentialist may claim that as a matter of empirical fact, situations such as the Trolley Problem and the Hospital Case rarely if ever occur, so they are not for practical purposes a problem for the theory. But it cannot be true that such cases *never* occur. They have occurred often enough in situations of war, for example. More important, cases such as Guidant and George and the CBW lab show that treating people fairly or acting with integrity can easily conflict with good outcomes in business- and work-related decisions. And, in any case, consequentialists must answer for the logical implications of their theory even if they are unlikely to occur in practice. The Hospital Case is no less horrific for being improbable, and a consequentialism that condoned organ harvesting would be discredited even if no one ever acted on it.

Utilitarians and consequentialists have another answer. They may accept that their theories contradict our common intuitions in some cases. But that is to be expected, they may say, since we have been indoctrinated from the beginning of our lives to believe certain moral codes. That does not make them right. A hundred and fifty years ago many people had strong intuitions that slavery was permissible and even required. Consequentialism shows that they were mistaken. The nonconsequentialist intuitions we keep clinging to today may be equally bad guides to morality, utilitarians can say. Like the beliefs that supported slavery, they are vestiges of irrational moral codes, superstitions that are proven wrong by a rational approach to morality. If our moral intuitions conflict with consequentialist deduction, it is our moral intuitions that have to yield.

This retort has the intellectual merit of being logically coherent. But it would have us discard anything that seems to cast doubt on consequentialism. That would be a high price to pay, for there would be an awful lot to discard, as the examples of perfectly sensible intuitions in this chapter show. Worse, this route requires total intellectual capitulation, elevating as it does the consequentialist principle to the status of axiomatic truth rather than asking whether, in the troubling cases, our nonconsequentialist intuitions indicate that an alternative theory is needed.

There is a final retort to which defenders of consequentialism can turn that is more promising than either assuming troubling cases away or defining away what is troubling about them. That is to opt for rule-consequentialism rather than act-consequentialism. Recall that rule-consequentialism maintains the criterion that the goodness of consequences is the only source of moral right and wrong, but instead of applying it directly to individual actions, this approach applies it to *practices* or rules of behavior. Rule-consequentialism asks: "What if everyone did that?"—or more precisely "What would the consequences be if everyone followed the general practice of acting this way in these circumstances?" Specific actions are then judged according to whether they follow the morally right practice, that is, the practice whose general adoption has the best consequences. John Stuart Mill compared this approach to using a nautical almanac: Rather than calculating the almanac's numbers every time they are needed for navigation, one simply relies on the prepared answers to set the course. Similarly, instead of calculating the consequences of any particular action, one relies on rules of thumb about which actions generally yield the best outcomes.

In the Hospital Case, for example, one would not ask: "Does killing the healthy person for his organs have better consequences than letting the five patients die from organ failure?" The right question, for rule-consequentialism, is: "Would a world where a rule was respected which allowed a healthy individual to be killed for his organs whenever that would save five people's lives be better than a world where a rule was followed that prohibited this?" The appeal of this approach is its promise to respect our intuitive reactions to the difficult cases we have considered. It is clear that in many cases, rule-consequentialism would avoid the embarrassing implications of act-consequentialism, and of act-utilitarianism in particular. In the Hospital Case the rule-utilitarian need not conclude that it is justified to kill the healthy person. In a single case, such killing may conceivably do good. But as a general practice, it would keep people away from hospitals and doctors for fear of ending up as involuntary organ donors. This would no doubt erode trust in the health system and the medical profession so badly that the consequences would be far worse (including fewer organs actually being donated). That there are no equivalent considerations in the Trolley Problem (if people were discouraged from venturing on to train tracks, that would be no bad thing) suggests that a rule-consequentialist theory could also respect our differential reactions to the two thought experiments.

More generally, rule-consequentialism accommodates much of what seems important about social roles and practices. It can justify many of the norms built into conventional social roles, at the same time as it can condemn those social conventions which, when generally practiced, reduce well-being. A rule-consequentialist approach to the argument between Carr and Solomon, for example, could settle it by pointing out that a generally respected rule of truth telling would probably lead to better outcomes than a general practice of deception.

There is a problem with rule-consequentialism, however. It is inconceivable that the acts prescribed by the rule *the general compliance with which* has the best consequences will in *each and every instance* have the best consequences of all the actions available. There will be exceptional situations where breaking the rule is better. There are *some* times when killing (or causing more deaths to happen) advances the common good. And on some occasions, we can be *certain* of this. On consequentialist grounds, how could it possibly be rational, let alone moral, to respect the rule on such occasions? In Mill's example, in a case where the almanac were *known* to be wrong, what reason could there be to follow it? That would amount to rule-worship, which, in the moral case, is precisely the kind of superstitious hindrance to human well-being that consequentialism was meant to get rid of in the first place. Surely if consequences are what matters, it is immoral to sacrifice the best available outcome for the sake of respecting a rule.

The philosopher J. J. C. Smart puts it the following way. The rule-consequentialist wants us to ask: "What if everyone did that?" The question can be interpreted in one of two ways: either as suggesting a *prediction*—my lying may make others lie—or as a merely *hypothetical* question which makes no assumption that others will in fact act as I do. If other people *actually* do something as a result of my having done it, that is, of course, a legitimate consequentialist concern; it is, after all, a consequence. But only in very peculiar situations will this change what I ought to do; more often, the possible effect on the conduct of others is an argument for doing things in secret, rather than for not doing them at all. In the hypothetical sense, in contrast, the consequences "if everyone did that" could clearly tell against an action. But how can a consequentialist justify being concerned with *hypothetical* consequences that do not, in fact, materialise? Consider Carr's defense of deception. A rule-consequentialist would respond by asking in the hypothetical mode: "What if everyone lied?" But the answer to this is straightforward: "Well, it would not be good, but that doesn't matter because everyone is *not* going to lie, or, at least, no one is more likely to lie as a result of my deception. I agree that generalized truth telling produces better outcomes than generalized deception, but *this* instance of deception (taken together with how everyone else is in fact going to act) produces better outcomes still."

The fact that such an answer is always available (provided the facts are right) casts serious doubt on whether rule-consequentialism is a tenable position. Any supposedly optimal system of rules can be improved by allowing for exceptions to the rules in well-defined situations (those where deviating from the rule would yield better consequences than sticking to it). But if the rule-consequentialist must decide in each case whether it warrants a departure from the rule, the theory collapses into act-consequentialism, in which case it does not escape the criticisms of the latter after all. The only alternative is to claim that the hypothetical "What if everyone did that?" matters for *other* moral reasons. At that point, however, the theory ceases to be purely utilitarian or consequentialist, since it would appeal to nonconsequentialist reasons for respecting rules and practices even in cases where doing so has suboptimal consequences. It is tempting to conclude that the best way to support intuitions about fairness, integrity, and directed obligations is indeed to give up on the consequentialist criterion as the sole foundation of morality. In later chapters, we shall examine defenses of the hypothetical "What if everyone did that?" in which the value of rules is not reducible to their instrumental value in bringing about good consequences.

Summary of the Argument in This Chapter

Taken as abstract principles, the premises of consequentialism and indeed of utilitarianism are difficult to disagree with; nevertheless, there are powerful inductive arguments against them. The Trolley Problem and the Hospital Case together showed two ways in which utilitarianism clashes with deeply held intuitions. First, it has to favor what looks like unfairly sacrificing the healthy patient to harvest his organs. Second, it has to exclude from the start the possibility that the right thing to do may be different in the Hospital Case and the Trolley Problem. Other forms of welfarist consequentialism do not fare much better. Paretianism only avoids endorsing the human sacrifice by refraining from drawing any conclusion at all about which outcome is better. And the Plasma case shows that even Paretianism can be charged with unfairness in how it allows Pareto-improving gains to be shared. Finally, no welfare consequentialism can adequately account for the intuition that the Trolley Problem and the Hospital Case are not morally equivalent, since they *are* equivalent as far as the consequences for well-being are concerned. The fundamental problem is that consequentialism cares only about how good the outcomes are and is indifferent to how they are brought about.

This stumbling block cannot be avoided by tweaking the content of any given consequentialist theory to make it fit the cases. Williams's thought experiments show that it is in the nature of consequentialism to focus on the impartially judged goodness of the outcomes *and nothing else.* Our place with respect to how the outcome is caused—including what we do as opposed to what we let happen, and including to whom we

do it or to whom we let it happen—has no moral significance by itself. This rules out giving intrinsic importance to any of the following considerations: backward-looking reasons for what we ought to do (the idea that we owe a specific duty to someone because of our past action, for example because we made a promise); relationship-specific reasons for what we ought to do (the idea that we have a special responsibility for people with whom we have certain relationships); and self-referential reasons for what we ought to do (the idea that it matters morally what *we* do; for example, it is not irrelevant to Jim's moral deliberation that if he shoots, *he* will be the one taking an innocent person's life). As the imaginary and real examples we have examined expose, this puts consequentialism at odds with our ordinary ethical thinking, to the point of seeming blind to our most profound moral values.

This does not prove consequentialism incorrect, but it does force us to make a choice. We can only accept consequentialism at the cost of radically overhauling how we usually think of morality. Some consequentialists say that this reveals the flaws in our intuitions, not in their theory. They would have us bite the bullet, treat the intuitions appealed to in this chapter as superstitions, and accept the need to free ourselves from them. Others deny that consequentialism has these unpalatable conclusions in the first place. But this rebuttal does not succeed. Such situations may be unlikely to occur, but it is not true they will never occur. In any case, rejecting the logical implications of the theory invalidates its premises even if those implications only apply in imagined (but possible) circumstances.

A more promising retort is to redefine the theory as *rule*-consequentialism; that is, to judge an action not by its *actual* consequences but by the consequences its general practice would have. Since the counterexamples on which the inductive arguments in this chapter are based are all in some way exceptional, a focus on general practices rather than special cases avoids many of act-consequentialism's more embarrassing conclusions. But if the move to rule-consequentialism rebuts the inductive objections, it falls afoul of the following deductive argument: On consequentialist grounds, it is *irrational* to focus on the hypothetical consequences of following rules and *immoral* to do so when breaking them would lead to better outcomes. Rule-consequentialism must either fail or resort to a nonconsequentialist argument to justify its approach. But then the sensible step is not to try to rescue a consequentialist construct from our many nonconsequentialist intuitions; it is rather to seek nonconsequentialist principles that justify them.

CHAPTER 8

Self-Evident Truths?
Imagining a World Without Rights

All the counterexamples to consequentialism we considered in the previous chapter had one thing in common: the intuition—which negative responsibility rejects—that we owe specific obligations to specific people, and that these directed obligations may depend on more than the overall consequences of our actions. In the Trolley Problem and in the Hospital Case, those threatened with being sacrificed for the greater good can demand, it seems, that the sacrifice (flipping the lever, taking his organs) be justified to *them*, not just to society at large. The Plasma case triggered a suspicion that not everyone had received what they deserved—a notion which presupposes that something specific is due to each one of them. And in Williams's thought experiments—where the obvious moral questions are whether CBW research is something *George* ought to take on, and whether shooting the Indian is something *Jim* may do to the person whose life he will thereby sacrifice—we grasp that asking these questions is not the same as asking which actions would produce the best outcomes.

All the examples, in short, suggest that there are certain ways people ought to be treated, regardless of consequences. The way we commonly express this thought is by saying that people have *rights*. Saying that someone has a right to be treated a certain way is claiming that producing a better outcome may not be sufficient to justify treating that person differently. Consequentialism cannot admit this. It sees individuals not as holders of rights that must not be violated, but as the vehicles of well-being (or whatever else defines good consequences)—as the arena, so to speak, on which morally valuable consequences play out. Some critics of utilitarianism have expressed this as saying that it does not "respect the separateness of persons," by which they mean that it ignores the separate claim every individual has to not being traded off against the interests of others without further justification. It ignores, in other words, the rights of individuals not to be treated as dispensable for the sake of the greater good.

The notion of rights helps to formulate the unease many feel about the case with which we started our venture into consequentialist reasoning: Guidant corporation's decision to withhold information about the defect in its defibrillators. We saw that, given reasonable assumptions about the facts, a strong consequentialist argument can be made in favor of the company's conduct. Yet this will not dispel the reservations that many retain about Guidant's secrecy. Their skepticism can be captured by the thought that Guidant's customer-patients have a *right to know* about any flaws in a device that is surgically implanted into their hearts—and that because of this right, Guidant has a duty to inform them even if society as a whole, and indeed the customers themselves, would be better off if they did not know. Appropriately generalized, the intuition that people have rights that protect them against being sacrificed for the sake of the greater good also helps express our intuitive resistance to consequentialist solutions in the other problematic cases we have considered.

Many of history's great political declarations haven taken the claim that people have rights as not just true, but as self-evidently true. Our task in this chapter and the next is to understand in better detail what the claim means and to establish what reasons we may have for thinking that it may be true.

SELF-EVIDENT TRUTHS?

In everyday usage, the term "right" often serves not to single out a certain type of moral claim, but as a shorthand for describing moral obligations of any kind. The thought that it is wrong to treat people in a certain way can be expressed by saying that people have a right not to be treated in this way. But the same thought can equally well be expressed by saying that there is a duty not to treat them in this way. Any "ought"-proposition phrased in terms of rights can be stated from the flip side, as it were, in the language of duties or obligations. This has been called the doctrine of the "logical correlativity of rights and duties": If someone has a right, this entails that someone else has a duty. Now in this general sense in which "right" is just the flip side of a duty, the promiscuous use of the word "right" in casual moral debate is unwarranted, since it adds no meaning to what can be stated exhaustively in terms of obligations. But there is a narrower sense of "right" that does add meaning, which becomes clear when we consider the correlation of rights and duties more closely. If a right always entails a duty and a duty always entails a right, then the two concepts are equivalent. But if the correlation only goes one way—if any right entails a duty but not every duty entails a right—then a claim that one person has a right is more than a redundant gloss on a claim that another person ought to act in a certain way. For this means that there are two kinds of duties: those that do and those that do not correspond to a right. Claiming that someone has a right is not then just the flip side of claiming that someone else has a duty; it is to claim that the duty in question is of the kind that corresponds to a right as opposed to one that does not.

This distinction between two types of obligations captures something that seems at the heart of morality and that, as we shall presently see, lies behind many of the objections we raised to consequentialism in the previous chapter. The striking feature of rights is that they *belong* to people. For there to be a right, it must be *someone's* right to something. This means that the pairing of a duty with a right and the lack of such a pairing establish different kinds of moral facts. The difference resides in whether the beneficiary of a duty can, morally speaking, *demand* it or *exact* it as something being *owed* to him. A common example of a duty that does not correspond to anyone's right—called an "imperfect" duty—is the duty of charity. If I am well-to-do, I may have a duty to help the poor. But there is no person who has a right to my charity. A beggar on the street cannot *demand* that I be charitable to *him*, and he has no standing to complain if I am not. There is no one who is wronged—whose rights are violated—if I do not give him money. I may choose how, when and to whom to carry out my duty to be charitable. But some other duties are (as the etymology of the term suggests) *due* to specific people. If a student scores perfectly on her exams and excels at all other requirements for receiving an A in the course, the teacher has a duty to give her an A. This duty is not simply a general obligation to give As to good students. The teacher owes a duty *to the student who has excelled* to give her an A; it would not just be wrong but unfair to *her* to give her a bad grade. The teacher's duty to give the student an A is a "perfect duty"—a duty of the sort that gives her the standing to *demand* an A and a legitimate moral reason to complain or demand redress if she does not receive one. In short, she has a right to an A.

The evident importance of whether a duty is *due to someone*, who is therefore uniquely entitled to demand its satisfaction, is why rights language is not redundant. A statement about rights is more specific than a claim that morality requires certain actions to be carried out. It adds an assertion about the moral standing of specific people to whom those actions are *due* as a matter of right. This explains why, when actions strike us as wrong even if they make outcomes better, we are prone to make assertions about rights. For in cases where an individual's interests are sacrificed for the greater good, our intuition is often that those individuals are not just harmed but *wronged*. They have been treated unfairly: Something that *they* are in a moral position to demand as their due has been denied to them. Thus, claims about rights function as claims to protection against being sacrificed for the greater good. If there are no rights—if duties are not owed to anyone in particular—it is quite reasonable to count the interests of each person with an equal weight in a calculation of the overall goodness of actions. Acknowledging rights pre-empts this treatment. So a right is more than an interest: If I have a right to something, that provides a moral reason against trading off my interest in that thing against the interests of others. Accordingly, some philosophers have described rights as "trumps" against consequentialist evaluation.

The most influential political documents in history have been precisely such assertions of moral protections or "trumps." The United States Declaration of Independence, for example, states that

> We hold these truths to be self-evident, that all men are created equal, that they are endowed by their Creator with certain unalienable Rights, that among these are Life, Liberty and the pursuit of Happiness.

Similarly bold assertions of the rights that people have are found in the French Revolution's Declaration of the Rights of Man and the United Nations' Universal Declaration of Human Rights. Whether their claims are true or not, they are hardly self-evident truths, as attested by the fact that people found it necessary to write them down. (Jeremy Bentham famously scoffed at declarations of inalienable rights, which he called "nonsense upon stilts.") None of what we have said so far shows that people have any of these rights, or even that they have rights at all; it even suggests that they may not. For saying that rights express that certain interests "trump" the consequentialist calculus immediately invites the question of why anything at all should trump the common interest. The answer is not obvious. If we respond that consequentialist conclusions are trumped because people have rights, we are obviously guilty of circular reasoning. Unless we can find a satisfactory account of rights to explain why people have them, we should revisit our intuitive presumption that people do.

There are three very broad questions such an account should address. The first is the broadest: what are rights? What precisely does it mean to say that people have rights, beyond that something is due to them? This first question in a conceptual analysis of rights is one that we must distinguish from claims about which rights people do in fact have, if any. We do not need to assume that anyone has rights in order to elucidate what it would mean to have them, any more than we need to assume that mermaids exist in order to explicate the concept of mermaids. It is only once we have a good understanding of the concept of rights that we can ask the second and third questions. The second is: Are there any rights? That is, do people have rights (at all)? If the answer is yes, the third question immediately poses itself: Which rights do people then have? We will devote this chapter to the first question; only with a proper account of what rights are in hand, will we be able to justify or refute specific claims that so-and-so has this-or-that right—including the historic rights declarations themselves.

A WORLD WITHOUT RIGHTS

In trying to understand the concept of rights, we can learn more from trying to describe what the *absence* of rights would be like than from attempting to posit a definition of what rights are. Philosopher Joel Feinberg followed this roundabout path of inquiry to probe the nature of rights through the following thought experiment:

> Try to imagine Nowheresville—a world very much like our own except that no one . . . has *rights*. If this flaw makes Nowheresville too ugly to hold very long in contemplation, we can make it as pretty as we wish in other moral respects. We can, for example, make the human beings in it as attractive and virtuous as possible without taxing our conceptions of the limits of human nature. In particular, let the virtues of moral sensibility flourish. Fill this imagined world with as much benevolence, compassion, sympathy, and pity as it will conveniently hold without strain. Now we can imagine men helping one another from compassionate motives merely, quite as much or even more than they do in our actual world from a variety of more complicated motives.[108]

In Nowheresville, people do not have rights, nor do they have the concept of a right (so they do not know that they do not have rights). Contemplating how Nowheresville is different from our own world—and, indeed, realizing how difficult it is even to contemplate a world without rights—helps show what rights are and what we value about them. First, note what is not different. Feinberg does not say morality does not apply to Nowheresvillians. They can act rightly or wrongly, and they have the concept of right and wrong. There are, therefore, things they ought to do and things they ought not to do (and because they have such unimpeachable moral motivations, they usually do what they ought to do)—in other words, they have duties. But since no one has any

---

[108] Joel Feinberg, "The Nature and Value of Rights," *The Journal of Value Inquiry*, 1979.

rights, none of these duties are obligations due to or owed to other individuals. That is, they are imperfect duties. Since perfect duties correspond to rights (belonging to whomever the duties are due to), such duties do not exist in Nowheresville. Every duty is an imperfect duty, and no one can claim anything as his due.

To our ordinary moral thinking, Nowheresville is a bizarre world. Consider our earlier example of grading the excellent student. A Nowheresvillian teacher may have a duty to give a top grade to the excellent students, but this is an imperfect duty akin to the duty of charity. He has no perfect duty to the excellent student to give her an A because she excels. If he does not, she will be disappointed—in the same way a beggar on the street is disappointed when the rich passer-by does not put a coin in his cup. But, like the beggar, the Nowheresvillian student cannot legitimately feel *unfairly treated* because she was not favored. She has not been wronged in a way in which the other students were not, because she cannot claim the A as *owed to her,* so she has no special moral ground from which to complain about the teacher's action as unfair *to her.* This incapacity of Nowheresvillians to make moral claims, to "stand up for themselves," shows what Feinberg sees as the essential nature of rights: the moral ground for *claiming* something as *due to you* from someone else.

TAXONOMY OF RIGHTS

In a general schema, we can characterize a right as follows:

> A right is a claim *to* something, *against* someone, that ought to be recognized as valid.

It is instructive to examine each part of this schema in turn.

A right is a claim *to* something

We never just have "a right"; a right-claim must specify what we have a right to. The specification could take two different forms. We could claim that someone ought to *refrain* from doing certain things to us. To say I have a "a right to life," in this interpretation, means claiming that no one ought to kill me. My "right to property" can be interpreted as the claim that no one ought to take my things away without my consent. So interpreted, these rights are *negative rights*—rights to be free from certain kinds of interference. But a right-claim could also be a claim that others *perform* certain actions; these would be *positive rights*. A positive "right to life" would entail not just that people must refrain from killing me, but that they must also keep me alive, perhaps by providing me with the means of subsistence. As another example, consider a "right to education." This is usually understood as a positive right: a claim to be provided with an education—and not just not to be prevented from receiving an education, which would be a negative right.

A right is a claim *against* someone

As we have pointed out, rights have correlative duties. If I have a right to something, that means someone else has a duty to act (if a positive right) or refrain from acting (if a negative right) in some way. The previous examples show this immediately. My negative right to life entails that others have a duty not to kill me. My right to my property entails that others have a duty not to take away my things without my consent. These are *negative duties*—duties not to do certain things. Similarly, there are *positive duties*—duties to perform specific actions. Thus, if I have a positive right to life, it must mean that someone has the duty to provide me with the means of subsistence. A (positive) right to education entails a duty, by someone to be specified, to provide me with an education. Both negative duties (to refrain from some action) and positive duties (to perform some action) are *perfect* duties; they are owed to the person to whose right they correspond. Such duties do not exist in Nowheresville.

Whose duties they are—whom they are owed *by*—must be specified or implied by the particular claim that someone has a certain right. In general, negative rights are likely to give rise to negative duties for *everyone*. My negative right to life corresponds to literally billions of duties, since it means that everyone has a duty not to kill me. Positive rights, in contrast, more naturally impose a duty on a specific person. The excellent student's right to a good grade, for example, may correspond to one single duty—the duty of her teacher to give her one (perhaps it also imposes positive duties on school officials to discipline a teacher who grades unfairly). In any case, the distinction between positive and negative duties, together with that between perfect and imperfect duties, allows us to formulate intricate webs of who owes what to whom, which are much better suited to capturing the relief of our moral landscapes than is utilitarianism's flattening reductionism and its implication of negative responsibility.

It is worth considering here the ways in which one may come to acquire a perfect duty, if the actual world is not like Nowheresville. If we believe the historic declarations of rights, the rights they proclaim belong to people *innately*: We have them just by the virtue of being human; they are not conditional on anything else. If that is true, then the duty to respect those rights must also apply unconditionally. In the case of other rights, we often think of their corresponding duties as arising out of certain choices. Most immediately relevant to business ethics are *contractual* rights. By signing a contract, I give you a right to my performance of a certain set of actions—such as those involved in delivering a product—at least this is how ordinary moral sense perceives it.[109] It is how we usually *think* of contractual obligations—as perfect duties corresponding to rights. Even if this is an illusion and the world is really like Nowheresville, it offers a conceptual example of how a duty corresponding to a right is assumed through the free choice of the person who takes the duty on by signing the contract. If we can justify the existence of such rights—which we may usefully call *special* rights, to contrast them with the *general* or fundamental rights everyone has in common—then they can account for the many *directed* duties we seem to have: duties owed to specific individuals and rooted in the special relationships we have with them.

Rights are claims that *ought to be recognized as valid*

The final part of the schema raises the question: According to *what* ought rights to be recognized as valid? The answers we give will differentiate the kinds of right in question. Feinberg mentions two types. *Legal* rights are claims whose recognition is called

---

[109] In Nowheresville, of course, there are no contractual rights. There, a contract may give rise to a moral obligation to perform what one has contracted to do, but that is not an obligation the other party to the contract can claim as *due to him*.

for by *the law*. That is, they are the rights that the law gives us and enforces, the claims which it would be *illegal* not to recognize and respect. But we have already pointed out that legality and morality are not the same thing. So something that is a legal right (and corresponds to legal duties) is not necessarily also a *moral* right (corresponding to *moral* duties), or vice versa. Moral rights, as our schema tells us, are claims whose recognition is required by morality, regardless of whether it is required by the law. The distinction between moral and legal rights is an important one that people very often fail to make in their assertions about rights. We need to be clear that one can have a moral right (or duty) that is not protected or enforced by the law and that one can have a legal right (or duty) that is not rooted in morality. The distinction is crucial, for example, to character-ize what is usually thought to be the moral problem with unjust states: namely, that their laws violate or fail to protect their people's moral rights. By extension, we cannot begin to develop an account of how business should operate in such states without dis-tinguishing between legal and moral rights and duties.

Legal and moral rights, recognized as valid according to the law and morality, respectively, are the most obvious kinds of rights people may have. But the conceptual schema allows us to talk about rights within any system of rules—including those that are conventional or institutional (and, therefore, not moral) but are not part of the *law*. For ex-ample, according to the rules that govern the membership of a particular club, a member may or may not have a right to bring in nonmember guests. This is obviously not a moral right; nor is it a legal right. If the club changed its rules, no moral or legal rights would (ordinarily) be violated. Still, we may call this an "institutionally defined right" since a member's right to bring in guests is one that ought to be recognized as valid, according to current club rules. Similarly, a culture's social norms may call for certain claims to be rec-ognized as valid, in which case it would make sense to call them "conventional rights" or "socially accepted rights."

The distinction between types of rights is often missed in a commonly heard turn of phrase: the statement that someone "should have a right" or "should not have a right" to this or that. Intended as moral claims, which they almost always are, such statements mean that *it is morally right or required* that someone have the right in question. Now, such a statement is meaningful enough if it refers to legal (or, more generally, nonmoral) rights. It would mean, simply, that there are moral reasons why the law (or other non-moral systems of rules) ought to recognize someone's claim to something as valid, that is, to make it a legal right. One such reason may be that the person already has a moral right to the thing in question, and that the moral right is so important that it should enjoy the protection of the force of law. But the meaning of the statement that someone "ought (or ought not) to have a right" is quite mysterious if the discussion is one of the *moral* rights that people "should" have. For morality either recognizes someone's claim as valid or it does not. If it does, then he has this moral right, and it is redundant to add that he should have this right. And if morality does not recognize his claim as valid, how can it be a right that he morally "should" have? In the case of moral rights, therefore, we had better simply say that the person has or does not have the moral right in question.

This is why the historic declarations of rights are precisely that—*declarations* of rights that people have, not rights that they "should" have. While some of these docu-ments may have some sort of legal status, they are primarily declarations of *moral* rights. And, notably, they are phrased as recognitions of moral rights that already exist, not establishments of new legal rights. Indeed, they claim that people have certain rights in virtue simply of being human—which means that they have them even in the absence of any legal rights. They are, that is, "fundamental human rights": rights that have moral force regardless what the law may be (for, as these declarations' drafters were keenly aware, the law could be unjust). Of course, declarations of moral rights provide the premise of an obvious *argument* for legal rights: If humans have certain fundamental *moral* rights, then lest their moral rights be violated, they must be protected by force of law through the granting of corresponding *legal* rights.

EXAMPLES OF RIGHTS

Although the concept of rights lends itself to analyzing claims recognized by a variety of possible systems of rules—legal, moral, social, and so on—we shall, from now on, focus on moral rights, since this is the kind that—if such rights exist—directly determines what we ought, morally, to do. This is so because of the correlativity doctrine: If someone has a moral right, someone else must have a moral duty to do something (or refrain from doing something). Establishing the existence of a moral right, therefore, by itself establishes that one ought morally to respect that right; for what else is it to respect a right than to fulfill the moral duty that one has in virtue of that right? In this basic sense, the question of whether it is morally required to respect rights, or more pointedly, whether it is wrong to violate rights, cannot, conceptually speaking, arise. Part of what it means to have a right is that it is wrong to violate it. There could, however, be a question of *which* right one should violate if one is in the tragic situation where one cannot possibly respect all the rights that bear on one's actions. The logical possibility of such a case—where all alternatives involve a moral wrong because each violates some right—is a feature of a rights-based view that sets it apart from consequentialism, for which tragic choices are unintelligible. When all the choices available to us involve some rights violation, a rights-based view may resolve our doubt by identifying the least wrong action, but this does not dissipate the dilemma, since the morally right action retains a residual of wrongdoing. In consequentialism, in contrast, dilemmas are impossible once the facts are known, for there is *nothing wrong* in the choice that leads to the best achievable outcome. The fact that it seems possible for an action both to be right thing to do, all things considered, and still be guilty of some degree of moral wrong, is another example of how uneasily our ordinary moral thinking sits with consequentialism.

Until now the dissection we have performed on the concept of right has had to remain at a rather abstract level. But the language of rights that we have developed offers a new way of rationalizing the moral intuitions sparked by the concrete cases we have discussed throughout this book—potentially a better way. While nothing we have said in this chapter yet constitutes an argument for thinking that people in fact have rights, many of the moral intuitions our cases have provoked are natural candidates for statements about rights. This becomes obvious if we take a new look at our examples from the perspective that people have moral rights which may not be violated.

Google in China as a case of negative rights to information

We saw that those who think Google acted wrongly in opening a censored Web site in China, such as Congressman Tom Lantos, cannot base their criticism on conventionalism; they must argue instead that engaging in censorship is morally wrong even if it conforms with local convention. Whether consequentialism can provide such an argument is doubtful. It judges censorship according to whether it produces a better outcome than the alternative. In this case, Google estimated that the absence of google.cn would drive Chinese Internet users to using local search engines more, as the government would continue to slow or block access to international ones such as google.com. Since local search engines would be subject to the same censorship requirements, Google's compliance would not make things worse, and could make them better, if more information is better than less. Therefore, the consequentialist could argue, it was morally right for Google to comply with the censorship demands.

To Google's critics, such an argument misses the point. The fact that "someone else would do it" if Google did not censor does nothing to exonerate Google's action if its wrongness lies not in the relative badness of its consequences, but in that it treats people in a way in which they ought not to be treated. That is an intuition the language of rights can formulate more elaborately. It can do so by saying that Google acted wrongly in violating a right not to be censored, and that the wrongness of the violation is not made lesser by the fact that others would have violated that right even if Google had not. Whether such an argument succeeds depends on how the right not to be censored is specified and defended. Whose right is at stake? What precisely is it a right to? And on whom does the right put a duty? Here, we can only sketch a tentative argument, but the lines along which the case would have to be made are not complicated. If censorship is wrong, then it is presumably because it wrongs Internet users; the right in question must, therefore, belong to Internet users or more specifically to any individual using a search engine. The argument would have to specify the content of the claim as some sort of "right to information." It would also have to characterize it as either a positive or negative right, since this affects whether the right can plausibly be thought of as imposing a duty on Google. A positive right to information would be a right to be provided with information. Could there be such a right? Perhaps citizens could have such a claim on their government; but surely it is far-fetched to say that Google has a *positive* duty to provide information. Otherwise it would be morally wrong of Google to decide to stay out of China altogether—but even critics of Google's behavior do not claim this. If there is any duty at all that Google violates by engaging in censorship, therefore, it must be a negative duty to refrain from censoring information on any search engine that the company chooses to provide, rather than a positive duty to provide a search engine whether it chooses to or not. So the critics must claim that China's Internet users have a negative right that the information they search for is not censored. Even if that claim can be backed by convincing moral reasons, this does not conclude the argument, for the corresponding duty not to censor information could plausibly be thought to be the duty of the Chinese government, not the search engine providers themselves. Once a (negative) right against censorship is established, however, the path is open to argue that even though it imposes a duty directly only on the government, it could also entail a derivative duty on others, including Internet companies, not to assist the Chinese government in violating *its* duty to its citizens. This allows one to make the plausible claim that even if Google acted wrongly, the greater wrong lay with the authorities that required it to censor. All of this, of course, stands or falls with the reasoning mustered to justify a right to uncensored information in the first place. We let this rest until the next chapter.

Guidant as a case of positive rights to information

Guidant's choice not to divulge the defect it discovered in its defibrillator had a solid consequentialist justification, since secrecy could reasonably be expected to save lives compared with the alternative. Consequentialists can readily admit that the action *harmed* those who, if they had known, would have chosen early replacement surgery but who instead suffered a malfunction. But they were not, according to consequentialism, *wronged*, since the harm to them could be expected to be more than outweighed by the benefit to those who would have died or suffered from risky replacement surgery that they would have chosen to undergo if they had been told of the defect. But we need not accept this implication of consequentialism—that the victims were harmed but not wronged—if we think that users of Guidant's devices had a *right* to know about any discovered defects. For if they had that right, then Guidant's secrecy *did them wrong* by violating that right, even if the consequences of what Guidant did were indeed for the best. Now if there is such a right, it presumably has to be some sort of *positive* right to information, as it corresponds (if the argument is correct) to a positive duty on Guidant to provide the information in question. It falls on proponents of such a claim to specify what information the right-holders have a morally valid claim to. The specification could easily become rather detailed: One may imagine a right specified by the long pages of definitional minutiae that characterize product warnings or commercial contracts. But why should rights not be so specific? There is nothing more untoward about highly detailed rights in the moral case than in the legal case, especially if they are derived as the more specific instances of simpler, more general rights. In this case, a right to one's medical information could be justified as an instance of a basic right to decide what medical treatment one undergoes, which is hard to do without the relevant information. Whether *such* a right exists, of course, remains to be established, as does how it comes about. A plausible account of how the right to medical information arises and imposes a positive duty on Guidant (as opposed to, say, the government) would presumably center on the moral relationship into which Guidant enters by selling a heart implant to a patient. That is, it would cast Guidant as *voluntarily assuming* certain duties through its actions—duties that give the buyers rights which Guidant's later secrecy would violate.

Kate's Dilemma as a case of assumed negative duties

If the thought of rights arising from our voluntary action seems strange, it is because the most conspicuous debates about moral rights concentrate on fundamental or innate rights, the rights we have by the virtue of being human. This is quite reasonable inasmuch as claims about such rights touch on the most consequential moral problems humans face—those problems that affect their most deeply held concerns and interests. But this does not mean that they exhaust the range of rights we could, in principle, have. Indeed, rights-claims grounded in our voluntary actions may be inconspicuous precisely because they figure so ubiquitously in the more pedestrian moral questions of everyday life that we take them for granted. They are, for example, how we usually think of an entire class of very common moral commitments, namely those we create by making promises. My act of promising something to someone is aptly described as granting someone a claim on me to the thing I promise them—a claim which morality recognizes as one I must respect. On the one hand, this is just a complicated way of saying that I ought, morally, to keep my promises. But it is also a way of saying that by promising I grant someone a right by putting myself under the corresponding perfect duty (to do what I promised).

Seeing promising as a rights-generating act gives us a way of expressing the intuition we acknowledged in Kate's Dilemma: that Kate ought to keep secret what Lucy told her because she had promised to do so. Once Kate has promised, we can say, Lucy has a right to Kate's confidentiality, and Kate has the corresponding duty not to tell. Her obligation is a *negative* duty—it is a duty to refrain from doing something (telling)—and it is a *perfect* duty owed to a specific person (Lucy)—it is not left up to Kate's discretion to choose when, how, and for whose benefit she discharges it (unlike, say, a duty of charity).

If we establish that Lucy has such a right, we would by the same token establish that Kate would violate a duty, and wrong Lucy, if she passed on the information. And she would violate a duty and wrong Lucy regardless of whether passing on the information would lead to the best outcome overall. Establishing a right thus provides a counterargument to the consequentialist reasoning that concludes that Kate ought to tell. It does not, however, settle the question. For someone could claim that even if Kate's telling would involve committing a wrong against Lucy, it would still be the right thing to do *all things considered*. It is easy, in principle, to find reasons why this could be; they could be grouped, first, into reasons for saying that the consequences of secrecy would be so awful that it is right to break the promise (that is, consequentialist considerations outweigh the alleged right) or, second, into reasons for saying that keeping the secret would *also* violate rights, and that it is more important to respect *those* rights than Lucy's right to confidentiality. Whether the latter claim can be defended depends, of course, on what these other rights are claimed to be and why they are supposed to exist. It would seem strange to say that an employer has a right to employees' not keeping their friends' secrets (stranger, at any rate, than seeing promising as right-creating). If employees have a duty of loyalty to their employer, that duty is often more convincingly characterized as an imperfect duty—which the employee has discretion over how and when to fulfill—than as a perfect duty. If this is so, the imperfect duty is unlikely to "defeat" the perfect duty. One can respect an imperfect duty without fulfilling it all the time in all ways possible. Not acting on a perfect duty, in contrast, always wrongs the person whose right it is, so one can avoid wronging someone only by respecting the perfect duty while temporarily ignoring the imperfect one.

Shareholder primacy as a case of property rights

We have already described two possible justifications for the shareholder primacy view that we first investigated in Chapter 2, and neither the social role-based nor the consequentialist defense could carry the burden of its conclusions. The notion of rights suggests a third line of reasoning (which Milton Friedman's own argument also employs), namely that managers who do not maximize profits violate shareholders' rights. This argument could claim that shareholders *own* the capital that the managers deploy—that is to say, they have a property right to the capital. A property right, if there is such a thing, is presumably a negative right; it confers on others the negative duty not to interfere with the owners' use of their property. Such an argument need not implausibly assert that property rights are "absolute" or that owners have a right to do anything they like with their property; as the classic example goes, whatever property right I have to my knife, I cannot have a right to drive it into your stomach. But as long as the alleged property right includes the right to deny others the use of the property in ways that the owner disapproves of, a limited argument can be constructed to the effect that *if* the company and its capital are the shareholders' property *and* the shareholders do not wish that capital deployed for anything other than profit-maximizing purposes, then managers act wrongly if they so deploy it.[110] A variant of the argument would say that when managers take on their jobs, they make a promise to shareholders to act according to their interests. While not a property right, this could be argued to create a right with the same effect. In either case the argument would say, for example, that as much good as Merck could do by sacrificing profits to fight river blindness, it is morally wrong to do so because it violates the rights of shareholders. Whether that conclusion can be sustained will of course depend on whether its proponents can satisfactorily establish the alleged right, and whether they can substantiate that shareholders' rights outweigh other rights or broader moral considerations.

In neither of these four short discussions has the point been to investigate whether either fundamental rights to information and property or rights created by promising outweigh the consequences of respecting them, defeat the claims of other rights, or even exist at all. The point is, rather, just to show that such investigations can be performed. Until we actually do so, the right-claims we have sketched in this and the previous examples remain idle and prove nothing at all about what is the right thing to do. But even as mere theoretical possibilities, they show how seeing moral assertions as claims about rights moves the conversation beyond where it may previously have stalled.

This explication of the concept of rights—of what rights are—does not answer the ultimately much more important question of whether people in fact have rights, and if so, which ones. But it does put us in a position to address that question, which we shall do in the next chapter. And it demonstrates—as the examples of rights-based reasoning applied to our earlier examples show—that we intuitively understand many common moral claims in terms of rights. This gives us a hint at what seems unnatural about Nowheresville. There, it would be incorrect to couch the strong intuitions that our example cases trigger in the language of rights. If there is anything morally troubling about Google's censorship, Guidant's secrecy, or Kate's telling—*if they did the things they did in Nowheresville*—no congenial explanation of *what* was troubling about any one of those actions would be accessible to us, because it would be ruled out by definition. In particular, Google's search users, Guidant's defibrillator customers, and Lucy would all be denied any special standing to complain that these actions wronged *them*. Rights language allows them to claim such a standing (whether justifiably or not is unimportant here; what matters before assessing the validity of such claims is that they be intelligible). Even before looking at reasons for thinking that people do indeed have rights,

---

[110] Except, of course, in cases where the owners themselves have no right to use the capital in the way that makes the most profits, for example if Mafia-type activities bring a greater return than any other business.

therefore, employing rights language clarifies our moral thinking. This strongly suggests that rights must indeed be part of our moral fabric. If they are not, it is no surprise that people have found it necessary to invent them.

Summary of the Argument in This Chapter

Many of the worries consequentialism raises—such as how it sacrifices one for the many or fails to recognize special moral bonds—spring from the same fundamental feature that is also consequentialism's strength: its unwillingness to treat individuals and their special relationships as morally important except insofar as how they account for human well-being (or whatever other measure of goodness of outcomes the consequentialist theory in question applies). But this unwillingness is difficult to accept; our moral intuitions drive us to assert that individuals must be respected in a stronger sense. They must be *treated fairly*, which means that they can demand that actions which affect them must be justified *to them* and not just with respect to the greater good. It is this assertion that claims about rights express, claims that pervade modern ethical thinking from the great historic declarations of human rights to many of our everyday moral arguments.

We gain an understanding of what it means to say someone has a right to something by imagining the opposite: Joel Feinberg's Nowheresville, where there are no rights. What is missing in such a world is individuals' standing to claim something as *due to them*. While there can be moral obligations without rights (*imperfect duties* to act in certain ways, but where those actions are not something other individuals can claim from us), there can only be *perfect duties* (obligations that others can exact from us as *due to them*) if there are also rights. Rights and perfect duties are "correlative"; they are flip sides of the same coin. A right, we can say, is a claim *to* something, *against* someone, that *ought to be recognized as valid*. It is the normative validity of the claim that grounds the corresponding duty.

The duty can be *positive* if the right in question is a claim to something being done or provided (a positive right); or *negative* if the right is a claim to something being refrained from or not interfered with (a negative right). Thus, a positive "right to life" imposes a more burdensome duty—perhaps to provide the means of subsistence—than a negative "right to life," which merely entails a duty not to kill. Just as a right is *someone's* claim to something, it also imposes a duty *on* identifiable persons. A negative right can in principle impose duties on *everyone*; there is nothing incoherent in the notion that a negative right is a protection against *anyone's* interference. But logic and practicality may dictate that positive rights impose more narrowly held duties. The positive duty to provide or do something specific is often not plausibly matched by a duty for *everyone* to do so, but for *someone* to do so. These modalities must be specified by the right-claim in question, and, more broadly, in the normative system by which the claim is recognized as valid.

Rights formulations are not unique to morality: We can discuss legal rights (claims that ought to be recognized as valid according to the law) just as well as moral ones (claims that ought to be recognized as valid according to morality), and, indeed, rights defined within any other possible system of normative rules. Since our interest is in morality, however, we shall focus on moral rights. Other kinds of rights may carry implications for what we ought morally to do (in ordinary cases, we ought *morally* to respect *legal* rights and duties even if they are not also moral ones). But whereas the question can be asked, "Do we have a moral duty to follow our legal obligations?" this question does not arise with *moral* rights and duties. For what it means to have a moral duty is that we ought morally to do it; what it means to have a moral right is that someone has a moral duty to respect it.

None of this proves that there are any moral rights and duties at all. But our examples show that establishing the existence of rights would significantly affect our moral conclusions. Even the possible existence of rights in principle opens up new routes for our moral reasoning, as the focus shifts to whether rights are ever outweighed by other considerations (which could be other, conflicting rights, or the negative consequences of respecting rights) as well as to what is owed to those whose rights are violated when this is the right thing to do, all things considered.

CHAPTER 9

The Case for Rights
Justifying Right-Claims

In 1993, when Western corporations were first streaming into China to set up factories or subcontract manufacturing, one company attracted much attention, and no little derision, for doing the opposite. Levi Strauss, the iconic maker of jeans, was at the time producing some three million pieces of garment annually through Chinese subcontractors, a small part of its worldwide output. It was a company that prided itself on taking ethics seriously: While Jack Welch was preaching shareholder value maximization, Levi Strauss devoted time and resources to analyze which business practices it deemed ethically required. In 1991, it produced two sets of rules that still govern its outsourcing operations today. The "Business Partner Terms of Engagement" ban outsourcing to companies that employ child labor, forced or prison labor; engage in corporal punishment; force workers regularly to work more than sixty-hour weeks; and fail to "respect the right to free association and the right to organize and bargain collectively without unlawful interference." The "Country Assessment Guidelines" are used to evaluate possible challenges to "the ethical principles we have set for ourselves"—most notably the "human rights environment in the country."[111]

Levi Strauss practiced what it preached. After it found child labor and forced labor in random checks at its Chinese supply factories, it decided to stop doing business there. The reactions, predictably, ranged from commendation to condemnation—as well a good deal of puzzlement. The company agonized as much over what moral business conduct requires as did Google over its predicament a decade later; Levi Strauss changed its mind in 1998, before it had even had time to phase out its presence in China completely. But however much the company wavered on exactly what responsibility it had for human rights—"Levi Strauss is not in the human rights business, but to the degree that human rights affects our business, we care about it," said a company

---

[111] *Levi Strauss & Co. Global Sourcing and Operating Guidelines*, available on http://www.levistrauss.com/library/levi-strauss-co-global-sourcing-and-operating-guidelines (accessed November 2010).

official[112]—Levi Strauss's reasoning never questioned the premise that humans *have* rights. This is surely significant. For if there are no rights, then not only is there no question of what those rights are and what we must do to respect them, it is also senseless to base rules for company conduct on the notion of respecting rights.

Having established in the previous chapter what it means to say that there are rights, we must now, like Levi Strauss, confront the question of whether people actually have rights, and if so, which rights they have. It is immediately clear that the answers depend on what kinds of rights we are talking about. If we ask, "Do people have *legal* rights?" the answer is obviously yes. That is an essentially descriptive claim about whether the law recognizes certain claims as valid. While a degree of interpretation is always involved in specifying the detailed legal rights that the law grants us, it is clear enough that wherever there is any formal law at all that is minimally enforced, at least some people have some legal rights. Many constitutions or bills of rights explicitly enumerate the basic legal rights of their citizens.

But looking to the law is not particularly helpful for companies which, like Levi Strauss, are concerned about respecting *moral* rights. When Levi Strauss included the following language in its Terms of Engagement:

> Use of child labor is not permissible. Workers can be no less than 15 years of age and not younger than the compulsory age to be in school.

the company knew full well that the legal minimum working age was less than fifteen in several poor countries. What the company was asserting was that children have a moral right not to be put to work if they are younger than fifteen, regardless of whether the law recognizes that as a legal right. But was Levi Strauss correct about this or about any of its other claims?

For many of us, it seems obvious that we have rights, and that the rights we have are roughly the kinds recognized in the political and corporate documents we have mentioned. As we have seen, some of our most deeply held moral notions can seemingly only be expressed in the language of rights. But these intuitions are not necessarily true. On some moral views, the world is like Nowheresville—there are things people morally ought to do, but it is inappropriate to claim them as *owed* to people. Those who hold such a point view might suggest that insisting on individual rights—that is, on claiming things as due to us individually—is too selfish and individualistic an activity to be the core of morality, as proponents of rights would have it. Anyone who asserts the existence of moral rights, therefore, has to give moral reasons why rights should be thought such an essential part of the furniture of morality. What these moral reasons can be is the subject of this chapter.

RELATIVISM AGAIN: THE ASIAN VALUES DEBATE

Since most countries in the world signed the United Nations Universal Declaration of Human Rights of 1948, human rights have gradually become a standard by which international politics is gauged, rhetorically if not substantively. Recently, it has also been

---

[112] Mark Landler, "Reversing Course, Levi Strauss Will Expand Its Output in China," *The New York Times,* 9 April 1998.

proposed that the concept of human rights can guide multinational business corporations through such initiatives as the U.N. Global Compact.[113] (Of course many individual companies have, like Levi Strauss, paid attention to human rights since long before the Global Compact came into being.) Now, if people do have fundamental rights, they evidently do not depend for their moral force on the Universal Declaration of Human Rights, the prescriptions of the Global Compact, or any corporation's code of conduct. These documents are not irrelevant—they can be of great help in combating violations of moral rights, including by encouraging the development of previously nonexistent legal rights to match and protect moral rights with the force of law. But the moral *validity* of rights is not something that declarations of rights generate. It is, at most, something they can acknowledge and pay tribute to.

This raises the question of whether any given declaration of human rights or a code of conduct that prescribes respect for them "gets it right." It obviously must fail to do so if there are no moral rights. It may fail to do so even if there are rights, if the rights it posits are not the ones people in fact have. As an illustration, consider that while some of the human rights asserted in the Universal Declaration of Human Rights seem indisputable—Article 3 asserts the right "to life, liberty and security of person"—others are more apt to leave one scratching one's head: According to Article 24, everyone has the right to "periodic holidays with pay." That this is a fundamental human *right* as opposed to something that it would be good for people to have is, if not inconceivable, certainly far-fetched. To defend it, we would at least have to point out whose duty it is to provide periodic holidays with pay. That in turn would require us to overcome the problem that many people live in such destitute conditions that no one is in a position even to offer jobs at decent wages, not to speak of paid leave, and where it would be frivolous to suggest we can identify someone on whom to pin a positive duty to provide these goods. Joel Feinberg has instead proposed to think of a claim such as this as "a special 'manifesto sense' of 'right'." It is better, he says, to describe the

> manifesto writers [who] identify needs, or at least basic needs, with what they call 'human rights' . . . as urging upon the world community the moral principle that *all* basic human needs ought to be recognized as *claims* . . . worthy of sympathy and serious consideration right now, even though . . . they cannot yet plausibly be treated as *valid* claims, that is, as grounds of any other people's duties . . . A person in need, then, is always 'in a position' to make a claim, even when there is no one in the corresponding position to do anything about it. Such claims [are] the natural seed from which rights grow.[114]

We can only agree with Feinberg to grant this "rhetorical license," however, at the cost of making the Universal Declaration of Human Rights say rather less than it claims to say, since some of the rights it asserts are then not to be taken as rights at all, just (at

---

[113] See http://www.unglobalcompact.org/ (accessed November 2010). The U.N. Global Compact, intended to commit companies to protecting human rights, is a mixed success, judging by the U.N.'s exclusion of more than a thousand companies in 2008–9 for failing to meet reporting requirements; see http://www.unglobalcompact.org/newsandevents/news_archives/2009_10_07.html (accessed November 2010).

[114] Feinberg, "The Nature and Value of Rights."

best) as morally worthy aspirations ("manifesto rights"). But if we need not take everything the Declaration says on its word, then it is a short way to questioning why we should believe any of it at all.

In fact, an influential argument, highly relevant to business, has been made that the human rights asserted by the U.N. Universal Declaration of Human Rights are not universal at all. In a speech to Cambridge University in 1995, the then prime minister of Malaysia, Mahathir bin Mohamad, began by warning that he would "offend . . . the many Western universalists who insist that there are only universal values, [and] no such thing as 'Asian values.'" The universalists are not only wrong, said Mahathir, but also arrogant:

> The demise of communism and the discrediting of Fabian socialism have not impressed the Western universalists on the need to be a little circumspect, on the need to be less insistent that the West is always right. They still insist that what is right for them is right for the world . . . The countries of the West have a right to their preferences. But they have no right to ram their preferences down anyone's throat . . . so far, it has not entered the mind of any Asian leader to threaten sanctions if any European country fails to put its house in order . . . If it is preposterous and mad for Asian leaders to threaten sanctions when Europeans fail to measure up to their standards and norms, could it not be a little preposterous for Europeans to threaten sanctions when non-evil and non-uncivilized Asian countries prefer their own standards and norms and not Europe's?[115]

The speech was one of many instances in the 1990s when Asian intellectuals and political leaders began to defend "Asian values" in response to western criticism of the human right records in fast-growing Asian countries.[116] It is a line of reasoning that has enjoyed some resurgence after the 2008 financial crisis showed the vulnerability of western-style capitalism.

Attacks on the western emphasis on individual human rights from claims of alleged "Asian values" take several forms. One is to denounce it—no doubt often justifiably—as a moralizing camouflage for economic protectionism, in cases where unions and activists in rich countries call for boycotts of goods allegedly produced under conditions that violate the workers' human rights. Another is to argue instrumentally that an excessive focus on rights is harmful to economic development. But from the perspective of moral reasoning, the strongest claim is that rights-based talk is simply *misguided*—that although such language may apply within the western societies that have developed and cultivated it, it has no place in Asian societies. According to Lee Kuan Yew, the long-time prime minister of Singapore, "the idea of the inviolability of the individual has been turned into a dogma . . . It makes the hopeful assumption that all men are equal, that people all over the world are the same. They are not."[117]

---

[115] Mahathir bin Mohamad, speech to the Senate House, Cambridge University, 15 March 1995, available on http://www.pmo.gov.my/ucapan/?m=p&p=mahathir&id=1584 (accessed November 2010).

[116] An overview of the Asian values debate can be found in Matt Steinglass, "Whose Asian values?" *The Boston Globe*, 20 November 2005.

[117] Lee Kuan Yew interviewed by Fareed Zakaria, "Culture is Destiny: A Conversation with Lee Kuan Yew," *Foreign Affairs*, 73(2), March/April 1994.

Defenders of the notion of individual moral rights have, in turn, pointed out that intellectual criticism of the idea of rights easily becomes an attack on rights themselves. Rejecting the notion of individual moral rights is not an idle intellectual argument; it has implications for politics—and for business. Appeals to "Asian values" have been used to excuse hardships caused by industrialization and fast economic growth. If the whole idea of individual rights is a mistake, then this is not a problem: One can hardly blame those who attack it for promoting the violation of rights that do not exist. If individuals do have moral rights, however, it is not just intellectually but morally important to refute the criticism of them.

The "Asian values" claim can be interpreted in two quite different ways, depending on what one means by saying that the belief in individual rights is mistaken. One could be saying—as suggested by Lee—that it is mistaken *everywhere*, including in the West. Alternatively, one could be making the more modest claim (or what may seem like the more modest claim) that Mahathir made in his speech: that the idea of rights may be appropriate for the West and in the West, but that it is not right for Asia and in Asia, because Asian values differ from Western values in general, and have little room for individual rights in particular. We shall consider this second interpretation first.

Taken as a purely empirical claim, the statement that "Asian values" differ from "Western values" could simply mean that the things most Asians think are morally right or good differ from the things most Westerners consider morally right or good. That may be true—indeed Mahathir, in the speech already quoted, referred to a survey purporting to find exactly this: While Westerners stressed values of individual independence, Asians ranked values of social order and harmony more highly. The descriptive claim that what Asians find morally valuable is not what Westerners find morally valuable, however, is not the same as the normative claim that what is morally valuable for Asians is not what is morally valuable for Westerners. And it is not certainly the same as that normative claim as it logically applies to rights—which, when we strip it down to its essence, says that while Westerners have individual moral rights, Asians do not (or they do not have to be respected, which means the same thing). But Mahathir seemed to propose something very close to this: that it is justified for Westerners in the West to insist that they have rights that must not be violated, but that it is wrong to impose on Asians an improper (for them) Western idolatry of the individual. A variation on this theme is to say that while everyone has rights, different peoples have different rights. For example, while Westerners have rights to freedom of speech, sexual orientation, or lifestyle choice, Asians have social or economic rights to economic well-being and an orderly community. Now it is true enough that in the case of legal rights, which ones people have depends on the jurisdiction. The question is whether the equivalent holds for moral rights.

A reason to be skeptical of these claims is that they are instances of the relativist argument we have already encountered. The relativist tries to impress on us the obvious fact that different cultures disagree about whether people have rights and about which rights people have. To the relativist this means that there are no fundamental moral rights, only culture-relative rights. But we have seen that we should not be impressed by this argument, since the fact of disagreement does not by itself show that there is no fact of the matter about the question on which people disagree. Assertions of rights, such as the declarations mentioned earlier, claim that there is a fact of the matter. They also specify what the relevant facts are: namely, that all human beings have moral rights, and that the moral rights include what the declaration in question says. They may be mistaken. But they are not shown to be mistaken by the fact that people disagree. Even if the champions of Asian values were correct to say that the notion of individual rights is alien to Asian intellectual traditions (which they are not);[118] or even if they are right to claim that Westerners try to force their beliefs onto the rest of the world (which, sadly, they often are)—how would this compromise the validity of whatever innate moral rights Asians may have? As moral reasons go, someone's belief that they do not have rights and others' conviction that they do are equally irrelevant for whether they are, in fact, innately owed anything.

There happens to be a very good reason to think that if there are innate moral rights at all, then they are innate to *all* human beings. For whatever reasons can be conceived to support the notion of innate moral rights, they will surely have to ground rights in innate human characteristics—characteristics, that is, which all human beings are born with. Or to reverse this thought, suppose a moral reason could be found that justified certain moral rights as belonging to some people but not to others. It is not believable that this could *also* be a reason to think of those rights as *human* rights in the sense of innate, fundamental rights. Amartya Sen has written that

> the idea of 'human rights' has to be properly understood. In the most general form, the notion of human rights builds on our shared humanity. These rights are not derived from citizenship in any country, or membership in any nation. They are taken as entitlements of every human being. These rights differ, therefore, from constitutionally created rights guaranteed for specified people (such as American citizens or French nationals). The human right of a person not to be tortured is affirmed independently of the country of which this person is a citizen, and also irrespective of what the government of that country—or any other country—wants to do. Of course, a government can dispute a person's legal right not to be tortured, but that will not amount to disputing what must be seen as the person's human right not to be tortured. [The] so-called Asian values that are invoked to justify authoritarianism are not especially Asian in any significant sense . . . The people whose rights are being disputed are Asians, and [the] case for liberty and political rights turns ultimately on their basic importance . . . [This] case is as strong in Asia as it is elsewhere.[119]

Once a conclusive reason for an innate right is given, no *further* reason needs to be given for that right's universality—if anything, a further reason would have to be given why its universality should be curtailed. Since rights correlate with duties, someone's *innate* moral right gives others a moral duty, made valid by the simple fact that this person exists. But if another person's existence is reason enough to place me under a duty to do or (more probably) not to do something to him (not to torture him, say), why would not the existence of *other* persons be reason enough to place me under similar duties to *them*? We arrive, then, at a specific instance of the observation we made in Chapter 1 that

---

[118] Amartya Sen has argued forcefully that the notion of individual liberty and other moral rights is as well grounded in Asian traditions as in Western ones. See Amartya Sen, "Human Rights and Asian Values," *The New Republic*, 14 and 21 July 1997.

[119] Amartya Sen, "Human Rights and Asian Values".

the structure of moral thinking by itself tends toward a universal form. That does not rule out the possibility that we ought to adjust our behavior to the culture in which we find ourselves; it would be absurd to think that we should not. But the justification for such differential behavior must ultimately be derived from moral reasons that apply universally. That is also true of any argument for differential moral rights: If a justification for rights can be found at all, then at the most basic level it must apply to everyone.

RIGHTS OR "RIGHTS"?

One can, of course, without contradiction both agree that a justification of rights can only be sustained if some part of it applies universally and at the same time deny that any such justification is possible. For this reason, refuting the simple relativism of a Mahathir leaves unscathed the more radical assault on the idea of individual rights of a Lee Kuan Yew. To assess that deeper criticism we must establish what exactly it is one rejects by adopting a wholesale skepticism about rights. In other words, what is special about rights? At what price does a moral theory reject the notion of individual rights altogether?

We should take care not to caricature the skeptic's position. One can reject the concept of individual rights without being committed to the absurd claim that anyone may behave in any way one likes. Reasonable proponents of "Asian values" or other detractors of individual rights do not say, for example, that it is right to torture people. They say, rather, that the wrongness of torture is not well captured by describing it as a violation of a right. The question, then, is whether we *need* the concept of individual rights as we have explicated it to account adequately for what morality commands. That is surely a question worth asking: Why do we need to cast moral rules—especially those on which widely disparate traditions agree—in terms of *rights* rather than some other moral concept? And once we raise *that* question, another one logically follows, namely that if we do not after all need the concept of rights to express what is ethically required of us, might it not be that framing morality's commands as right-claims *distorts* our understanding of the morally valuable by turning, as Lee Kuan Yew would say, "the idea of the inviolability of the individual [into] dogma"?

We have already contemplated a morality shorn of rights: It is the ethics that governs Nowheresville. Although Feinberg offered it as a thought experiment to highlight reasons to think that there are rights, it is a surprisingly good schematic representation of what the moral world is actually like according to several thoughtful theories that deny the existence of rights as we have defined them. These theories insist that we do not need the concept of rights that Nowheresvillians lack: Their lacking it is no shortcoming, because there are better alternatives to rights for explaining our deepest moral intuitions. The moral philosopher Alan Strudler contends that one such theory can be based on the Asian tradition of Confucian thought:

> Suppose that you are an American manager representing a firm that until recently had all its operations in Massachusetts; now the firm has put you in charge of a new manufacturing plant operating in an Asian community, where government officials express skepticism about rights. Your employees, unhappy with their working conditions, gather in the firm's parking lot, assessing their grievances and devising a strategy for redress. Your

Massachusetts experience suggests that fairness requires that you let these people meet and formulate their views, and that you then remain open to negotiating with them. But local government officials . . . say that you are wrong to allow the employees to congregate and complain, that the employees, by claiming these rights, insult the local values on which the community is built . . . [It] would be a mistake to dismiss these accusations as simple expressions of cynicism. Many distinguished Confucian scholars with no ties to government or ulterior motives make arguments reminiscent of [these]. They contend that Confucian culture contains the moral resources to say every thing morally worth saying, even though individual rights form no part of its vocabulary, and that appeal to rights actually compromises the integrity of Confucian culture.[120]

The implications of Strudler's thought experiment for real-life cases such as Levi Strauss's are obvious. Strudler's point is twofold. First, the fact that the government denies any right to organize does not entail that the workers' situation need not be addressed (nor, indeed, that the government thinks they need not be addressed). Like in Nowheresville, there may well be a moral obligation to address it. Second, therefore, it is misguided to think that a denial of rights either undermines arguments for the company's responsibility for its workers (let alone the responsibility of the government or the wider community) or necessarily frustrates its ability to fulfill that responsibility. A Confucian theory that values a harmonious community and secure livelihood for all of a community's members can easily require the kind of managerial responsibility for workers that some early industrialists in the West also endorsed, not as a matter of workers' rights but as a paternalistic obligation to provide for their welfare. But this can be done (indeed, Strudler suggests, Confucians have powerful reasons to claim that it must be done) without encouraging the socially harmful activity of claiming supposed rights:

> The Confucian sees people as having many obligations, roles, and duties, but no rights generally, and no workplace rights in particular. Even if one were to accept this perspective, it would not follow that one should not do what one can to see that employees get a just and fair wage, along with decent working conditions. It would follow, however, that in providing this kind of aid, one should not facilitate employees in pressing rights against one's firm or otherwise adopting an adversarial posture.

The point is that insisting on redress as a matter of right—claiming a change as one's personal due—is a misguided, even preposterous way for the workers to express the problem. The reason is that the adversarial position in which the notion of individual rights puts the presumptive claimants perverts their relationship with the larger community of which they are part: "[A Confucian] may contend that it is . . . selfish and disloyal for the disgruntled employees to press their felt rights against their employer . . . To the extent that one sees one's relations in terms of rights, one has a reason to see fellow group members as rivals in a contest for whatever scarce goods are available to

---

[120] Alan Strudler, "Confucian concern about workplace rights," *Business Ethics Quarterly*, 18(1), 2008.

the group, and hence one does not see them as sharing a collective interest."[121] It would be wrong to encourage or reward the moral vices of selfishness and disloyalty, just as it is wrong to indulge and act on those vices.

Strudler, who does not believe that a business firm can constitute a community in the sense required to ground a Confucian obligation for the manager to care for workers, in the end concludes in favor of workplace rights to protect workers' interests. But by acknowledging the strength of a Confucian theory that denies them, he leaves the road open for an argument that a firm ought to be such a community. Such an argument could allow a Confucian theorist to assert managerial obligations while denying the existence of (and decrying the insistence on) moral rights.

This excursion into Confucian thought—limited, unrepresentative, and far too brief to do justice to that rich tradition—should not be confused with the orientalist canard that assertions and denials of individual rights track an East-West divide. Many Asian thinkers have asserted the importance of individual rights or liberties, and the Western philosophical tradition contains important theories that reject them. We have already encountered the most important—utilitarianism—and its position on rights bears examining here. Despite the many differences between utilitarianism and Confucian thought, their skepticism of rights have something in common.

We have seen that utilitarianism has little room for rights as we have understood them. Certainly act-utilitarianism does not: If the standard of rightness for each individual act is its effect on the sum total of human well-being, individuals can have no inviolable claims that ought not be sacrificed for that goal. Thus Jeremy Bentham, the father of classical utilitarianism, was admirably consistent when he famously exclaimed: "*Natural rights* is simple nonsense: natural and imprescriptible rights, rhetorical nonsense—nonsense upon stilts."[122] Now the rather obvious retort against Bentham's disparagement of natural rights is that it clearly is a good thing for human well-being that people treat each other in the ways that correspond to what we commonly think of as respecting natural rights. This is the argument that John Stuart Mill made in his short but seminal book *Utilitarianism*. Not only is utilitarianism the best explanation of our intuitions that people have rights, Mill says, it is also the only *possible* justification for these intuitions. He points out that our common rules of justice and rights, such as the security of the person and property, are crucial preconditions for human well-being. A society in which rules against killing, assault, and theft were not generally observed could most likely not subsist for long; or if it could, it would be one in which the human lot would be miserable. The behavior required by granting people the common list of rights, therefore, must in general be required by a utilitarian morality.

Indeed, it is precisely the fact that this behavior is such an important precondition for human well-being, says Mill, that endows us with such strong intuitions that individuals have inviolable rights in the first place. If "rights" seem like a qualitatively distinct moral category, it is because of their enormous quantitative effect on how happy our lives are:

> . . .the sentiment itself does not arise from anything which would commonly or correctly be termed an idea of [utility, but] whatever is moral in it does . . .

---

[121] Ibid.

[122] In his *Anarchical Fallacies*, a commentary on the French Declaration of the Rights of Man.

> To have a right [is] to have something which society ought to defend me in possession of. If the objector goes on to ask why it ought, I can give him no other reason than general utility. If that expression does not seem to convey a sufficient feeling of the strength of the obligation, nor to account for the peculiar energy of the feeling, it is because [it] derives its intensity, as well as its moral justification, from the extraordinarily important and impressive kind of utility which is concerned.[123]

So we should not, Mill argues, think that our intuitions that people have rights stand in opposition to utilitarian concerns. On the contrary, it is because they are fundamental for achieving the utilitarian goal of the greatest happiness for the greatest number that our intuitions that people have inviolable rights are generally correct about what we ought to do. Indeed, that is the only thing that justifies those intuitions.

We should be clear about what this means. If Mill is correct, people have "rights" in the sense that there are certain ways we must treat people. These treatments are so morally important that they warrant a special word, precisely because so much suffering would ensue if they were not respected. Our conviction that we have a "right" not to be killed or assaulted expresses how extremely heavily considerations of utility weigh in favor of our bodily security; our intuition that we have a "right" to property is warranted because of how miserable we would be if we could not rely on controlling certain things as belonging to us. Thus, utilitarianism in its indirect or rule-utilitarian form *mimics* rights-based views. Asking, "What would the consequences be for human well-being if people did not generally respect the common lists of 'rights'?" supports our intuitions of individual inviolability.

But, as Bentham saw clearly, and as Mill acknowledged, these "rights" are not rights as we have defined them in the sense of a separate and foundational moral category. They do not deserve recognition in virtue of a moral force of their own, which is independent from and could at least in principle outweigh the common good. Millian "rights" cannot be called valid individual claims at all, for they grant none of the individual prerogative inherent in a valid claim, namely the moral ground on which the person whose right it is has a special standing to exact his due. Rule-utilitarian "rights" do not denote something due to individuals but something that it would be good for society (in terms of its aggregate happiness) that those individuals be granted. At best, rule-utilitarianism can conclude that *society* is due the satisfaction of those "rights," and that therefore, as Mill says, society may exact it from those with the corresponding duties. But such "rights" are a far cry from rights as we—and evidently the rights declarations—conceive of them: *individual* claims whose moral validity is independent of what may be good for society.

Does this matter? It does in the cases where respecting "rights" would *not* contribute to social well-being, but on the contrary detract from it. Even act-utilitarians say that it is usually wrong to kill or steal, because usually killing or stealing diminishes overall well-being. But by definition, those are the only times act-utilitarianism can condemn those actions. Since it is at least hypothetically possible for an act of killing or stealing to *add* to social well-being—Raskolnikov's murder and Robin Hood's thievery come to mind—if rights are to have any function at all, it must be to ban some such

---

[123] John Stuart Mill, *Utilitarianism*, Chapter V.

cases as immoral. But this is precisely what act-utilitarianism cannot do. And therefore, nor can rule-utilitarianism, which we have seen collapses into act-utilitarianism (unless it appeals to non-consequentialist principles). For how is rule-utilitarianism to defend Raskolnikov's or Robin Hood's victims, when violating those victims' "rights" will be beneficial for society's happiness? Within any utilitarian theory, only the utilitarian criterion can ultimately adjudicate between social utility and individual claims; and it will always rule in favor of the former. If "rights" are a useful rule of thumb for the utilitarianly most significant obligations we have, that is also all they can be. However closely rule-utilitarian "rights" resemble real rights in terms of their content, their foundation and therefore their validity could not be more different.

RIGHTS, DIGNITY AND CONSENT

There is a common sense in which these two otherwise very different approaches—Confucian and utilitarian—take rights seriously even though they ultimately reject them as an independent source of moral justification. Rather than dismissing a concern for individual rights out of hand, they try to *defuse* it by showing that although our intuitions that we have rights are false, there is *something* that is true in those intuitions, and that whatever is true in them is something their theories can account for. Specifically, they claim that the moral requirements on how we ought to treat people that rights-based theories call respecting their rights can be rescued, even if the concept of rights itself (understood as the fundamental moral category we have analyzed it as) cannot be maintained. Pseudo-"rights," in other words, can do all the valuable justificatory work that the concept of fundamental moral rights provides; and at the same time they avoid that concept's undesirable baggage of adversarialism. Rejecting superstitious beliefs in rights and instead focusing on "rights"—that is to say, what is in truth morally valuable in the idea of rights, be it the conduct conducive to a flourishing harmonious community or to a maximum amount of happiness and well-being—is an advance in moral reasoning.

What are we to make of this? The answer clearly depends on the extent to which the alternative theories reproduce the practical conclusions of a theory that does acknowledge individual rights.[124] In principle, it is of course *possible* that a non-rights-based theory could end up justifying exactly the duties that correspond to the common lists of fundamental human rights. It may be possible to identify Confucian or other communitarian reasons for doing the things that we tend to identify with respecting people's rights, as Strudler suggests. It may be true that acting as if people have rights is what in general best promotes human well-being, as Mill argues. These approaches, and no doubt many other ones, could with a reasonable expectation of success be pursued to establish that giving up rights does not necessarily change much, because we always have "rights."

But even if this is true, and our concern for individual rights can be defused, would we not feel somehow *cheated* by such theories? It would seem too coincidental

---

[124] Such a judgment, if it is at all detailed, will vary from one specific theory to another—wide differences exist among both rights-based and rights-denying theories. While not denying the undeniable pluralism in both camps, however, the views that affirm individual rights have enough family resemblance to make rough generalizations fruitful.

for comfort that such different theories should so closely track each other in their practical conclusions. It would smack of *rationalization*, of indulging our intuitions while refusing to call them by their name. For our thought is not just that we ought to act in certain ways (which "rights" can rationalize), but that we owe it to specific people to act in those ways, and that they may demand as their due that we act in those ways. If denying this made no difference to how we ought to behave, it would indeed make little sense to insist on rights rather than "rights"—but one might as well question why some Confucians, utilitarians, and others bother to *deny* that there are rights. The correct answer is surely that it *does* matter whether or not we have rights rather than "rights"— which is why "defusing" our worry seems like cheating. Underplaying the difference between rights-affirming and rights-denying theories hides from view precisely what is most important about both, which is their distinct position on what, ultimately, matters most morally. Rights and "rights" differ in how obligations are justified, and this difference in turn shapes both the content of obligations and their relative priority should several apparent duties conflict.

Rights and the source of moral value

The difference between rights and the pseudo-"rights" accorded by alternative theories is that "rights" are always instrumental—to the good of the community, its harmonious order or its greatest happiness. In contrast, the value of rights as fundamental moral "trumps" is intrinsic. It lies precisely in the individual inviolability that critics such as Lee Kuan Yew find dogmatic. Having rights enables us to claim as our individual due the things that we have a right to; rights provide individuals with a moral ground to stand on to make such claims.[125] Feinberg's Nowherevillians or people in a Confucian (as Strudler describes it) or rule-utilitarian moral universe, have no such ground. They cannot claim things as their moral due; "even when they are discriminated against invidiously, or left without the things they need, or otherwise badly treated, [they] do not think to leap to their feet and make righteous demands against one another"[126] (or if they do, they will either not be understood or they will come across as petulant children). It is not that people without rights cannot *complain*. Moral theories without rights still consist of rules that impose duties and obligations, and anyone may complain against those who transgress the rules. But the very fact that *anyone* can complain is what makes a society without rights different. *I* have no special standing, which others do not share, to complain about your transgressions against *me*. Nor do I have any stronger moral reason than others do to demand that you stop mistreating me; this is not something I can claim as owed by you to me. Strudler gives the example of "Ed, a victim of repeated spouse abuse, who happens to live next door to another victim of spouse abuse . . . In a Confucian regime he has no more reason to complain about his plight than he would have to complain about the plight of his neighbor. As a victim he has no special standing. All he can do is identify the wrong. And the wrong committed by his neighbor is exactly the same as the wrong committed by his spouse. If Ed focuses his complaints on his own case rather than his neighbor's, one might

---

[125] In much the same way as legal rights provide individuals with the *legal* ground for claiming.

[126] Feinberg, "The Nature and Value of Rights."

understand the prudential basis for his doing so. But Ed cannot claim a moral basis for his action."[127]

This lack of moral ground for claiming something as our due should strike us as more than a mere inability; it seems a *dis*ability, the loss of a morally valuable function. The activity of claiming, Feinberg suggests, is a prerequisite for a certain form of dignity, the dignity that comes from being able to "stand up for oneself" and "look others in the eyes"—that is, from the ability to consider oneself in an important moral sense as the equal of others, as someone who not only ought to treat others in certain ways, but who can demand to be treated similarly in return:

> respect for persons . . . may simply be respect for their rights, so that there cannot be one without the other; and what is called 'human dignity' may simply be the recognizable capacity to assert claims. To respect a person, then, or to think of him as possessed of human dignity, simply *is* to think of him as a potential maker of claims.[128]

Note that the fundamental moral significance is in the potential claim, not the actual claim. The individual's moral dignity of which his rights are the manifestation is secured by his *ability* to engage (intelligibly and validly) in the activity of claim-making, whether or not he actually makes any claims. (Psychologically, too, his felt dignity may also depend as much on the knowledge that he can claim as on his actual claiming.) For it is a special feature of rights that their exercise is in general *voluntary*; the need to fulfill the perfect duties which derive from them can be waived at the right-holder's discretion. Thus, an owner is free to allow people access to her private property; a creditor is free to forgive his debtors; and in Kate's Dilemma, Lucy is free to release Kate from her promise.[129] Indeed, this freedom is what gives moral life much of its richness. If an individual's moral dignity is bound up with his rights, the quality of his moral character expresses itself in his judgment on when to refrain from pressing his rights and when to insist on getting his due.

These thoughts lead naturally to the notions of consent and of free will. If moral dignity depends on the ability to claim, and the moral importance of having a valid claim consists at least in part on one's being free to choose whether or not to press it, it must be because free choice is itself a deep repository of moral value. Our view of moral rights, in other words, will reflect the importance we attribute to whether people consent to the way they are treated. Rights-denying theories, of course, can find consent valuable because it makes the achievement of moral goals such as communal harmony or societal well-being more probable. What distinguishes a view of rights as fundamental, in contrast, is that it treats individual consent as intrinsically and not just instrumentally valuable.

---

[127] Strudler, "Confucian skepticism about workplace rights."

[128] Feinberg, "The Nature and Value of Rights."

[129] The right-holder's freedom not to enforce his right may be termed a "moral freedom." It simply means that he has no moral duty to enforce it. It does not follow, of course, that he is "free" in a broader social sense. It may not be the case, for example, that he can choose not to enforce his right without excessively negative consequences for himself.

Dignity and the content of obligations

The following remarks about the Asian values debate were given by the political philosopher and rights theorist Ronald Dworkin to an audience in Beijing:

> [T]he human rights commonly recognized in Western democracies rest on two fundamental principles: first, that the fate of every living human being is equally important, and, second, that nevertheless one person has special responsibility for the success of each life—the person whose life it is.
>
> The first principle . . . forbids sacrificing some people for the sake of others or for the sake of the community as a whole, as any government does that arrests and tortures political opponents to intimidate others, or as the Chinese government has done in concentrating investment and wealth in its commercially important coastal cities to the neglect of the rural population, which has not been allowed to share in China's recent prosperity.
>
> The second principle requires that government respect the rights that individuals need to direct their lives: the right, among others, to practice any religion freely, to speak their minds on matters of political and moral conse-quence, and to choose political positions and associates for themselves. China violates that second principle because it jails political dissidents, for-bids any political activity outside the Communist Party, and persecutes the Falun Gong, a religious movement with no political aims but with a remark-able ability to organize mass meetings and demonstrations in defense of its religious practices.[130]

Dworkin's second principle—the idea that each individual has a special responsi-bility for living her own life well—contains the kernel of what must be denied by the radical interpretation of the "Asian values" claim and indeed by all moral theories that reject moral rights as a fundamental moral category. Our argument has led us to con-trast the intrinsic value of individual consent with "rights" that, at best, treat consent as a useful instrument for achieving other goals. In light of Dworkin's remarks, what those pseudo-rights miss is that there is inherent moral value in each person's life being shaped by that person's own free will. Respecting that moral value, conversely, requires not subordinating people's ability to direct their lives autonomously to concerns that those lives should be happy, harmonious, or otherwise successful.

Placing the dignity of an individual's free will at the heart of morality helps justify the "trumps" that we suggested rights constitute against the claims of conventional social roles or of the common good. This is still of course, merely a foundation; the whole work of deriving, from this basis, the content of people's rights and duties remains. But even the mere foundation gives us a tentative perspective on possible rights-based arguments about the cases we have examined:

- In the dispute over corporate social responsibility, the claim of shareholders gains new luster. Not taking their wishes into account is to violate the moral dignity manifested in their choice about how their capital is to be used. But at the same

---

[130] Ronald Dworkin, "Taking Rights Seriously in Beijing," *The New York Review of Books*, 49(14), 26 September 2002, available on http://www.nybooks.com/articles/15692 (accessed November 2010).

time, this cannot justify pure profit maximization, for the same moral dignity that requires shareholders' consent to how to use the funds they have provided may well require other stakeholders' consent to how those funds are deployed in ways that affect their lives. A rights analysis of Texaco in the Amazon, for example, would have to take into account that if Amazonians have a right to their environment not being sullied (a right that the theory would have to justify), then shareholders' rights do not include a claim to profits gained from polluting. In contrast, respecting the rights of Merck shareholders may require not paying to develop Mectizan (if that is what shareholders want) unless the duty to help victims of river blindness is a perfect duty and not merely an imperfect one.[131]

- Grounding moral dignity in consent would seem to favor Kate's keeping the promise to Lucy. Holding Kate responsible for her free choice requires seeing it as possible for her to enter binding moral relations—including the one in which Kate has a duty to keep her promise and Lucy has the right that Kate should keep it. Similarly, respecting Lucy's moral dignity is a reason to leave it in her discretion whether to insist on her right or release Kate from the promise.

- A rights-based theory grounded in the moral value of free will puts into doubt a view that Guidant's ultimate responsibility is to maximize the health—and in our case, minimize the deaths—of its customers. Instead, the principle of respecting their dignity and holding them responsible for directing their own lives argues in favor of a right to access information relevant to one's own health. Given such a right, Guidant's duty was to release the information regarding the defective defibrillator.

Resolving conflicts of rights

Finally, locating moral value in the dignity of free consent suggests a new way of thinking about conflicting moral reasons. We recognized from the beginning of this book that we need a moral theory because we face moral dilemmas—situations where there are moral reasons for choosing several mutually exclusive acts. Within rights-based theories, the dilemmas may often be expressed as conflicts between a right-claim and other important moral concerns (a theory can recognize rights as a fundamental category of moral reasons without claiming that it is the only such category) or as conflicts between different rights. How we resolve such conflicts will depend on our detailed theory of ethics. But we should notice here that a moral theory based (in part) on rights will treat conflicts in a different way from consequentialism, because of the directional element of rights and their correlative duties. A right, as we have said, is a claim on a specified *someone*, and that specification will often, if not always, help to resolve conflicting claims.

Recall Bernard Williams's example of Jim and the Indians. On any consequentialist view, it i obvious that Jim should take the offer of shooting one Indian, so that

---

[131] Thomas W. Dunfee has argued that such duties may well be perfect ones, in which case there is no moral freedom not to extend help. See his "Do firms with unique competencies for rescuing victims of catastrophes have special obligations?", *Business Ethics Quarterly*, 16(2), 2006.

nineteen others could be saved. This is even true for a view sometimes called rights-consequentialism, which acknowledges the presence of rights, but says that we should act in the way that minimizes the number of rights violations.[132] A more fundamental rights-based view, however, will emphasize the directional relations between the rights and duties in question. All the Indians have a negative right not to be killed; and everyone has a negative duty not to kill them. The captain is preparing to violate twenty of these rights and duties; this is clearly wrong. But Jim's choice is between accepting the captain's offer, by which Jim will violate one Indian's negative right not to be killed, and declining it, which will result in the captain's violating twenty. Now it makes sense to say that twenty rights violations, from an impersonal point of view, are worse than one. But the twenty killings would not involve *Jim's* violation of *his* duty not to kill. If he takes up the offer, however, *he* is the one who violates the rights of the one Indian he kills. So, in one case, though the outcome is much worse, *he* has not wronged *anyone*, while in the other, though the outcome is better, he has. This surely matters (one way it could matter is in what we may think Jim owes the one Indian's relatives).

Now this is hardly conclusive; keeping one's own hands clean cannot always come above avoiding horrific outcomes. But what the directional aspect of rights language points out is the need to establish a connection from pointing out that an outcome is bad to saying that someone specific has a duty to do something to make it less bad. Among other things, this means a rights-based theory avoids the mistake of unlimited negative responsibility. In Jim's case, the connection could take the form of arguing that the consequences at stake are so severe as to be more important than his own duty not to kill or that another duty—a positive duty to prevent killings by others—prevails here. In either case, the rights perspective highlights two considerations that consequentialist reasoning tends to obscure. The first is the need for arguments identifying *who* has duties to do what. The other is that even if it is required, all things considered, to violate someone's right, that violation still constitutes a wrong for which the violator can be held accountable. The same will hold in business ethics dilemmas, such as Google's choice to censor for its Chinese search engine. If censoring does indeed violate Chinese Internet users' rights, then it is insufficient for Google to point out that without Google's presence, even more rights violations might be committed by other companies. Even as it acted for the best, Google would be committing a wrong; and it would remain morally liable with respect to those it wronged.

If we think that morality is essentially about treating humans with dignity, and if we agree with Feinberg about the importance to human dignity of the ability to make claims, we shall have to agree that rights are a necessary component of morality. To grant individuals the moral ground for claiming their rights is to see moral value inherent in individual consent. The fact that rights protect an element of choice and control over how the right-holder's life goes suggests that a theory of rights can ultimately be founded on the *moral value of free individual choice*—in which rights are justified because they carve out a sphere of inviolability within which that moral value can be realized.

---

[132] A more nuanced view would weight the number of rights violated by the gravity of the violation and the importance of each right, and tell us to minimize the weighted sum of rights violations. But that, too, would tell Jim to take up the captain's offer.

Identifying individual free choice as the source of moral value is only the first step toward constructing such a theory, but it is a momentous step, as it will, among other things, lead us to reject the Confucian or rule-utilitarian substitutes for rights. To see if that step can be justified, we shall devote the next chapter to the most influential account of the moral value of choice: Immanuel Kant's moral theory.

Summary of the Argument in This Chapter

We turn from the formal question of what rights statements mean to the substantive question of whether they are correct. The battle over rights is split between proponents whose most ringing statements are the historic declarations of human rights and opponents who argue that the whole notion of individual rights either distort what is morally valuable in moral intuitions that have a grain of truth or elevates outright immoral behavior. In the skirmish over "Asian values," several prominent Asian leaders have claimed that the insistence on rights is both misguided and dangerous, as it encourages an antisocial and adversarial emphasis on the individual. Such arguments all denounce the Western emphasis on rights as camouflaged protectionism or aggressive interference with the value systems of others. But they also differ subtly from one another.

One claim is that while rights may be fine for Westerners, they only apply within Western cultures. There may be rights, but not universal rights, and one should not try to impose them where they do not fit. This claim, however, we should recognize as an untenable instance of moral relativism, which we refuted in Chapter 4. A stronger claim recognizes that if there were individual rights, at least some of them would have to be universal or "human" rights—but denies that there are such rights at all. Instead, whatever is morally valuable in our intuitions about

rights can be more soundly expressed by non-rights-based theories. In the Asian values debate, one such theory can be developed from a Confucian tradition rooting duties in the need to protect a harmonious community. But there is nothing particularly Asian about rejecting rights. The Western tradition of utilitarianism also claims that while rights intuitions are a way to express important moral truths, thinking that rights are in any way fundamental is, at best, to miss the point, and, at worst, a fetishism that leads us morally astray.

The argument, therefore, comes down to whether what is special about rights is morally fundamental. What rights do, which the "as if"-rights mimicked by other theories cannot do, is give us moral grounds for claiming our rights as our due and demanding their satisfaction *at our discretion*. They give us, that is, the moral authority to choose to claim something and also to refrain from claiming it. Rights theorists see this equal standing to freely claim as what gives human beings their dignity as individuals. The notion of moral rights, therefore, is ultimately the development of a principle that individual free choice is of fundamental moral value. Other theories can treat consent as valuable insofar as it is instrumental to other valuable goals. But if consent and free individual choice are *intrinsically* morally valuable, then respecting their value will, at least in part, involve acknowledging moral rights.

CHAPTER **10**

Ethics as Equal Freedom
Respecting Each Person's Dignity

The arguments developed over the last few chapters have led us to say that the best way to understand the intuitive importance of fundamental moral rights—and to establish what these rights are—is to see them as expressing the deep moral value residing in every person's free will. This may strike some as a grotesquely libertarian view, of the kind that naïvely celebrates untrammeled profit maximization. But that would be a misperception of the sort of moral conclusions that a concern for everyone's free choice will actually support. An example of where a concern for free will is not necessarily "pro-business" is *marketing*, a business activity whose goal is to make consumers choose certain things and not others—that is to say, to change people's will. Any view locating ultimate moral value in free will must take seriously the question of whether choices influenced by advertising are free, and it is not at all obvious that a plausible analysis will answer in the affirmative.

The most influential theory based on the ultimate moral value of individual freedom is that of Immanuel Kant, the eighteenth-century German philosopher. In this chapter, we shall explore his theory as he develops it in his *Groundwork for a Metaphysics of Morals*, and consider how it applies to questions of business ethics. Kantian theory comes at the value of free will in a rather roundabout way: Kant starts not with the concept of freedom but with that of *duty*.[133] He denies that consequentialist moral theories can account for moral duty—if an action is morally required, he says, it cannot be its consequences that make it so. An action that is good because of its consequences has an *instrumental* moral value that is *contingent* upon two conditions: The goal (consequence) toward which it is a means must itself be morally valuable; and the action must in fact have the desired instrumental effect—it must be a good way to achieve the morally valuable goal. Unless these conditions hold, clearly, the action has no value if

---

[133] His argument that freedom and duty are linked is complicated but should not unsettle us—as we have seen, duties are logically connected to rights, and it is a short way from the concept of a right to the concept of freedom.

it is only valued for its consequences. But value that is *contingent*, says Kant, cannot be enough to justify a moral *obligation*. This is true even of the value that everyone presumably desires: happiness or well-being, the consequence so prized by utilitarians. Utilitarians say that I ought to do X because X leads to the greatest sum of human happiness. But suppose that I ask, "Why should I value the sum of human happiness?" What can the utilitarian reply? That I ought to value human happiness? Then what is the source of *this* obligation? We cannot, of course, answer that valuing human happiness leads to the greatest sum of human happiness without being guilty of circularity. If Kant is right, then if *anything at all* is morally required, there must be some ultimate source of noncontingent value that is unrelated to the required action's instrumental power. Only this can make a moral requirement a *duty* rather than a piece of advice for how to reach certain outcomes that we happen to value, but which we are morally free not to pursue.

Now this does not show that there is actually anything at all that we ought morally to do. But we saw in Chapter 1 the extreme price one would have to pay for radical moral skepticism. And as soon we accept that there are *some* moral constraints on what we may do, Kant's argument applies, albeit in the conditional mode: If there are moral requirements at all, they cannot in the ultimate analysis depend on the consequences of the required actions, but must take the form of *absolute duties* (though these can in principle be duties to pursue certain consequences). A large part of Kantian theory is built on developing from the concept of duty itself what the content of our specific duties must be. This makes it a *deontological*, or duty-based, theory of ethics (from the Greek word for duty, *deon*), belonging to the third great tradition of Western moral thought besides virtue ethics and consequentialist ethics.

THE SOURCE OF MORAL WORTH

Consider a shopkeeper who always gives his customers the right change. He is undoubtedly doing the right thing. Suppose we find out that he never does so because he thinks it is right, only because he knows that customers who are shortchanged will stay away and tell other customers to stop patronizing his shop. If a child, too young to count the change correctly, came alone to his shop to buy sweets and the shopkeeper did not think the parents would find out, he would return too little change to the child. What does this do to how we judge the shopkeeper's normal tendency to return the correct change? That is, of course, still the right thing to do, but are we not justified in withholding our approval—and certainly our moral praise—from his actions?

Consider a second example. A man jumps into a cold river to rescue another man who is drowning. With no other knowledge of the situation, it seems like an extraordinary act of bravery, indeed a case of going beyond one's duty. But suppose we find out that the rescuer only jumped in because he recognized the drowning man as a famous billionaire, and was motivated solely by the prospect of a rich reward. That does not make the action wrong—it is not that the rescuer should not have jumped after all—but it does seem to take away all reason to treat it as morally praiseworthy.

Whatever it is that makes these actions right, it seems clear enough that it is not the prospect of gain, since what is morally valuable in them evaporates once that motive is revealed to us. The right *motivation*, then, is where moral value must ultimately spring from, says Kant: "[Nothing] can be regarded as good without qualification, except a *good will*."[134] Instead of an action being morally required because of its consequences, what gives an action its moral worth is the character of the will that chooses it. In Kantian theory, therefore, morality becomes a question of how the will is determined. In very simplified terms, we can group the determinants of the human will into two kinds of influences. The first consists of our wants, desires, instincts and inclinations—what we may call our animal or nonrational nature. The other influence is our reason. As rational beings, we have the ability not to be blindly driven by our inclinations, informing our choices and decisions by reason instead. But since we are only imperfect rational beings, our will remains influenced by both sides of our nature—inclinations and reason:

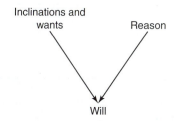

Our nonrational nature influences the will by making us desire things or actions—where "desire" covers the full range of emotions, from those that repulse (such as disgust or fear) to those that attract (lust, greed, admiration). Reason influences our will by making us aware that there are things we ought to do—by issuing to the will "imperatives," which is what Kant calls reason's commands to the will. They are expressed by "ought"-sentences ("You ought to stop") or, as the name suggests, the imperative verb tense ("Stop!"). Imperatives, then, are not inclinations (though they may coincide with them); they are, rather, how reason tells us to do things that we may have no inclination to do.

Reason can issue its orders, Kant says, "hypothetically" or "categorically." A *hypothetical imperative* is a command to will the means required to achieve your ends, whatever they happen to be. For example, suppose studying is necessary to get a good grade. A hypothetical imperative is then:

"You ought to study (in order to get a good grade)." [ought-sentence]

    or equivalently

"(In order to get a good grade,) study!" [imperative tense]

Reason tells you to study, but it does so hypothetically, that is to say, *contingently* on a good grade being something you value. If you do, then reason tells you to study—it is irrational not to. If not, then reason does not tell you to study.

---

[134] Immanuel Kant, *Groundwork for a Metaphysics of Morals*.

A *categorical* imperative, in contrast, commands not contingently but categorically or unconditionally. Its validity does not depend on anything else. For example:

"You ought not to lie."

   or

"Do not lie!"

We can use this terminology to rephrase what we said before. *If* there are any moral requirements, Kant claims, they must take the form of categorical imperatives—absolute duties. If there is anything morality requires us to do, it must require us to do it *unconditionally*, rather than because it leads to something we happen to desire. It is not because customers will leave if shortchanged that shopkeepers have a moral obligation to return the right change. It is not because we might receive a reward that we ought to rescue drowning people. The fact that an action has good consequences for us may, of course, give us a reason to do it. But that is only a hypothetical imperative, not a moral reason.

As we have already pointed out, however, even if the shopkeeper and the rescuer act only in pursuit of the consequences they want, that does not make their actions *wrong*. So we need to distinguish between two ways of characterizing an action—by its moral rightness or wrongness, and by the moral worth of the motive from which it is done. On the one hand, an action can be right or it can be wrong. On the other hand, we can perform an action *from inclination*—motivated by a hypothetical imperative, because we want to do it—or we can perform it *out of duty*—motivated by a categorical imperative, because it is the right thing to do.

Rightness/wrongness and motivation are not equivalent. An action could be right even if it is not performed *because* it is right but because an inclination moves us to do it. Kant calls this kind of action "in accordance with duty, but not out of duty." The shopkeeper and the rescuer act in accordance with duty (they do the right thing) but not out of duty (they do not do it for the sake of doing the right thing). Put differently, they act on hypothetical imperatives, not categorical ones. That, says Kant, means that their actions have no "moral worth": They do what they should do but from morally worthless motives.

The implication of Kant's stark claims for business is immediate. Most companies engaged in "corporate social responsibility" take pains to justify ethics as being ultimately good for profits. They are hardly the first to do this, as the old saying that honesty is the best policy makes clear. But being honest because it is the best policy, or pursuing CSR because it is good for the bottom line, seem no different from our self-interested shopkeeper and rescuer. CSR initiatives may be the right thing to do—but if they are done for the sake of profitability or any other desired outcome, then the businesses in question are acting on hypothetical imperatives. What then is their moral worth? If moral value lies in acting on categorical imperatives, then CSR initiatives are morally worthless. Only if the motivation behind them is to "do the right thing"—that is, only if the businesses in question see CSR as a categorical imperative, something they should do whether it benefits them or not—only then, according to Kant's reasoning, can their action be said to have moral worth.

UNIVERSALIZATION AS A SOURCE OF DUTIES

Suppose I am in need of money. I know you will lend it to me if you are confident I will return it. But I have no plans to pay back the loan. (I may even have a strategy for avoiding any legal repercussions, perhaps by setting up a sophisticated company structure that will sign off on the loan and pay me a salary before I take it into bankruptcy to cancel the obligation to repay you.) Aside from what the law says, it is *immoral* for me to try to make you lend me the money by falsely promising to pay it back. It is no surprise that Kant agrees that it is immoral to make false promises. What is instructive about this example is the reasoning by which he arrives at this conclusion. That reasoning involves how the two concepts we have just examined relate to each other.

Consider the possible combinations of an action's rightness or wrongness and its motivation by duty or inclination. We can sum up the combinations in a matrix:

| | | Motivation—action is done out of: | |
		Inclination	Duty
Action is morally:	**Right**	"In accordance with duty": compatible with CI but motivated by HI— **no moral worth**	"Out of duty": motivated by and compatible with CI— **moral worth**
	Wrong	"Contrary to duty": incompatible with CI— **no moral worth**	

Look at the left column. For the reasons stated previously, an action that is done out of inclination (left column, top row) could be right—"in accordance with" our duty. Even so, Kant argues that it has no moral worth. It could, alternatively, be straightforwardly wrong—as it is when we act on an inclination contrary to what we ought to do (left column, bottom row). Such an action is clearly morally worthless as well, as it *must* have been done out of inclination on the Kantian analysis. For if a will chooses an action in violation of a categorical imperative, then it cannot have been the categorical imperative that directed it to do so. Instead, something else must have swayed that will away from the categorical imperative—a desire, perhaps, or an error of judgment. On the Kantian psychology, this influence on the will can only have come from the nonrational part of our nature, which means that the choice can only have been motivated by a hypothetical imperative. But then it cannot be said to have been done "contrary to duty, but *out of* (motivated by) duty." This is why the lower-right box is blacked out.

What this implies—now looking at the table row by row—is that for an action to be morally right it must be at least *possible* for it to be performed out of duty rather than out of inclination (an action can only be in the top row if it possible for it to be in the right-hand column). This is not to say that it *must* actually be done out of duty in order to be right. The self-interested shopkeeper and rescuer are both doing the right thing even though they are not acting out of duty. But their actions are right because they *could* be done for the pure sake of doing one's duty. This is a conceptual, not a psychological, condition. The moral rightness of an action depends on the logical possibility of the action being motivated by duty, not on a psychological ability to be motivated in such a way. So for an action to be morally right, it must be logically possible to will it independently of any inclinations it would satisfy, which means that it must be possible for reason *alone* to order the will to perform it.[135] Put differently, for an action to be right, it must be possible for it to be required by a categorical imperative, not just a hypothetical one.

But what, then, are the categorical imperatives? They are what can be commanded without any reference to what we (contingently) happen to want or value—what reason can direct the will to do in the absence of any inclinations. But this seems to argue us into a void. If we strip away everything in our nonrational nature and leave the will determined by reason only, then we are left with no reasons for willing anything in particular. It seems that we have pursued Kant's moral reasoning to the point where it can produce no substantive commands. One thing, however, is left intact by this untethering of morality from any substantive goals: the purely formal moral requirement that an action must be compatible with reason itself. But for this requirement to be satisfied, the action must be compatible with reason for *anyone* in the same situation. Something that reason alone can direct the will to do must be something it can direct *all* rational wills to do; unencumbered by particular inclinations, two purely rational beings would decide to act in the same way. But that means, Kant says, that only actions that can be willed by all rational beings are morally right.

All of Kantian morality, then, comes down to one formal requirement. There is *only one* categorical imperative, and it is that actions must be compatible with pure reason, which means that it must be something that reason could command universally:

> Act only on that maxim whereby you can at the same time will that it should become a universal law.

This is the first formulation of Kant's categorical imperative, and it captures the reasoning we have developed up to here (we can paraphrase "maxim" by "intention" or "principle"): An action is morally right if and only if you can rationally—without contradiction—will it to be universally done. Kant gives a second formulation:

> Act as if the maxim of your action were to become through your will a universal law of nature.

which says the same thing (since a law of nature is something everyone must follow). Kant's formulations show that the categorical imperative is a *universalizability test*. It determines whether an action is right by asking: "What if everybody did that?" More precisely, it asks if you can, without contradiction, will both the action you are proposing and the universalized practice of that action. If you cannot, then the action is wrong. If you can, then it is not. In this sense, the moral is for Kant coextensive with the rational: The things we ought not to do are the things it would be *irrational* for us—as pure rational wills—to do. If we fully understand what rationality requires, we will know which actions are right.

---

[135] Kant acknowledges that on his analysis it may be that nobody ever did an action out of duty, so that there was never any moral worth in the history of humanity. But this does not stop us from describing what it would be for an action to have moral worth, any more than the possibility that no perfect circles have been found in the world stops us from describing the properties of circles.

We may now return to the case of false promising, in which Kant famously put the universalizability test to work. When I consider making a false promise, the maxim of my action is:

F1: "I will to make a false promise when it benefits me"

This entails, among other things:

F2: "I will that my promises be believed"

What is the universalization of the maxim F1? It is:

U1: "I will that one should make a false promise when it benefits one"

but, clearly, a necessary consequence of the universalized practice is that no one would ever believe a promise. So U1 entails:

U2: "I will that promises should never be believed"

Comparing F2 and U2, it is easy to see the logical contradiction. You cannot rationally at the same time will that your promise be believed (which is why you are making the false promise in the first place) and will that promises in general never be believed. If you did, your will would be contradicting itself. What you really intend by making a false promise is to make an *exception* for yourself; what you will includes that promises be believed in general—and in particular that *yours* be believed—and for this you will that promises in general be kept. But making an exception for yourself cannot be universalized; your desire to benefit from something not everyone can benefit from is not something that pure reason could alone command. It can only be rationalized by appeal to your inclinations, as a hypothetical imperative—but since it violates the categorical imperative, it is wrong.

We may here compare Kant's universalizability test as set out in the first formulation of the categorical imperative with two other universalizability tests: rule-consequentialism and the Golden Rule ("Do unto others as you would have them do unto you"). The Kantian test checks if universalization is something you could will to happen without contradiction with your willing the particular action you are resolving to perform. Rule-consequentialism, in contrast, asks if the universalization would have *good consequences*. This question would of course also lead to the conclusion that it is usually wrong to make false promises—not, however, because you cannot rationally will everyone else to do it while at the same time doing it successfully yourself, but because a society in which promises were not believed would be worse than one in which they were believed. The Golden Rule asks a similar question—"What if somebody did that to you?" Here, what is asked for is not whether the consequences would be the best for everyone, but whether they would be good for *you*. For example: "Would you want other people to make false promises to you?" In a Kantian perspective, both these approaches make the same mistake. The mistake is to base the moral judgment of an action on the goodness of its consequences—in the first case, for society at large; in the second, for your individual wants. That makes the answers empirically contingent in a way that Kant says cannot ultimately justify a categorical imperative. The Golden Rule, for example, cannot condemn a fraudster who says: "I am permitted to defraud others, for I am willing to accept that others try to defraud me (because I think I am smart enough to defend myself from it)." Also, these are *hypothetical* universalizations, and as we have said, it is deeply unclear why consequentialist theories should care at all about hypothetical consequences rather than actual ones.

In the Kantian universalizability test, in contrast, the consequences themselves are not of ultimate moral importance. Its version of "What if everyone did that?" is, roughly, "What if everyone did that, is that something you could really will without contradicting your willing the action you are proposing for yourself?" If not, you are making an exception for yourself. The problem with this is not that it would be bad if everyone did the same (although it probably would be); the problem is that since making an exception for itself is something a perfectly rational will cannot do, you are *contradicting* yourself (that is, your *rational* self). The only justification you can have for making such an exception must be something in your nonrational nature that makes you different from other rational beings in the same situation. But that means that this is an action you could never will to do simply because it was the right thing to do. And the condition for an action's moral justification is that it can logically be willed for the sake of duty alone. In Kant's universalizability test, the hypothetical consequences of universalizing the action matter, but they only matter because they reveal whether this condition is satisfied.

The contradiction involved in universalizing false promising is a *logical* one. There are other actions we seemingly have a duty to perform but where, Kant admits, it is not logically impossible to universalize the maxim of not performing them.[136] In the case of charity—our duty, if we have one, to help those less well off than ourselves—one could logically will the universal breach of this duty. A world in which no one helped the unfortunate would be brutal, but it is not irrational to will such a world for someone who, like our amoralist from Chapter 1, thinks he would do rather better than others in an each-to-his-own scramble. But there is a *practical* contradiction, Kant asserts: No one does *in fact* will both their own noncharity and the universalized practice of nobody being charitable. For no one can, in practice, avoid having some substantive goals; and there are *some* conceivable situations in which even the most self-reliant would want the help of others (namely when their own goals, be they as basic as physical survival, can only be realized with such help). Kant aligns *logical* contradictions in the universalizability test with perfect duties and *practical* ones with imperfect duties. In the case of the former, therefore, the categorical imperative establishes rights as well as duties: Making a false promise violates the rights of those to whom you promise. In contrast, although we have a duty of charity, nobody in particular has a *right* to our benevolence, the breach of which is "merely" a practical contradiction in the will, not a logical one.

Arriving at rights as the correlates of duties arising from logical contradictions in the universalizability test may strike some as unsatisfying. This method seems to justify rights almost as an afterthought, which does not do justice to their intuitive primacy. It also appears to ignore the *directionality* of rights-based relationships. We typically think of our perfect duties to others as deriving from the rights that they have, not the other way around—a directionality that is all the more important if the moral value of consent is indeed at the heart of a proper theory of rights. This appearance notwithstanding, Kant's theory does recognize the centrality of consent and freedom; we are now ready to see how.

---

[136] Kant is not always persuasive in what he designates as contradictions. For example, he claims that it is contrary to duty to commit suicide to end one's suffering. This is wrong, he says, because we cannot without contradiction will it to be a universal law of nature to destroy oneself. But why not? While it is unlikely that anyone would, as a matter of fact, want everyone who suffered to commit suicide, it seems neither impossible nor inconceivable for a rational will to endorse this. But if Kant sometimes fails to convince, this does not incriminate the Kantian method. Rather, it simply suggests that it was possible for Kant himself to misapply it, and indeed that applying the universalizability test properly is an effective way to refute his more far-fetched conclusions.

AUTONOMY AS A SOURCE OF RIGHTS

Kant locates morality in *acting rationally* in his very specific sense of doing only that which we could without contradiction will to be universalized. So for Kant, the ultimate source of moral value, from which every moral action gets whatever moral worth it has, is rational agency. But since acting rationally is to make choices unbiased by wants and inclinations, it is a short step for Kant to identify *acting morally* with *being free.* Wresting control of our will from blind wants and inclinations to the direction of reason, says Kant, *is* just what constitutes individual freedom, or as he calls it, *autonomy* (from the ancient Greek for "law unto itself"). When we act morally—that is, according to the categorical imperative—our reason "sets a law" for itself and for the will. The alternative is for our will to be ruled by something else, namely our nonrational nature (the failure of autonomy is *heteronomy*—"law of another"). Rational autonomy, then—the will freely directed by reason—is the fundamental moral value: It is what moral action is and it is also what freedom is. Acting against morality is to act against reason and, therefore, to be unfree, in thrall to one's inclinations.

The value of autonomy leads Kant to a third formulation of the categorical imperative, often called the "mere means principle":

> Act in such a way that you treat humanity, whether in your own person or in the person of any other, always at the same time as an end and never merely as a means.[137]

In light of what we said previously, we should amend this formulation to specify that it is "rational agency," not just "humanity," that we must never treat as a mere means. For what is morally valuable in humanity, in Kant's view, is rationally autonomous action. (Among the more eccentric implications of Kantian theory is that if rational alien beings exist, it would apply to them as much as to humans.) Treating something as an "end in itself," in Kantian parlance, is to see it as having intrinsic moral value that must be respected and to refrain from subjecting it completely to other ends (other valuable goals) that are not its own. The mere means principle, therefore, tells us to respect the autonomy of every person's rational will, which, in turn, means to respect their ability to pursue their own freely chosen ends and refrain from manipulating that ability as an instrument of the will of others.

It now becomes clear how individual rights, far from an afterthought, find a firm foundation in the categorical imperative. The mere means formulation forbids using other people merely as instruments for our own purposes and exhorts us to respect them as autonomous choosers of their own ends. We should emphasize the "merely." Kant does not say that you may never treat someone else as instrumental to your own goals; that would rule out most business and, indeed, a lot of innocent nonbusiness

---

[137] Note that Kant sees these three formulations of the categorical imperative as statements of *the same rule*—he thinks that they are logically equivalent expressions of the same unique principle. It is far from obvious that he is right, and many philosophers have disagreed with this claim. It is not something we need to address here, however; whether or not Kant is right, we can acknowledge the intuitive centrality to moral thinking both of universalizability and of not treating people as mere means to our ends.

human interaction. In any market exchange, the participants seek something from their counterparties to benefit themselves. What the principle says is that you may never treat others *merely* as ways for you to reach your goals. You may interact with them for your own self-regarding purposes, but you must also treat them as autonomous wills worthy of respect—which means, in part, that you must acknowledge the legitimacy of their pursuit of goals which you may or may not share. This almost immediately entails the most basic individual rights—such as those to "life, liberty and the pursuit of happiness" that are enumerated in the historic declarations of rights. Killing someone is clearly a violation of autonomy, since it puts an end to their ability to make free choices. Enslaving another human being violates autonomy in an even more insidious way, since not only does it constrain the slave's exercise of her will, it also subjects her actions and choices continuously to the will of another.

We can now see that the actions that violate rights under the mere means principle are the same actions that breach our perfect duties as demonstrated by the universalizability test. When you make a false promise, you undermine someone else's rational autonomy, using it simply as an instrument for your own benefit. By deceiving the person you make the promise to, you try to ensure that when they think they are exercising their autonomy in pursuit of their own ends, they are in fact advancing yours. You are "hijacking" their autonomous use of their reason for your own purposes. Contrast this with the case of charity, which is no perfect duty. The absence of charitable acts does not amount to an outright use of another's rational agency merely as a means—so it does not violate anyone's rights. It is, however, a failure to *advance* their ability to achieve their ends. This suggests that we can read the mere means principle's demand to "respect" autonomy as two complementary requirements. First, we ought not to undermine or interfere with the rational autonomy of others, which would violate their rights and which we have a (negative) perfect duty not to do. Second, we ought to *promote* their rational autonomy. This is an *imperfect* duty (not corresponding to a right) which we have some choice as to how to fulfill. We may to some extent balance it against our own interests, and in any case it must come second to not violating anyone's rights. Within those limits, however, the categorical imperative calls on us to choose actions that most "harmonize" with the full development of everyone's rational autonomy.

THE KANTIAN COMPANY

In addition to a basis for arguing that people have rights, then, Kant's ethical theory equips us with a method for addressing which rights people have. We can assess the content of any particular right-claim by asking whether the purported right protects the claimant's rational autonomy. A right to organize would seem straightforward to defend on this basis; a right to periodic holidays with pay, in contrast, much more dubiously so. We can similarly begin to determine the content of our imperfect duties by considering, in the situations we are likely to find ourselves, which action would not merely respect the autonomy of others but actively promote it. In this light, periodic holidays with pay start to look more plausible; they could be a possible fulfillment of an imperfect managerial duty to give workers the opportunity to develop their own capacities and pursue their autonomously chosen goals.

Applying the Kantian apparatus to business decisions has profound implications for what it means to do business ethically. A fully articulated Kantian theory of business ethics would have to apply the categorical imperative in its various formulations, as well as the reasoning behind it, to the types of moral dilemmas and relationships that occur in business life. That is a task that needs much more detailed reasoning and investigation than we can give it here—and that would have to be carried out not only in the abstract but also as part of the ongoing decision making inside real companies. We can, however, sketch the rough contours of what such a theory would look like and point out some directions it might take.

Charitable giving

One insight the Kantian perspective offers is that what many business practitioners think the moral responsibility of business consists in—"corporate social responsibility," understood largely as charitable giving—is neither necessary nor sufficient for ethical business conduct. As we have seen, the duty of charity is in ordinary cases an imperfect duty, and it is left to our discretion how, where, and when we discharge it. There is in general little reason to think that anything else applies in the business context.[138] What this means is that no one can demand from a company that it engage in charitable giving. Indeed, Milton Friedman makes a strong case that dividends should be prioritized over charitable giving, leaving it to individual shareholders to choose how to fulfill their duty of charity. And although we pointed out in Chapter 2 that some corporate charitable contributions can be justified instrumentally—improving the company's image among consumers, providing public goods for the local community from which its workforce is drawn, or making employees proud of their workplace may all add to profits—it is clear that on a Kantian view, charity performed for *that* reason merits no moral applause. In short, a focus on corporate charity, while it can do some good, is little more than a distraction from the more consequential moral constraints on business activity.

Autonomy in the workplace

Among those constraints is the requirement to fulfill one's *perfect* duties; in other words, respecting the rights of people within and outside the corporation. This moral concern, if applied comprehensively, could drive a profound transformation of how business is commonly carried out. Consider how managers would have to organize their company internally to make it a truly ethical workplace on Kantian lines. A Kantian workplace, clearly, is one that respects the dignity and rational autonomy of everyone who works there. What does this mean, practically speaking? At the very least, that management must treat workers as more than "human resources" merely to be disposed of as means befitting the company's ends without taking into account the ends held by the workers themselves. An abundance of popular culture criticizes such practices for undermining human dignity— think of the factory Taylorism that sees workers as so many substitutable parts to be slotted into an assembly line, depicted in films such as Charlie Chaplin's *Modern Times* or Fritz Lang's *Metropolis*, or consider its post-industrial equivalent of the *Dilbert* cartoons'

---

[138] As Thomas Dunfee has argued, it may turn into a perfect duty when we are the only ones in a position to offer desperately needed help. Merck and river blindness may be such as case.

office cubicle dreariness. In contrast, Kantian business ethicist Norman Bowie has argued that Kantian ethics

> would require companies to provide meaningful work . . . For a Kantian, meaningful work:
>
> - is freely chosen and provides opportunities for the worker to exercise autonomy on the job;
> - supports the autonomy and rationality of human beings; work that lessens autonomy or that undermines rationality is immoral;
> - provides a salary sufficient to exercise independence and provide for physical well-being and the satisfaction of some of the worker's desires; enables a worker to develop rational capacities; and does not interfere with a worker's moral development.[139]

One example of treating workers as rational autonomous beings, Bowie suggests, is "open book management":

> Under open book management, all employees are given all the financial information about the company on a regular frequent basis. With complete information and the proper incentive, employees behave responsibly without the necessity of layers of supervision . . . The adoption of practices like open book management would go far toward correcting the asymmetrical information that managers possess, a situation that promotes abuse of power and deception . . . Open book management also enhances employee self-respect. Employees at Springfield Manufacturing Company [which pioneered the practice] use Kantian 'respect for persons' language when describing the impact of open book management on working conditions.[140]

Job security

Beyond how managers ought to treat workers who are part of a company, implications of the Kantian perspective may extend to what right workers have to their employment itself. Conventions about how long employees can expect to work for one employer and about how secure their position should be vary widely across sectors, countries and time. In the United States, the contractual norm is "employment at will" in which employee and employer are both free to sever a work relationship at their say-so. In continental Europe, the moral presumption and legal requirement of job security are much stronger, and some East Asian societies have a tradition of employment for life. Apart from family, few relationships are more important for our material and mental ability to be in charge of our own lives than our professional relationships, so there is clearly a lot to say about what respect for rational autonomy means for the issue of job security— particularly for managers of multinational corporations who have to adjudicate claims made in this regard by clashing local conventions. Two possible arguments readily

---

[139] Norman E. Bowie, "A Kantian Approach to Business Ethics," in Robert E. Frederick (ed.), *A Companion to Business Ethics* (Oxford: Blackwell Publishers, 1999).

[140] Ibid.

present themselves. On the one hand, one may think that for workers to truly consent to how they are treated (presumably a central part of worker autonomy) they must be reasonably confident that being "difficult" by resisting what managers want does not jeopardize their jobs. From this perspective, autonomy requires a rather firm degree of job security. On the other hand, the contract at will may be seen precisely as an expression of autonomous choice. It is a mutual agreement between two unforced parties, and respecting the autonomy of each requires letting them come to whatever agreement they see fit. How the conflict between these views should be resolved will no doubt depend to a large extent on background facts, such as the availability of adequate alternatives outside this particular work relationship (are there enough other jobs to get for the worker; and can the company easily find other employees) or the nature of the demands managers generally make on workers. The point here is not to solve this matter but to point out how Kantian ethics defines the terms by which it must be solved. As Bowie points out, "by framing the issue in terms of whether or not [a violation of autonomy] has occurred, one has adopted a Kantian approach to business ethics."

As a finishing remark, it is worth noting that there are a host of management theories that say that it is good for business to respect workers as rationally autonomous beings. In contrast, Kantian ethical theory argues that respecting autonomy is morally required, whether or not it helps the bottom line.

THE KANTIAN FIRM IN THE MARKETPLACE: REVISITING DECEPTION

We may again return to Albert Carr's argument. Kantian ethics can refute Carr's insufficiently qualified claim that business bluffing is morally permissible whenever—as in poker—the conventional "rules of the game" permit it. Is lying universalizable? Clearly not, for the liar wants others to believe what he says, and if people did not generally tell the truth, words would never have any credibility. So what the liar proposes to do (the "maxim of his action") is to tell a lie in an environment where people do not generally lie. He wants to make an exception for himself to benefit from his violation of a rule he wants to be generally respected, and this is immoral. The third formulation of the categorical imperative describes the same wrongness from the perspective of the person lied to. The victim of a lie has her rational autonomy undermined because the liar willfully induces her to believe false information on which she will base her choices. This sabotages her ability to pursue her autonomously chosen ends; her rational decision making has, in a word, been *manipulated*—treated as a mere means rather than an end in itself, worthy of respect. But this characterization is not restricted to outright lying. If deception is to make someone else believe a statement one oneself believes to be untrue, then even nonmendacious deception commits the wrong of lying, which is to manipulate the rational decision making of another. If outright lying is immoral, then so is making true but intentionally misleading statements.

Does this Kantian argument against deception succeed? To do so, it must refute Carr's poker analogy and show that the categorical imperative treats bluffing in games as different from lying. Otherwise, it would founder on the absurd conclusion that poker is inherently immoral. But this is a distinction Kantian reasoning makes readily. For the poker player's intention when he bluffs is not, as with lying, to induce a false belief by exploiting a general convention of honesty. It is, rather, to induce a false belief among people who have consented that others may try to induce false beliefs in them. Not only does the presence of consent make the maxim unproblematically universalizable; it also removes any failure to respect the autonomy of others. It is because such consent is *not* generally present in business life that the poker analogy fails to justify business deception. Bluffing is indeed permissible in poker, but poker is no analogy to business.[141]

The following three cases bring into relief the factors that determine whether business choices are deceptive in the sense Kantian ethics condemns as immoral.

Enron

The energy trading company that became a byword for corporate accounting fraud went bankrupt in a spectacular scandal in 2001 after investors realized that its reported financial results were to a large extent illusory. Enron's top executives were later found guilty of securities fraud in court. But beyond their legal culpability, did Enron's management commit the *moral* wrong of deception? Journalist Malcolm Gladwell has argued that the facts about Enron were hiding in plain sight:

> [Wall Street Journal reporter Jonathan Weil's] conclusions were sobering. In the second quarter of 2000, $747 million of the money Enron said it had made was 'unrealized'—that is, it was money that executives thought they were going to make at some point in the future. If you took that imaginary money away, Enron had shown a significant loss in the second quarter. This was one of the most admired companies in the United States . . . and there was practically no cash coming into its coffers . . . When Weil had finished his reporting, he called Enron for comment . . . The Enron officials acknowledged that the money they said they earned was virtually all money that they *hoped* to earn. Weil and the Enron officials then had a long conversation about how certain Enron was about its estimates of future earnings . . . It was all very civil. 'There was no dispute about the numbers . . . There was only a difference in how you should interpret them.' . . . The prosecutor in the Enron case told the jury to send Jeffrey Skilling to prison because Enron had hidden the truth: You're 'entitled to be told what the financial condition of the company is,' the prosecutor had said. But what truth was Enron hiding here? Everything Weil learned for his Enron exposé came from Enron, and when he wanted to confirm his numbers the company's executives got on a plane and sat down with him in a conference room in Dallas.[142]

---

[141] This reasoning is somewhat hasty; two possible complications are of interest. One is that in real poker games, it is not always true that every participant has exercised an autonomous choice to expose himself to the possibility of being taken in. People can be driven to poker by addiction, naïveté, or desperation. The other is that in some business contexts—most obviously negotiations with competitors—all sides may indeed consent to the possibility of being misled. But these plausible counterfactuals do not embarrass the Kantian argument sketched in the main text. In the former case, the conclusion must be—against Carr, it would seem—that it is *not* ethically permissible to play poker with people who play from heteronomous motivations. In the latter, the Kantian position may well admit—and will ring more true as a result—that "bluffing" is permissible in certain types of negotiations where such permission is indeed a shared understanding of the "rules of the game"—and, importantly, that it is a game everyone has autonomously chosen to participate in. That still rule out a swathe of possible deceptive practices vis-à-vis consumers, employees, and others. We return to this argument in the final chapter.

[142] Malcolm Gladwell, "Open Secrets," *The New Yorker*, 8 January 2007.

If investors could have found out what Weil found out, in what sense were they deceived? Gladwell claims that in investing, the problem may often be too much information rather than too little: The fog of numbers coming out of legally required corporate reporting is so thick that the essential facts about a company's financial condition can hardly be discerned. If that is indeed the situation, are executives morally to blame if investors think more highly of their company than they should? On a Kantian view, executives would be violating investors' rights if they tried to deceive them, that is, tried to manipulate them into flattering but unwarranted beliefs about the company which they would not otherwise have held. But perhaps Enron's management, rather than actively undermining investors' rational decision making, simply did not do anything to promote that rationality. In a Kantian analysis of Enron, that question would determine whether its executives violated anyone's rights or merely failed to adequately fulfill an imperfect duty—a failure investors could not claim had morally wronged *them*.

Subprime mortgages

In the 2008 global financial crisis, an avalanche of losses in investment banks was set off when bonds backed by U.S. subprime mortgages—that is, loans to relatively uncreditworthy house buyers—plummeted in market value. The reason was that loan default rates hit unexpected levels, in large part because American subprime borrowers had taken on debt they could no longer service when U.S. house prices stopped rising in the summer of 2006. Some of the mortgages that later went sour had been issued to financially unsophisticated borrowers who did not understand the implications of the loan documents they were signing. Many of these loans were arranged by mortgage brokers who would earn a commission on the transaction and who had no stake in whether the borrower would repay. Some of the banks who actually lent the money had no stake either, since they quickly sold the loans off to other investors whose demand for mortgage-backed bonds at the time seemed insatiable. The incentive was to make as many loans as possible:

> Lenders were off to the races. They created slick new mortgage products with low 'teaser' interest rates that ratcheted up significantly after two years or so. They devised loans that required only the payment of interest, not principal as well. They extended mortgages to 50-year terms to reduce monthly payments . . . But according to experts on lending practices, the products devised to propel homeownership did so only as long as housing prices kept rising . . . On a $250,000 loan with a current interest rate of around 8 percent, a prepayment penalty would be $10,000. Because many subprime borrowers do not have that kind of money lying around, lenders typically offer to roll the amount into the new loan offered in a refinancing. Tacking on such penalties to new loans makes it even harder for borrowers to pay them off . . . subprime loans with low initial rates that reset at much higher rates almost force refinancings, generating fees for lenders but often putting borrowers in a hole . . . While subprime borrowers try to climb out of the holes they fell into, those who sold and packaged the loans are laughing all the way to the bank.[143]

---

[143] Gretchen Morgenson, "Home Loans: A Nightmare Grows Darker," *The New York Times*, 8 April 2007.

Did these lenders and brokers act immorally? To the extent that they tried to induce in their customers a belief they knew to be untrue (that they would be able to afford the payments) the Kantian answer, for the reasons outlined above, would be that they committed a double wrong. First, if the teaser rates and prepayment fees served to make mortgages look less costly to borrowers than they really were, then they were instances of deception. Second, if this deception served to make money from customers' misguided decisions, the mortgage issuance treated borrowers merely as means to lenders' and brokers' pursuit of profit.[144]

Advertising

If the wrong of trying to induce false beliefs in someone is the same as the wrong of lying, what are we to make of advertising or marketing? In 2007, the company TWS Marketing, which produces HomeMaker orange juice, equipped the cartons of HomeMaker Premium Florida Squeezed juice with this grammatically unhappy declaration across the top in boldface:

Made With <u>Not</u> From Concentrate Juice

This did not, contrary to what some customers may have thought, literally mean that the juice did not come from concentrate. Indeed, it also said in smaller print at the bottom:

Blended with Valencia Orange Juice. From Concentrate

What the carton actually contained was a mix of fresh juice with juice reconstituted from concentrate. The confusing statement on the top of the carton was compatible with this. But the only plausible reason to put such a contorted statement on the carton is that it would lead some consumers—with little time to read the fine print before picking a carton of juice in the supermarket—to believe that the juice was of a higher quality than it really was. If so, there seems to be a strong moral case against the company for disrespecting consumers' rational autonomy.

But this, detractors will point out, seems to incriminate virtually all advertising and marketing. For what is the purpose of marketing, they will ask, if not to improve consumers' impression of the product? If that counts as violating their rational autonomy, it seems all marketing is immoral from a Kantian point of view—and this, they may add, casts more doubt on Kantian ethics than on the practice of marketing. In answer to this, one would need to point out that some advertisements pose no problem for the Kantian concern with autonomy. Purely informative types of advertising, which just convey factual descriptions of a product, may serve to enhance consumers' autonomy by improving the information upon which they base their decisions. Other marketing techniques, however, aim at sidelining or undermining rational decision making in order to increase demand—whether by reinforcing irrational beliefs that the products bring qualities that consumers already desire (such as sex appeal or material success),

---

[144] An advisor recommending the mortgage without a financial stake in it issuance, in contrast, would only violate borrowers' rational autonomy in the first of these two ways.

or by trying to influence what consumers ultimately value. Kantians may plausibly consider such efforts manipulative of consumers' rational agency, and—depending on their severity and the ability of consumers to avoid exposure to them—morally impermissible. Since a single advertisement may at the same time provide information and try to manipulate desires and beliefs, whether it passes muster ethically will hinge on whether its overall intention and effect are balanced toward enhancing autonomous and rational decision making rather than disarming it.

We concluded the last chapter with the need both for an argument why we should believe people have rights and for a method to determine what those rights are. The last illustrations show that from the principle that ultimate moral value resides in rational autonomy, Kantian theory provides both. Only by conforming to the categorical imperative do we adequately respect rational autonomy wherever we encounter it; and the categorical imperative equips us with a method for establishing what duties we have and the rights to which they correspond. They are what it takes to protect everyone's ability autonomously to choose and pursue their own goals (in the case of rights and perfect duties) or to promote that ability (in the case of imperfect duties). This introduction to Kantian ethics completes a survey of the three major traditions of Western moral thought. As we shall see in the concluding chapter, the Kantian approach can be developed further into the social contract theory of ethics, which promises to bring on board some of the valuable intuitions of the other traditions while addressing questions they do not answer satisfactorily. Before we do so, however, we shall pause to examine what the reasoning we have pursued so far has to say about one of the moral questions most fundamental to business: the challenge of distributive justice.

Summary of the Argument in This Chapter

Whereas utilitarianism identifies an action's moral value with the amount of well-being it brings about, Kant locates it in how the will is determined—the motive behind the action. The human will, in the Kantian psychology, is under the influence of reason and of nonrational factors or *inclinations*. The desirability of consequences, naturally contingent on our inclinations and what we happen to desire, can only support *hypothetical imperatives*— reason's commands to will the means necessary for the ends we happen to have. But since the necessity of choosing the means is contingent on the value of the end, hypothetical imperatives can never justify *intrinsic* value in any action. That, however, is what moral obligation presupposes: If something is a duty, then reason commands it *categorically*, regardless of whether we are inclined to fulfill it. If we are under any moral duty at all, then, it must be a *categorical imperative*, and

the categorical imperative, in turn, must be a command that reason could issue regardless of which contingent inclinations happen to weigh on the will.

From this purely formal analysis, Kant develops a test for the morality of actions. Since moral duty is independent of anything in our nonrational nature, it must be something that any purely rational will could command. The categorical imperative, therefore, states that one ought to act only on such motives that one could, without contradiction, will everyone else to act on as well. This first formulation of the categorical imperative is a *universalizability test*: An action is moral if and only if it is one whose universalization you can will consistently with your willing to perform it yourself. If you cannot universalize what you are proposing to do, your intention is to immorally make an exception for yourself. Thus, it is wrong to make a false promise, for when you promise, you will that your promise be believed—which is inconsistent with willing a universal practice of making false promises.

The universalizability test is derived from the more basic principle that moral value resides not in our contingent inclinations but in letting reason determine our will. We may also apply that principle directly. If the ultimate source of moral value is a will determined by reason rather than irrationally swayed by inclinations, morality must direct us to respect rationality free of interference— whether from the person's own inclinations or from the outside. This suggests another formulation of the categorical imperative, which tells us always to respect *rational autonomy* in ourselves and in others and never to treat their wills as *mere means* to our goals.

The categorical imperative provides a foundation for testing moral claims by submitting them to the universalizability test: If an action can be universalized without contradiction, it is morally permissible; otherwise, it is not. In its mere means formulation, the categorical imperative also provides a direct foundation for moral *rights*. For the wrongness of violating others' freedom to choose their goals as their reason tells them, or to make rational choices in pursuit of those goals, corresponds to their moral right not to be interfered with in the exercise of their rational autonomy. In addition, the mere means principle places on us an imperfect duty to advance or promote the rational autonomy of others.

The detailed implications of a Kantian business ethics would have to be developed for the specific concrete dilemmas of commercial life. What is clear from the start is that such an analysis will be powerful, with a systematic and principled theory to back up its various conclusions with a unified argument, and with a rich story to tell about what business people ought to do. While it will justify many common business practices, it will require others to be thoroughly transformed. On the one hand, the Kantian company must go to great lengths to give employees opportunities to make autonomous choices about how their lives go—including within the workplace. Externally, it must treat those affected by its activities in similar ways—it must, for example, refrain from practices that deceive or otherwise manipulate consumers' rational decision making. On the other hand, the Kantian perspective shows that some of the things often demanded of companies, such as charitable giving, are not moral duties at all—at least not perfect ones.

CHAPTER 11

Fair Shares
Dividing the Value Added

Business, when done well, creates economic value. The value that business creates accrues to different groups: some to shareholders as dividends; some to employees as salary and other compensation; some to consumers and suppliers in the form of better prices; and some to governments in the form of taxes. Different ways of doing business changes the distribution of the surplus value among these (and other) groups. The distributive effects can be negative as well as positive, since business destroys value at the same time as it creates it. Business activity that increases economic value in the aggregate can at the same time hurt specific groups, such as when the success of Japanese car manufacturers in Alabama leads to job losses in traditional U.S. car plants in Michigan. And conversely, even business activities that destroy economic value overall—such as a factory that only makes a profit because it does not cover the costs that its pollution imposes on others—shift value from some people to others. Business decisions cannot avoid affecting the distribution of incomes and wealth.

Once we appreciate the distributive consequences of business activity, it becomes clear that our general question—"What ought people in business to do?"—subsumes a narrower (yet still vast) field of moral investigation into the question: "Who ought to get what share of the value that business creates?"—and, for that matter: "Who ought to bear what share of the loss when business destroys value?" To answer these questions, we need a theory of *distributive justice*, which is the subject of this chapter.

Questions of distributive justice arise inside firms—for example in decisions about compensation, or in disputes about whether shareholders are wronged when a company uses "their" money on non-profit-making activities. Challenges also arise in evaluating the distributive effects of companies' outward conduct—either in specific transactions, such as Plasma's allocation of economic value between blood donors, customers, and shareholders; or at the systemic level, where we may ask whether market capitalism produces just or unjust outcomes. In either case, moral reasoning must address which distribution is morally required—or whether morality requires any particular distribution at all. These are questions in which the theories we have already examined have rich implications. A consequentialist, for example, may care not just about the total amount of well-being in a society but also about how that well-being is distributed. And the last few chapters' reasoning about rights logically prompts us to ask whether individuals have rights to specific shares of the wealth creation they participate in. The arguments we have already developed, then, are ripe for being applied to distributive questions. Doing so will reveal how extraordinary fertile in strong intuitions this specific subfield of ethics—the morality of distributions—is.

A PARTICULAR RIGHT-CLAIM: FAIRNESS AND EXECUTIVE COMPENSATION

Here are a few facts about income inequality in the world:

- Incomes vary enormously between countries. The *per capita* national income of the U.S. in 2009 was $46,730, as measured by the World Bank. That of Nigeria was $1,980 (when adjusted for price differences), so the average U.S. citizen enjoyed an economic income 24-fold larger than that of the average Nigerian.
- Within countries, some individuals gain a much larger share of that income than others. In both the U.S. and Nigeria, the highest-earning 10 percent of the population receive one-third or more (in some years much more) of their nation's total income. From the opposite perspective of the income scale, 84 percent of the Nigerian population lived on less than two dollars per day in 2004.
- Income distributions change over time. In the 1920s and 1930s, the share of the U.S. national income going to the highest-earning *one* percent of Americans was between 15 and 20 percent. After World War II, that share dropped dramatically; for about three decades it hovered around 8–9 percent. In the mid-1980s, it shot back up, hitting 14 percent in 1990 and 20 percent a decade later. It has never been below 16 percent since; in 2007, it was almost 23 percent—of which 12 percent went to the top *one-tenth of a percent* of the population.[145]

These inequalities are factually indisputable; they may or may not also be morally unproblematic. It is implausible, however, to take them as morally *irrelevant*. Most people feel a tugging need to morally *justify* such differences in economic well-being—and they may quite legitimately agree on this need even as they vehemently disagree on whether the differences are in fact justified. Moreover, criticism of private business is often grounded on the claim that large inequalities render either capitalism as a whole or the business practices of individual companies immoral. There are good reasons, then, to examine what sort of moral argument is needed to justify or condemn economic inequalities.

Business most directly affects income distribution through choices about compensation—how much is paid to different types of employees, but also more broadly how new wealth is shared between rewards to employees, dividends to shareholders, and other purposes. Among these decisions, the most contentious are those about executive pay. The evolution of U.S. income inequality mentioned above reflects how

---

[145] For international data, see http://data.worldbank.org/indicator (accessed November 2010). For the US income distribution, see http://www.irs.gov/taxstats/indtaxstats/article/0,,id=133521,00.html (accessed November 2010).

extremely large incomes at the very top—often taken home by executives of large corporations, to copious public opprobrium—have ballooned since about 1980. One such executive was Lee Raymond, the former chief executive officer of the oil company ExxonMobil, who retired from his job at the end of 2005 after more than 40 years with the company. In his final year of work, he received a salary and bonus of about $9 million. That, however, was only a fraction of his total compensation, which also included restricted stock awards worth $32,087,000. Although these stock awards came with risks—Raymond could not sell the shares immediately, so they could lose value or be cancelled—he had accumulated enough restricted stock by 2005 that just the (unrestricted) cash dividends in that year amounted to more than $3 million. To top it off, Raymond received a lump-sum pension payment of $98,437,831 when he retired two weeks into 2006. In comparison, oil field workers are paid from $50,000 a year and up. Was it morally right—was it *just*—that Raymond should take home such vast rewards, when others receive so much less?

Debates about pay fairness in general, and about executive compensation in particular, have a curious tendency to turn into disputes about empirical facts. They often center on whether or not the people in question are paid their "market wage." More specifically, they may turn on whether companies need to pay what otherwise seem like obscenely large rewards in order to attract or motivate the best people, or whether people are compensated in proportion with the contribution they make to their employers, clients or society at large. Thus companies often justify outsize executive pay packages with reference to compensation committees' analysis of what are prevailing market rates. Critics often counter, in John Kenneth Galbraith's memorable words, that the "salary of the chief executive of the large corporation is not a market award for achievement. It is frequently in the nature of a warm personal gesture by the individual to himself."

Consider a specific form of executive pay: tying "incentive payments" to the company's stock price through options or restricted stock grants. This practice, which took off as part of the "shareholder value" movement in the 1980s and 1990s, is justified by some management theorists on the basis of the principal-agent model. The principal-agent model points out that shareholders can neither effectively monitor the executive officers nor, even if they could, would they be able to second-guess their strategic choices for the company. Those are, after all, meant to be the executives' expertise. The risk, therefore, is that executives will act in their own interests rather than in those of the shareholders. The solution, according to the model, is to align their interests by tying executive pay to the outcome that matters for shareholders, namely the stock price. But in their influential critique of executive pay, Lucian Bebchuk and Jessie Fried dispute that this is how incentive payments are designed in practice:

> . . . in the beginning of the 1990s, prominent financial economists such as Michael Jensen and Kevin Murphy urged shareholders to be more accepting of large pay packages that would provide high-powered incentives. Shareholders, it was argued, should care much more about providing managers with sufficiently strong incentives than about the amounts spent on executive pay . . . Unfortunately, however, much of the additional value provided to executives has not actually been tied to their own performance . . . managers have used their influence to obtain higher compensation through

arrangements that have substantially decoupled pay from performance. Firms could have generated the same increase in incentives at a much lower cost, or they could have used the amount spent to obtain more powerful incentives. Executive pay is much less sensitive to performance than has commonly been recognized.[146]

For instance, firms have failed to filter out stock price rises that are due largely to industry and general market trends and thus are unrelated to managers' own contribution to shareholder value.[147]

This is not the place to settle these empirical considerations. We should note, however, that even if they can be convincingly settled, they may distract from the moral question more than they help to answer it, because they take for granted a certain position about what makes a compensation scheme acceptable. The assertion that enormous rewards for executives improve shareholder returns invites us, at least implicitly, to think that this is a moral justification for them. Likewise those who claim that executive pay is in fact not all that aligned with shareholder interests present this as a reason for thinking such schemes unjustified. Presupposed in both positions is an unacknowledged moral premise: that being aligned with shareholder returns contributes to making an executive compensation scheme fair. But this premise is something for which the empirical discussion itself cannot establish any support. Facts about the nature and effects of specific pay schemes can only be inputs into moral arguments about the fairness of how economic value is distributed; they cannot tell us which sort of distribution morality requires. Only a theory of distributive justice can do that, by specifying which empirical factors *make* a distribution just or unjust. It may well be true that Lee Raymond would have left ExxonMobil had the company paid him any less, so that his compensation in fact benefited his shareholders. Even if so, more would need to be said to deem his compensation just. For it could be, for example, that he was demanding an unjust amount of money for staying, and that shareholders had no other choice but to pay him this unjust amount. And a theory of distributive justice, by establishing what moral requirements attach to distributions of rewards, can cast a morally tinged reflection back on the empirical facts themselves. If we were persuaded that Raymond's pay were unjustly generous, his supposed unwillingness to work for less than $45 million would look rather less like an impersonal market phenomenon to be accommodated and more like an unjustifiable hold-up.

THE PROBLEM OF "DESERVINGNESS"

Did Lee Raymond *deserve* $45 million? That is how our pre-theoretical thinking about distributive justice is typically framed. We may have in the back of our mind an intuitive "distribution of moral deserts" that more or less vaguely specifies what each person deserves, against which we then compare the actual distribution of gains. But on

---

[146] Lucian Bebchuk and Jessie Fried, *Pay without Performance: the Unfulfilled Promise of Executive Compensation* (Cambridge, MA: Harvard University Press, 2004), p. 6.

[147] Ibid., p. 7.

closer inspection, we shall find that the concept of "deservingness" is much less fruitful than ordinary moral thinking supposes it to be.

One meaning of "Raymond deserves $45 million from ExxonMobil" is simply that it is distributively just that the company should give Raymond $45 million. In this sense, saying that people have the wealth they "deserve" is *synonymous* with saying that the wealth distribution is just. For that reason, it cannot be an explanation of what *makes* it just. A tentative explanation could be, say, that Raymond's having $45 million maximizes the sum of well-being in society; or that the conventional understanding of the social role of oil company executive requires that he be paid this much; or that he has a moral right to this amount. All of these are plausible grounds for counting his reward as just, one he "deserves" to have. But none refers to his "deserving" his reward as a *reason* why the distribution is just; that would be circular, since "deserve", in this sense, just means to get what justice requires. So used in this way, the term "morally deserves" is superfluous; it says nothing more than what we already know. In particular, it would be meaningless to defend a distribution as just *because* it gives people what they deserve.

There is another sense of "morally deserves" which denotes something conceptually separate from distributive justice itself, and in which it can serve as an independent argument for deeming certain distributions just. The notion of moral desert, in the non-superfluous interpretation, rests on the idea that there are some benefits that properly accrue to us as rewards for something we are or something we have done. A fine artistic performance deserves acclamation, the best candidate deserves the job, or an act of courage deserves admiration. To use "deserve" in this sense is to assert a kind of *moral fittingness* between some characteristic of the person (the basis of desert) and that person's possession of something (the object of desert). That fittingness, in turn, is taken as a moral reason why, morally speaking, the person should have the thing in question. It is in this sense of moral fittingness that the concept is frequently used in claims that someone does or does not "deserve" the rewards they earn in the market: not a mere synonym for justice, but something that may help establish that a distribution is just.

But on what basis could anyone be thought to morally deserve any specific level of income or wealth? There are, of course, plenty of characteristics and choices that are correlated with monetary rewards. Other things being equal, greater abilities and harder effort may lead to better pay—but so may greater beauty, sharper elbows, and a knack for being in the right place at the right time. The characteristics most often thought of as bases of moral desert can be roughly grouped into abilities, effort, or contribution to society. Treating them as bases of desert, however—to say that a person's being more able, exerting more effort, or causing society to be provided with more are moral reasons why that person should earn more money—quickly runs into two problems: whether we can deserve anything at all; and if we can, whether there can ever be any close link between what we deserve and how much we earn.

Some of the personal characteristics that bring wealth fail to satisfy what seems like a basic condition for being a basis of moral desert, namely, that we are *responsible* for it or that it is something, as we often say, that we can take credit for. Most obviously, we clearly cannot take credit for our luck. If two friends each buy a lottery ticket, and one wins while the other loses, there is no *characteristic of the winner* that constitutes a moral reason why he should have the prize, for the prize should go to the holder of the winning ticket *whoever that is*. So there is nothing about the friend who happens to win that makes him more deserving of winning than the friend who loses. But if this is intuitive enough, we have to wonder whether we can take credit for anything at all, at least as far as income and wealth are concerned. For few of the determinants of our wealth have been primarily up to us to mold. Our innate talents—such as smarts or beauty— are by definition something we are born with. The same is true of the socioeconomic opportunities we are offered from the family or the political state we are born into. More plausible bases of desert are the choices and efforts we have made to cultivate and apply whatever innate skills and abilities we may have—for instance, by pursuing education. But even this is difficult to take credit for. For how easy we find it to make these efforts, or how congenial we find the habit of patiently cultivating innate talents, will itself be hugely influenced by our genes, our family background, and the cultural backdrop of our upbringing. Birth order, for example, is a strong determinant of educational success: First-born children are overrepresented in Ivy League universities, yet being a first-born child is hardly something one can claim responsibility for. Even if we can take credit for our efforts, this still does not show that we deserve the monetary rewards they command, for these are determined not by ourselves but by the market or other social forces beyond our control. Certainly the 24-fold difference between the incomes of the average American and the average Nigerian has almost everything to do with the different opportunities offered by the two countries, and vanishingly little to do with anything the American or Nigerian can have done to deserve a high or low income, respectively. Virtually all the determinants of socio-economic differences, then, are, in John Rawls's phrase, "arbitrary from a moral point of view." Since they resemble most of all the prizes in a natural lottery, they cannot serve as bases for claiming that those differences are morally deserved.

Not everyone will agree with the claim that we cannot deserve anything; the concept of desert is deeply engrained in how we understand our moral lives, and its use captures something important in the examples we have given in the last few pages. It is hard to believe that we can take no credit for how our choices shape the talents and abilities we now possess and the effort we currently exert. One may also challenge the requirement that we can only deserve that which we have been responsible for. If it is natural to think that morality incorporates a certain structure of reciprocity, it makes sense to think that someone could deserve a reward for contributing something to society that others value, even if he can take no credit for that contribution. That is, it is not inconsistent to agree that we have little responsibility for our talents and abilities, or even for our efforts, and yet assert that we deserve to be rewarded in proportion to how much those talents, abilities, and efforts benefit society.

But even if we hold on to a view that certain characteristics of persons make them morally deserving to possess certain things, it is still hard to argue that people morally deserve their incomes and wealth. Such a view would undoubtedly be forced to conclude that almost nobody ever gets what they deserve in a market where rewards are at least in part a result of individual choices. For, whatever plausible basis of moral desert we are prepared to countenance—be it abilities, efforts, or contribution to society—it will bear, at best, an extremely weak connection with actual monetary rewards, one far too tenuous to justify them as morally deserved. This may be true of most social mechanisms for allocating incomes and wealth; it is certainly true of reasonably free markets.

Business ethicist Nien-hê Hsieh writes that "in the market, desert claims are often illegitimate not because people cannot be morally deserving, but because the market . . . does not guarantee any meaningful proportionality between what a person receives and what he is said to deserve."[148] When Lee Raymond received $45 million in 2005, ExxonMobil stockholders had enjoyed a 45 percent return over the previous five years. Even if making money for shareholders is a plausible basis of moral desert for corporate executives, this return is hard to attribute to anything for which Raymond can take credit, since other oil companies had similar returns over the same period. Oil company stocks are so strongly influenced by market expectations of oil prices, that stock prices may never bear much of a relationship with what an executive could be said to deserve. ExxonMobil could, of course, change the way it determines executive pay: It could try to filter out from the performance measures everything that executives cannot take credit for.[149] But such fixes will never be enough to fill the gap between market determinants of pay and plausible bases for moral desert. For the market sets compensation—as it sets all prices—by an equilibrium in which the marginal benefit of what is sold equals the marginal cost of producing it (with adjustments for whatever market imperfections or government intervention may be at play), and there is no reason whatsoever to think that these *marginal* values should correspond in any systematic way to the factors we may envisage as grounds for desert, such as producers' effort or contribution to social well-being:

> lack of proportionality . . . reflects a fundamental fact about the market. The basic difficulty in grounding desert claims is not that imperfections in actual market operations undercut the relationship between what the producers receive and what they otherwise deserve to receive . . . Instead, the market operates according to a principle of maximization so that the prices that a consumer pays for goods are determined by the benefit that some consumer derives from consuming the last unit of those goods. Our intuitions about a producer's contribution, however, relate his contribution to the overall benefit that consumers derive from consuming his goods. Because there is no necessary relationship between a consumer's marginal benefit from consuming a good and the overall level of benefit that she derives from consuming that good, the market does not guarantee any proportionality between what a producer is paid and his contribution . . .

and, for the same reason,

> profit is not solely determined by effort, meaning that there is no meaningful proportionality between profit and effort.[150]

---

[148] Nien-hê Hsieh, "Moral Desert, Fairness and Legitimate Expectations in the Market," *Journal of Political Philosophy*, 8(1), 2000.

[149] One way to do this would be to only look at stock returns adjusted for how similarly situated companies have done, and use only the excess return over competitors as a performance measure.

[150] Hsieh, "Moral Desert."

What all this means is that even if we think that people can morally deserve things in virtue of their effort, abilities, or contributions to society, such moral desert claims are insufficient to conclude anything about the justice of the market's distribution of income and wealth. As it happens, it is also unnecessary. Recall the lottery example: Whatever intuitions we have about the possibility of moral desert, it seems clear that two otherwise equal buyers of lottery tickets are equally deserving of the prize, regardless of who happens to win. But, of course, it is the actual winner who should receive the prize; it would be unjust to deprive him of it. We can justify his receiving the prize as a matter of fairness without resort to desert—for deserving or not, the winner is fairly entitled to the prize—and this shows that we have no need for claims about what people deserve in order to establish what it is morally right that they should have. We can, that is, establish what distributive justice requires without establishing what people deserve.

This does not mean the characteristics commonly proposed as grounds for morally deserving this or that amount are irrelevant. There is something in our intuitive beliefs that ability, effort, and contribution play *some* role in determining what it would be morally right for people to have. But theories of distributive justice developed without reference to moral desert may well do a better job of rationalizing these intuitions. For such theories could well say that a just society is one whose just distributive mechanisms naturally lead people to expect that their rewards will in fact depend on these characteristics. If people act on such expectations and "play by the rules"—and the rules that they play by are just—the expectations take on a degree of legitimacy, and morality may require us to acknowledge someone's legitimate expectation as a moral reason (if not an overriding reason) why the person should obtain what he legitimately expect. This may be as solid an account of moral desert *qua* moral fittingness as we can hope for, and it is everything we need. In this sense, then, people may be said to "deserve" the rewards that they can legitimately expect, and a legitimate expectation of some reward is an expectation that is rational to hold for those who "play by the rules" of a distributive system that is itself morally justified. What one can legitimately expect to earn for one's abilities, efforts, or social contributions (and for that matter for one's beauty or luck) in a just system of rewards depends, of course, on what systems can be morally justified. That is something our earlier theories have answers to; we start by examining those given by utilitarianism.

UTILITARIANISM AS A THEORY OF JUSTICE

Notwithstanding the weaknesses of utilitarianism as a moral theory, the fact that it remains a leading normative framework for guiding both policy and business decisions (especially in the form of cost-benefit analysis) makes it necessary to explore its implications for distributive justice. As we ask what monetary rewards people can legitimately expect under utilitarianism, we must start by noting that within utilitarianism, "justice" and "fairness" are not their own moral categories, conceptually separate from utility or well-being. Just as utilitarians must use the term "rights" to refer simply to treatments that it is especially important to respect in order for the most aggregate well-being to be enjoyed, so they may call a distribution of income and wealth fair or just precisely according to whether it produces more aggregate well-being than any other achievable distribution. There is an important sense, then, in which utilitarianism ignores distribution altogether. Most basically, because it has no *direct* concern with income and wealth at all—well-being (or "happiness") is the only morally valuable currency it recognizes—and also because it measures well-being by *additive aggregation*, treating the same sum total of well-being as having the same moral value regardless of how it is distributed across individuals. One could, of course, see this as expressing a particular distributive attitude: a radical egalitarianism in which everyone counts the same so that it does not matter morally who enjoys a unit of extra well-being. But that would invert the logical sequence of utilitarian moral valuation. It is because more well-being is always better that it does not matter who enjoys it, rather than the other way around.

This indifference to distribution in the utilitarian *principle*, however, does not mean utilitarianism does not have distributive *implications*. For how things are allocated—and, in particular, how income and wealth accrue to different individuals—will affect how much well-being there is to be enjoyed in society overall. Utilitarianism, clearly, must say that income and wealth should flow to those who gain the most well-being from it, since this maximizes the sum total of well-being in society. (So utilitarianism can be said to distribute on the basis of *need*, if we measure someone's need for something by the amount of well-being forgone by not receiving it.) Which distributive recommendations this entails will depend on facts about the world, both psychological facts regarding the effect of money on well-being and economic and sociological facts about the incentive effects of various distributive systems. These are, needless to say, enormously complex empirical questions, which large swathes of the social sciences are devoted to answering. But some simple conjectures can give us a sense of what utilitarians are likely to conclude regarding policies of compensation and distribution.

Other things being equal, we would expect that the richer anyone becomes, the less additional well-being they gain from a given increase in their income or wealth. (We may want to say that they have less need of extra money, in the sense that they benefit less from the increase and suffer less from its absence.) This is known as the assumption of *diminishing marginal utility of money*. If money has diminishing marginal utility, a shift of income and wealth from the better off to the worse off would, other things being equal, increase the sum total of social well-being. Diminishing marginal utility being a plausible assumption, utilitarianism in effect has a certain egalitarian bias: It should in many cases advocate redistribution from the rich to the poor. Indeed, in many situations, utilitarianism must defend a radical redistributive program. Given the average income differences between Nigerians and Americans, for example, no one can doubt that more aggregate well-being would result from increasing Nigerian incomes at the cost of cutting U.S. ones—even cutting them by much more than Nigerian incomes would increase. Utilitarians may, of course, legitimately doubt the ability of any redistributive mechanism actually to make this happen, but they would still have to endorse such income transfers *in principle* if they were possible. Diminishing marginal utility also means that by utilitarian lights, many features of compensation policy in general, and executive pay in particular, do not pass moral muster. To justify Lee Raymond's compensation package in utilitarian terms, ExxonMobil's compensation committee—and Raymond himself—would have to claim that each dollar of his $45 million compensation package would generate as much well-being by being given to him as by any other use, including returning it to shareholders in the form of dividends; reducing oil and gas prices to consumers; or offering higher compensation to lower-ranking employees. That claim is, to put it mildly, implausible.

We should be clear that utilitarianism's tendency to egalitarianism because of diminishing marginal utility of money remains an efficiency argument. Redistribution is only "just" in utilitarian terms because a dollar is more efficiently put to work in its moral task of producing well-being if it is given to the worse off. This egalitarian bias is balanced by other efficiency considerations. These include utilitarianism's sensitivity to incentive effects, in particular the possibility that behavior conducive to greater amounts of social well-being (such as the production of desired goods) is best encouraged by unequal monetary rewards. No less plausible than diminishing marginal utility is the conjecture that the incentive effects of redistribution would outweigh the well-being gained by redistributing wealth well before it was fully equalized. For this reason, utilitarian "distributive justice" (that is to say, the happiness-maximizing distribution) will never realistically involve anything near full equality, since this would be inefficient.

Yet, two things need to be said about this point. First, this remains an empirical trade-off, and a utilitarian argument for or against a particular income distribution cannot simply assume that one or the other tendency predominates. This obvious point needs to be made insofar as assertions about the benefit of incentives are sometimes grotesquely exaggerated. The *New York Times* columnist Nicholas Kristof's lampooning of one particular executive is a case in point:

> Last year, Barry Diller [head of IAC/Interactive] took home a pay package worth $469 million, making him the highest-paid chief executive in America . . . [The company] said that the package was necessary to 'motivate Mr. Diller for the future.' Goodness, this man needs a lot of motivation! He required about $150,000 every hour just to get motivated—suggesting that he may be the laziest man in America.[151]

Second, while incentives arguments can justify inequalities on utilitarian grounds, they cannot justify all the actions that make such incentives necessary. In the case of executive pay, compensation committees may be right, on utilitarian grounds, to accept outsize executive pay because of the empirical requirement to "incentivize" executives who will otherwise refuse (so it is asserted) to do things in their power that bring about more than enough extra well-being to make the price worth paying. Individual executives, however, have no access to that utilitarian argument, since what incentives they need is within their control. Accept for the sake of argument that only under Lee Raymond's leadership could ExxonMobil so efficiently produce oil that profits and the sum of social well-being would be maximized. Even so, if Lee Raymond refused to provide that leadership for less than $45 million, that was something Lee Raymond could himself have changed by accepting to work for less. And if it were really true, as the premise of the argument asserts, that his leadership produced more than $45 million worth of well-being (or, more generally, more than it cost in forgone well-being for him to provide that leadership), then on utilitarian grounds he would be morally wrong to refuse to provide it. A utilitarian approach to distributive justice, therefore, may well have to condemn the need to

[151] Nicholas D. Kristof, "America's Laziest Man?" *The New York Times*, 7 November 2006.

"incentivize" executives with outsize pay as a mere artifact of unjust demands made by the executives themselves.

That utilitarianism can answer questions about distributive justice is no surprise; one of the theory's great appeals is its exhaustive ability to settle any moral question (so long as the facts are clear). That does not make its answers good ones; indeed, we can recognize in its analysis of justice many of the problems that we earlier identified in the utilitarian approach generally. Utilitarianism displays its unconcern for the individuality of persons in the way it evaluates distributive effects simply by its social consequences. As we have already said, this clashes with the need to respect a certain personal sphere. The most consistent utilitarians are clear about this:

> Given the present conditions in many parts of the world . . . we ought, morally, to be working full time to relieve great suffering of the sort that occurs as a result of famine or other disasters[152]

Although there are admittedly limits to how much we may merely look out for ourselves, however, those limits cannot be so tight that we must make all our decisions—including about what work we will do for what salary—solely so as to maximize the social benefit. A utilitarian theory of distributive justice, like utilitarianism generally, ignores the moral importance of people's responsibility for their own lives.

ENTITLEMENTS: NOZICKIAN LIBERTARIANISM

Some hold the diametrically opposite view—that we need not justify our incomes with respect to their beneficial consequences at all. This is *libertarianism*, and it says that we are entitled to whatever income and wealth we manage to earn in a free market, no matter how unequal a distribution of income and wealth may result. A libertarian view opposes redistribution regardless of whether it benefits society (or indeed the rich: Libertarianism does not admit as a justification for redistributing money even the possibility that everyone would be better off with redistribution, for example because a more egalitarian society would be a more harmonious one). How can such a view be justified?

Any plausible theory of distributive justice must to some degree accommodate the intuition that people are entitled to what they expect to get if they "play by the rules." No system for allocating the products of wealth-creating activities can be well-functioning, let alone just, if it does not allow the participants to have at least minimally reliable expectations about how they will fare from how they choose to apply their talents and efforts. The question is what the rules determining income and wealth distributions ought, morally, to be. That in turn will depend on the underlying theory. Utilitarianism, as we have seen, is more likely to be excessively biased toward egalitarian than libertarian conclusions. Instead, moral desert is sometimes proposed as a foundation for libertarian distributive justice: If people morally deserve what they receive in the market, it is just that they should keep what they earn. But we have already seen that if moral desert claims can be sustained at all, they will in general fault

---

[152] Peter Singer, "Famine, Affluence, and Morality," *Philosophy and Public Affairs* 1(1), Spring 1972.

rather than justify the market's distribution of rewards, so desert-based libertarianism is destined to fail.

The most promising—and prominent—defense of libertarian justice is one based on *rights*. If rights express the moral value of consent and free choice, then it stands to reason that rights-based theories of distributive justice should to a considerable degree respect the distributive outcomes of free choices. Robert Nozick has pushed that view to its logical limit with his "entitlement theory" of justice, according to which *any* distribution of income and wealth is just if it results from individuals' freely chosen actions, and that any redistribution not consented to by those affected is an immoral violation of their rights. This explicitly rejects what Nozick calls *time-slice principles* of justice, which "hold that the justice of a distribution is determined by how things are distributed (who has what) as judged by some *structural* principle(s) of just distribution." Utilitarianism is a time-slice principle of justice since it assesses the justice of distributions by comparing their sums total of well-being; so are other consequentialisms, which pay as little heed as utilitarianism does to how the distributions came about. "In contrast," Nozick writes, "*historical principles* of justice hold that past circumstances or actions of people can create differential entitlements or differential deserts to things." Time-slice principles will necessarily violate these entitlements. Nozick famously illustrates his argument with the example of legendary basketball player Wilt Chamberlain:

> . . . suppose a distribution favored by [a time-slice principle of justice] is realized. Let us suppose it is your favorite one and let us call [it] *D1*; perhaps everyone has an equal share, perhaps shares vary in accordance with some dimension you treasure. Now suppose that Wilt Chamberlain is greatly in demand by basketball teams . . . He signs the following sort of contract with a team: in each home game, twenty-five cents from the price of each ticket of admission goes to him . . . The season starts, and people cheerfully attend his team's games; they buy their tickets, each time dropping a separate twenty-five cents of their admission price into a special box with Chamberlain's name on it. They are excited about seeing him play; it is worth their admission price to them . . . [Is Chamberlain] entitled to this income? Is this new distribution, *D2*, unjust? If so, why? There is *no* question about whether each . . . was entitled to the control over the resources they held in *D1*; because that was the distribution (your favorite) that (for the purposes of argument) we assumed was acceptable . . . If *D1* was a just distribution, and people voluntarily moved from it to *D2*, transferring parts of their shares they were given under *D1* (what was it for if not to do something with?), isn't *D2* also just? If the people were entitled to dispose of the resources to which they were entitled (under *D1*), didn't this include their being entitled to give it to, or exchange it with, Wilt Chamberlain? Can anyone else complain on grounds of justice?[153]

Nozick's example makes two different and important claims about justice. One is that a *transfer* of possessions, if it satisfies certain moral criteria, cannot create an injustice

---

[153] This and the foregoing quotes are from Robert Nozick, *Anarchy, State, and Utopia*, BasicBooks, 1974.

where none existed before. Whatever arises from a just distribution via just means is itself just (Nozick calls this the principle of justice in transfer). Nozick's entitlement theory says that, *provided* initial entitlements are justified (to be determined by what Nozick calls a principle of justice in acquisition), distributive justice is a matter of the history by which possessions move from one person's control to that of another—"the means of transition from one situation to another specified by the principle of justice in transfer are justice-preserving, and any situation actually arising from repeated transitions in accordance with the principle from a just situation is itself just."[154] As the Chamberlain example suggests, the obvious criterion for a just transfer is that it not violate anyone's rights, which, on its face, any *voluntary* transfer satisfies. The second claim is that *because* of this, all time-slice principles are flawed. For no distributive pattern that such principles may require could conceivably be maintained under a continuous practice of voluntarily transferring and exchanging things. Since such a process will alter the distribution of income and wealth without violating justice in transfer, one simply cannot say from looking at the distribution at any point in time that it is unjust, even if it no longer satisfies the asserted time-slice principle. Nor can we be sure, conversely, that justice in transfer has *not* been violated simply because the time-slice principle *is* satisfied.

According to Nozick, justice simply requires that people have what they are entitled to, and they are entitled to whatever has been voluntarily transferred to them by people entitled to make those transfers. The upshot of Nozick's libertarian theory is to sharply limit the scope for morally criticizing inequalities resulting from business activity. Of course, rights-based libertarianism condemns inequalities caused by violations of rights—theft and fraud are the most obvious examples—although even in those cases it is not the inequalities themselves that are objectionable, but the unjust transfer of income and wealth. (Robin Hood is no less a perpetrator of injustice, on a Nozickian view, than the ordinary highwayman.) The mere fact of inequality in the allocation of value created by business, no matter how extreme, is morally irrelevant. It follows, for example, that the highly unequal sharing of the economic surplus generated by Plasma— where the blood suppliers' and consumers' respective willingness to accept a pittance and pay a fortune left the lion's share to Plasma's shareholders—was perfectly just insofar as no one's rights were violated. Nor was there anything unjust in Lee Raymond's $45 million yearly compensation and the $98 million pensions package, assuming that ExxonMobil's revenue was money that the company was entitled to. If Nozick's arguments hold, one can only challenge these distributive outcomes on grounds of justice by proving that the parties in the transactions were not entitled to make the transfers in the first place. That, in turn, would require showing that Plasma's counterparties committed rights violations in acquiring the money they willingly paid with or—implausibly— the blood they freely sold; or that Exxon Mobil's profits constituted ill-gotten gains. Such claims could conceivably be substantiated. But even if they were, they would seem so far removed from the intuitions of those objecting to Plasma's profits or Raymond's pay as to make it doubtful whether they are still arguments for moral concerns about *distribution.*

---

[154] Ibid.

JUST AND UNJUST INEQUALITIES:
RAWLSIAN SOCIAL CONTRACT THEORY

Nozick's libertarian reasoning and its respect for autonomous choice has obvious appeal for anyone concerned with rights. Yet, the short shrift it gives to the distributive effects of choice takes the value of consent to the point of fetishism. For even if no possessions are acquired or transferred unjustly in Nozick's sense—that is, by actions that violate people's rights—the distribution of material holdings is affected by a host of circumstances which cannot, on any plausible interpretation, be deemed to have been autonomously chosen. Such circumstances include the distribution of natural talents (which is determined genetically), the demand for and market price of those talents (which varies with a community's level of economic development, culturally influenced tastes, and social and legal institutions such as the form of property rights), and society's inherited technology, institutions, and state of accumulated knowledge, which affect the opportunities for various forms of productive activity. Even if our rights are perfectly respected, our fortunes are largely determined by the kind of society we find ourselves in; and virtually all that we can expect to achieve in the free exercise of our rights is made possible by the aggregate effects of social cooperation. In light of this, the connection between rational autonomy and the distributive outcomes of free exchanges begins too appear too tenuous to provide the necessary moral justification of the inequalities we see. To the extent that market distributions of income and wealth reflect choice at all, it is not so much individual choices as aggregate choices about how society is structured—or rather the absence of such choices, if Nozickian policies are followed.

If we care about autonomy, therefore, we must care about the degree of our autonomous influence on social structures. John Rawls has suggested that we should see society as a "cooperative venture for mutual advantage"—one characterized by conflicting as well as common interests. The mutual advantage of society's members lies in the fact that we are all infinitely better off by pursuing our goals within society than by going it alone; the conflict is that the many ways in which society can be organized benefit its members differentially. Defining justice simply as the result of free individual choices excludes from considerations of justice the ways in which the organization of society *shapes* the choices that are open to us and thereby determines the range of possible outcomes from those choices. If autonomy is the fundamental moral value, then surely a theory of justice cannot be indifferent to how much more our lives are hostage to these unchosen factors than to our choices themselves:

> the primary subject of justice is the basic structure of society, or more exactly, the way in which the major social institutions distribute fundamental rights and duties and determine the division of advantages from social cooperation . . . [The basic structure defines] men's rights and duties and influence their life prospects, what they can expect to be and how well they can hope to do. [It] is the primary subject of justice because its effects are so profound and present from the start. The intuitive notion here is that this structure contains various social positions and that men born into different positions have different expectations of life determined, in part, by the political system as well as by economic and social circumstances. In this way the institutions

favor certain starting places over others. These are especially deep inequalities. Not only are they pervasive, but they affect men's initial chances in life; yet they cannot possibly be justified by an appeal to the notions of merit and desert. It is these inequalities, presumably inevitable in the basic structure of any society, to which the principles of social justice must in the first instance apply.[155]

This suggests a counterargument to Nozickian libertarianism: Respecting rights cannot mean simply "letting things take their course" and not interfere with voluntary exchanges from a supposedly natural starting point. This is not only because there is no natural "pre-social" starting point outside of society's basic structure (although that is true) but because, even if such a "natural" basis of comparison could be imagined, it would be in no less need of moral justification. Yet the question of which (if any) inequalities are compatible with respecting rights evidently cannot be settled before we establish how such a rights-based theory can assess specific distributions of income and wealth at all, given that they will in large part be determined by forces beyond anyone's individual autonomous choice. The solution will lie in explaining how, even so, some possible basic social structures can be said better to respect individual autonomy than others. Though a rights-based theory of justice must be rooted in consent, the consent it must require need not be consent exclusively or even primarily to individual *transactions*. It can instead be based on consent to the social organization that shapes the possible or probable outcomes of those transactions from the outset. The basic structure of society itself, then, can be justified on rights-based grounds if it reflects the expression of the rational autonomy of its members.

In this approach to justice, "we are to imagine that those who engage in social cooperation choose together, in one joint act, the principles which are to assign basic rights and duties and to determine the division of social benefits."[156] In seeing justice as the result of an agreement by free individuals on the principles that shall govern their interactions, Rawls adopts the *social contract* approach to moral and political reasoning, a tradition that encompasses Thomas Hobbes, John Locke, Jean-Jacques Rousseau, and Immanuel Kant. Social contract theories ask us to imagine all members of society coming together, in an "original position," to decide in advance the rules by which they are to regulate and coordinate their pursuit of their personal goals and adjudicate conflicting claims on the benefits that this coordination produces. Whatever principles they would agree on in the original position are what actual social interaction in the real world must satisfy in order to be just; these principles, the theory says, are what justice *is*. Conversely, if a society satisfies the principles that its members would freely agree to in the original position, the way its benefits are distributed respects their rational autonomy.

Social contract theory, then, promises to yield specific principles of distributive justice—we shall discuss presently what they are—but it also offers a *methodology* for establishing and justifying those principles, which is to show that rational people would freely choose them in the original position.

---

[155] John Rawls, *A Theory of Justice*, 2nd ed. (Cambridge, MA: Harvard University Press, 1999), §2.

[156] Rawls, *Theory of Justice*, §3.

Two features of the social contract approach must be quite clear. First, the social contract is *hypothetical*; it does not depend on a historical claim about some actually occurring constitutional convention. The argument is not that people in some real or mythical past *in fact* agreed to certain principles. It is that everyone *would* agree to them who was, hypothetically, put in a situation of having to decide. One may ask, as we did of rule-utilitarianism's appeal to hypothetical consequences, why this matters. How could a *hypothetical* contract have any normative force? The answer is that it is not unreasonable to think that hypothetical consent may reproduce the moral value that rights-based theories attribute to actual consent, that is to say, respect for rational autonomy (in a way that hypothetical *consequences* do not exhibit the moral value that utilitarianism claims for actual consequences, that is to say, an actual increase in human well-being). The reason has to do with the second feature of social contract theory. The hypothetical social contract must be entered into under conditions that would be genuinely conducive to rational autonomy—conditions that the facts of society as it exists prevent any real contracting situation from ever perfectly fulfilling. The original position is, quite appropriately, an *idealized* contracting situation; one from which the agreement that results can be said to be an agreement by free and equal rational individuals. They are free in that their agreement is autonomously given; they are equal, so that their consent is not the heteronomous product of unequal power. A social contract theory of justice, then, requires principles of distribution that rational individuals would agree to in a contracting situation that is fundamentally *fair*. This is why Rawls calls his theory "justice as fairness"; and it is why hypothetical consent has normative force—it respects rational autonomy in a way that actual consent may never fully do, contaminated as the latter must be by the social conditions of the actual world in which freedom and equality are at best approximate.

For this reason, Rawls designs his original position so as to remove the sources of unfreedom and inequality that mar the actual world:

> Among the essential features of this situation is that no one knows his place in society, his class position for social status, nor does anyone know his fortune in the distribution of natural assets and abilities, his intelligence, strength, and the like. I shall even assume that the parties do not know their conception of the good or their special psychological propensities. The principles of justice are chosen behind a veil of ignorance. This ensures that no one is advantaged or disadvantaged in the choice of principles by the outcome of natural chance or the contingency of social circumstances . . . [given] the symmetry of everyone's relations to each other, this initial situation is fair between individuals as moral persons, that is, as rational beings with their own ends . . . The original position is, one might say, the appropriate initial status quo, and thus the fundamental agreements reached in it are fair.[157]

---

[157] Rawls, *Theory of Justice*, §6.

We may note here the analogy with Kant's categorical imperative. Just like duty, in Kantian theory, is whatever can be rationally willed when we strip away all contingent inclinations and heteronomous influences on the will, so justice, in the Rawlsian formulation, is whatever rational parties can agree to when all their morally arbitrary differences are removed from view.

What, then, would people agree to in the original position? Behind a veil of ignorance, rational persons must guide their agreement by the little they do know. Their knowledge includes that they will have certain differential abilities (but not which ones), that they will wish to pursue certain differential goals (but not which ones), and that the form of social organization they choose will shape the degree to which their abilities and choices are likely to achieve those goals. Under such radical uncertainty, Rawls argues, one must rationally worry about the worst-case scenario. All parties will want to avoid a social system that, if they are unlucky, puts them in an unnecessarily bad position. First, this means that they will agree on an expansive set of *rights*. No one will take the risk of having their life or their liberties sacrificed to what may turn out to be in the interest of the majority—even if the risk of being so sacrificed is lesser than the risk of ending up in the majority that would benefit from the absence of such protections. Second, Rawls thinks that the same reasoning must apply to deciding how the material benefits are to be distributed. Worrying about the risk of being deprived of those benefits, Rawls argues, will lead the parties in the original position to accept, in addition to securing the maximal possible set of basic rights and liberties that can be extended to everyone, the following distributive principle:

> social and economic inequalities are to be arranged so that they are both (a) reasonably expected to be to everyone's advantage, and (b) attached to positions and offices open to all[158]

where "to everyone's advantage" is further specified by Rawls as the *difference principle*: Inequalities are only permitted if the worst off in society are better off with the inequalities than they would be were the inequalities eliminated. Put differently, justice requires material egalitarianism except for inequalities that benefit the poorest— through the economic activity that they encourage—or at least leave them no worse off.

What are the implications of the difference principle for business ethics? The principle does not specify which economic activities should carry which reward, only that the overall distribution of rewards must make the poorest as well off as they can be. In a society where the difference principle is realized, people are fairly entitled to (we could say that they "deserve") whatever income and wealth they can expect to achieve by following the system's rules. Conceivably, this could allow large inequalities to remain, but that is something that would need to be established empirically. If it is not satisfied, however, then the distribution of income and wealth is unjust; business may then be morally required to play a role in reducing, or at least to play a role in avoiding the perpetuation of, that injustice. The specifics of this obligation would

---

[158] Rawls, *Theory of Justice*, §11.

depend on the particular nature of the injustice. But it could presumably include, within a company, a duty to counteract unjust effects of the social structure at the level of company compensation patterns—a duty to avoid gender or racial differences in pay, for example, even when social convention leads to such inequalities in general (perhaps especially then). Vis-à-vis the outside world, companies in an unjust society may have a combination of duties to remedy injustice through charitable giving (as may individual recipients of unjustly high rewards); and not to frustrate efforts to render society more just, such as tax and labor market reforms. If these duties can be defended, they clearly amount to requiring radical change of many common corporate practices.

We end by briefly mentioning two objections to justice as fairness. The first takes Rawls to be too redistributive, because (so it argues) it is not rational to be as risk-averse in the original position as he assumes. Rather, everyone would agree to some more inequality, accepting the risk of being at the bottom for the chance of greater rewards if one ends up at the top. The second objection, in contrast, faults Rawls for not being redistributive enough. By appealing to incentive effects to select the difference principle rather than a more ambitious egalitarianism, Rawls justifies extortion on the part of high-earners, or so the objection goes. For as we mentioned in our discussion of Lee Raymond's compensation package, incentives have the assumed effects because high earners make it so; and this is something parties in the original position, if they consistently apply the reasoning Rawls attributes to them, would want to rule out.[159] We shall not address these objections here, beyond pointing out that they both operate *within* the social contract approach he describes. Thus, they illustrate that it is possible to agree with Rawls's methodology of deriving principles of justice from what rational parties would agree to in the original position, while disagreeing with the particular conclusions he draws regarding what those rational parties would settle on. Whether or not one or the other objection succeeds against Rawls's own conclusion, they illustrate that the theory itself is an extraordinarily fertile tool for thinking about what justice requires.

The theories of distributive justice that we have surveyed, with the exception of utilitarianism, were not developed to answer question about how individuals ought to act but to judge the distributive characteristics of the "basic structure" of society, in Rawlsian terminology. This is worth keeping in mind, as it means that applying them to business decisions is to make them answer questions they were not designed to address. There is, however, no reason to think they cannot be so used, as long as one takes the appropriate extra steps. This could just mean respecting the theories' original focus on overall justice in society, and build a complementary theory of business ethics to answer the question of what business ought to do when it operates in a society that is more or less just. But more ambitiously, it can mean taking the methods of reasoning that a theory applies to questions of distribution and seeing what insights they can produce for a more general moral theory of how we ought to act. The social contract approach employed by Rawls readily lends itself to such a project. In our final chapter, accordingly, we shall examine how the Rawlsian method offers not just a theory of justice, but a social contract theory of business ethics.

---

[159] Gerald A. Cohen, "Where the Action is: On the Site of Distributive Justice," *Philosophy and Public Affairs*, 26(1), Winter 1997, pp. 3–30.

Summary of the Argument in This Chapter

We have so far postponed the question of how gains (and losses) from commercial activity ought to be distributed. Yet this is of the first order of importance. Striking inequalities between the poorest and the best paid are directly or indirectly the result of business activities. To answer whether this matters morally, we need to develop a theory of *distributive justice*.

Pre-theoretically, distributive justice is often framed as a matter of *moral desert*—of what incomes and wealth different people deserve to receive, and, in particular, whether they deserve what they receive in capitalist markets. But desert is a poor foundation for a strong theory of justice. Partly this is because there is no reliable proportionality between what people make in the market and commonly asserted bases of moral desert, such as talent, effort or contribution to society. But more fundamentally, because even the most plausible factors on which to base desert claims are much less under our control than we commonly think. Talent is partly innate, opportunities for cultivating one's abilities are constrained by socioeconomic status, and the propensity for effort may be both genetically or culturally dependent—in sum, the determinants of our income and wealth are largely due to factors that are, in John Rawls's words, "arbitrary from a moral point of view." Rather than seeing people's characteristics as making them inherently deserving, a theory of distributive justice had better see them as morally entitled to the rewards they can legitimately expect *in a just system*, given their individual characteristics. But what makes a system just must be established separately.

We can straightforwardly apply the utilitarian criterion to obtain a *utilitarian theory of distributive justice*. It would say that incomes should be distributed so that the resulting social sum of well-being is maximized. Even though this criterion has no inherent concern for equality, the plausible empirical conjecture of *diminishing marginal utility of money* makes it very likely that it will justify radical redistribution compared to existing income distributions—although not as far as complete equality, since incentive effects would make this inefficient. Given the tremendous problems of utilitarian ethics, however, it is hardly a satisfactory basis for the theory of justice.

Instead, we may construct an account of distributive justice based on moral rights. Robert Nozick's *libertarianism* starts from the inviolability of individual freedom to argue that if some initial distribution is just, then *whatever* new distribution results from an arbitrary series of non-rights-violating agreements between free individuals must also be just. Since there is no logical limit to what sort of distributions could arise from such exchanges, no *time-slice principle* of justice can be correct: Whether a distribution is just or not depends on how it came about, not its structural features at a point in time. For many (but not all) of the most striking inequalities capitalist business produces, it is difficult to argue that the exchanges leading to them were involuntary, so if Nozick is correct, most such inequalities are indeed morally just.

But we need not accept this conclusion. An informed respect for individual rational autonomy must take seriously the fact that the distribution of income and wealth is much more profoundly determined by a society's technology, its physical and human capital, and its forms of social and political organizations than it is by anyone's individual choices. So, if, as a proper rights-based view must require, the distribution of income and wealth ought to reflect autonomous choices, then these social factors must reflect them, too. While they cannot reflect anyone's rational autonomy *individually*, they can be required to respect our autonomy as members of a "cooperative venture for mutual advantage." The thought that what Rawls calls society's *basic structure* must itself be seen as being chosen by us inspires the *social contract theory* of justice. In Rawls's version, we are to imagine all members of society meeting behind a "veil of ignorance"—without knowledge of their particular position in life and the advantages it gives them—in an *original position* of having to agree to the basic constitutional rules to govern society. The veil of ignorance ensures that the resulting hypothetical agreement is *fair*. The social contract embodies the rules that would have been accepted by all if they met under conditions that ensured equal freedom by making it impossible to exploit individual advantages to get a better deal for oneself.

Rawls himself argues that the parties in the original position would take as their greatest concern the risk of ending up in a disadvantaged place in society, with few means for autonomously choosing and pursuing goals. Therefore, they would agree on the strongest possible set of universal political rights. They would also aim for egalitarian distributions of income and wealth, with one important exception. The *difference principle* says inequalities are just if and only if they can be justified to the worst off because they improve their situation from what it would otherwise be (because of incentive effects). We need not agree with Rawls's conclusions to accept the social contract approach. We can argue, without inconsistency, that he is mistaken about what would be chosen in the original position but that this method of moral analysis is correct. Indeed, we may expand the social contract approach, and use a hypothetical agreement between free and equal contractors in an original position as the justificatory device not just for distributions of economic advantage, but for rules to govern business activities generally.

CHAPTER 12

Just Business
Fulfilling Social Contracts

The previous chapter's excursion into the morality of distributions showed that respect for rational autonomy—of not treating people merely as means—can constitute the foundation of a fertile theory of justice, by requiring income and wealth inequalities to satisfy principles to which free and rational persons would consent if they did not know the morally arbitrary factors that influence where in that distribution they end up. Now, this Rawlsian reasoning need not be restricted to distributive matters, or to the broader foundational constitutional questions to which Rawls applies it. It is rational for the parties in the original position to take an interest in other matters as well; specifically, it is rational for them to care about business conduct, beyond its distributive impact. If we ask what rules they would agree should govern business behavior, we have opened the possibility of a *social contract theory of business ethics.*

The social contract approach presents a particularly promising solution to the need we identified early in this book. Once we acknowledge that business behavior must be morally justified and that mere social convention about norms cannot provide that justification, we recognize the need for principles, external to socially defined norms, that can adjudicate the truth and falsity of the claims those norms imply about what business ought to do. The metaphor of contract, the archetypal form of human intercourse in the economic realm, should be particularly congenial to those seeking answers to the ethical dilemmas in *business* in particular. Contract theory has the practical appeal of offering a general method for thinking about specific problems by focusing on what principles rational persons in an appropriate contracting situation would endorse. That is also its moral appeal: Unlike utilitarianism, social contract theory formalizes the need to justify morality's commands to all affected individuals. It does so because whenever it limits someone's pursuit of his self-interest, it justifies this to that individual by pointing out that *he would himself accept the principle* that requires the limitation, if he did not seek to make an exception for himself. Similarly, whenever the social contract theory permits someone to pursue his self-interest in ways that harm the interests of others, it justifies this to them by showing that they themselves would have endorsed the principle permitting the conduct in question had they thought they had an equal chance to be in a position to benefit from doing the same. In this sense, social contract theory arrives at moral conclusions via arguments that respect individuals as a free and equal persons whose ability to rationally choose what is important must not be sacrificed or manipulated for the purposes of others.

Of course, for this justificatory strategy to work, the social contract approach must show persuasively which rules and principles would be agreed to in the appropriately described social contracting situation. That, in turn, depends on how it is appropriate to describe the social contracting situation in order for the hypothetical agreements made within it to carry moral force.

A SOCIAL CONTRACT THEORY OF BUSINESS ETHICS

Rawls's theory was designed to establish the political rights and duties citizens should enjoy and the distributive rules that should govern economic outcomes. Accordingly, he had the imaginary contractors gather to decide how to regulate the "basic structure of society." The ethical questions we are looking to answer are different: They are the ethical dilemmas faced by business people in the world of commerce. Whether to manage their business in the sole interest of shareholders or to treat stakeholders as intrinsically important; whether Guidant should divulge the defect in its defibrillator; whether Plasma needed to share the surplus of its blood sale business more equally across suppliers, consumers, and shareholders—these are a selection of the dilemmas we have investigated in the course of this book, and a drop in the sea of problems that a business practitioner could conceivably encounter. If a social contract theory is to address these, it must be a social contract theory of business ethics rather than one of social and political justice. This means that the original position must be appropriately recrafted from the way we set it up in the previous chapter. Rather than deciding a political and social constitution, the contractors' task in our investigation is to agree on ground rules to govern their commercial interactions—in other words, on business ethics itself.

It follows that we must modify both the contractors' identity and their knowledge compared to what these are in Rawls's original position. We have argued that a theory of business ethics that respects rational autonomy is one whose principles can be justified to those affected by the actions it endorses or requires. It stands to reason, then, that we must identify a social contract acceptable to contractors in an original position who represent participants in real economic transactions: people in their capacity as owners, managers, employees, customers, suppliers, and so on. Now it seems probable that virtually every human being participates in economic transactions in some or other capacity. Every human being, therefore, must be represented in the original position in which the rules of business ethics are to be settled, just as every human being is represented in Rawls's original position set up to decide the constitution governing society's basic structure. But the social contract theory of business ethics will differ from a Rawlsian social contract theory of political and social justice in this: When the original contractors assess the possible agreements they can strike, they do so from their vantage point *as economic actors*. That is to say, in identifying rules for economic transactions, they must be allowed to keep in mind the purposes for which they may be pursuing business.

To secure that the bargaining is fair, the contractors will, as in Rawls's theory, be placed behind a veil of ignorance, although what the veil lets through and what it hides from view will have to be tailored to the task at hand. They will, at the very least, need to know the facts about how business is and can be done—the possible technological, institutional, and cultural solutions for organizing production and exchange. At the same time, to make the bargaining *fair,* the veil of ignorance must ensure that all the participants are respected as free and equal, so it must exclude information about individual characteristics that are arbitrary from a moral point of view and the knowledge of which would allow contractors to press for rules that would favor them at the expense of others.

What does this mean concretely? The authors of the best-developed social contract theory of business, Thomas Donaldson and Thomas Dunfee, propose to specify the original position as follows:

> . . . a contract providing a foundation for economic ethics acceptable to a diverse set of imaginary contractors . . . who represent the varied attitudes of the modern world. We assume that these contractors are rational, i.e., not afflicted by inconsistency or logical confusion, and that they are knowledgeable, i.e., they know the range of facts accepted at the time as being true. We do not assume, as Rawls does, that these hypothetical contractors are ignorant of all facts concerning themselves. They may or may not know that they are Christian, Muslim, of a risk-adverse [*sic.*] or risk-prone personality, etc. We assume only in this regard that they do not know of what economic communities they are members. For example, they do not know that they work for XYZ corporation, participate in country N's economic system, pay dues in worker union K, or ply their trade in profession P or industry Q. These facts about their economic membership are hidden from them. In a similar way, their level of personal wealth is obscured. They are ignorant of whether they possess a massive fortune, or nothing at all . . . We do not assume, as again Rawls would, that the contractors are ignorant of their economic and political *preferences* . . . Finally, we assume that the contractors do not come to the table entirely bereft of moral principles . . . We assert that rational contractors would accept a limited set of core assumptions in framing their search for a common economic ethics, where 'economic ethics' refers to the principles establishing the boundaries of proper behavior in the context of the production and exchange of goods and services.[160]

In Donaldson and Dunfee's social contract exercise—which for reasons that will become clear they call the *integrative social contracts theory* of business ethics (ISCT)—the principal information shrouded by the veil of ignorance is in which "economic community" the social contractors will find themselves, although they know the kinds of economic communities that exist.[161] The Rawlsian logic for this is straightforward enough. It is less clear why they want the contractors to be aware of their preferences—in particular the moral values that may inspire or constrain the way they want to go about business. One danger of including such information is indecision. If the social contract of

---

[160] Thomas Donaldson and Thomas W. Dunfee, *Ties that Bind: A Social Contracts Approach to Business Ethics* (Boston, MA: Harvard Business School Press, 1999), pp. 27–28.

[161] By economic community they mean, it seems, any group of people with partially coinciding interests who are connected through their economic activity, within which local norms might develop.

business ethics has to gain the consent of both Gordon Gekko and Mother Teresa, deadlock is certain—at least beyond a uselessly minimal set of ground rules. If instead, following Rawls, contractors did not know their personal preferences, then they would keep in mind the *possibility* that they have the preferences of a Gordon Gekko or a Mother Teresa, but also the much larger probability that they would have the preferences of the moderate majority, who largely prioritize themselves and their families, but also have moral beliefs that motivate them to share, assist, and generally behave decently toward others. They would find agreement, therefore, on a set of rules that would allow people with this sort of moderate preference to flourish. Another risk of allowing the contractors knowledge of their own actual preferences is conventionalism, for actual preferences are not infrequently hostile to individual autonomy. If existing moral attitudes are brought into the original position, unequal treatments that are widely practiced in the world and may be culturally internalized even by those they harm—such as limiting the opportunities of women or discriminating on the basis of ethnicity—will undermine the free and equal standing of all the contractors, and the outcomes of the contracting process can no longer be considered fair.

The alternative is to operate with a thicker veil of ignorance and a correspondingly thinner store of personalized knowledge available to the contracting parties. The contractors will still know the range of reasons people may have for entering business—including their possible moral, religious or other motivations beyond self-interest as well as different degrees of risk tolerance—but they will not know which personal goals are theirs. Such an approach builds in more respect for the freedom to choose one's own goals and therefore avoids the risk that people are treated, or treat themselves, as less than fully autonomous under the influence of cultural traditions or social pressure.

This concern about the specifics of the Donaldson-Dunfee approach is not one we have to resolve here. Indeed, we cannot resolve it on a purely theoretical basis. To specify the original position of a social contract theory of *business,* our reasoning must surely be informed by the experience of the people to whom the theory is meant to provide useful advice, that is to say, business practitioners. The social contract approach, and the thought experiment of the original contracting situation, is one that business practitioners must apply themselves to, drawing on the background knowledge they have about how business works. What we *can* usefully do in terms of pure theorizing is to point out how different constructions of the original position may support different conjectures about the principles on which the hypothetical contractors would agree, and in particular, about whether some principles would arguably gain consent across a wide range of assumptions about the what the contractors know.

Parties in the original position would, at the very least, be interested in agreeing on framework rules that guarantee a minimum of *efficiency* in the pursuit of economic success, for this is a goal they share even if they are divided both by their specific conceptions of what constitutes success and by their motivations for seeking it. Whatever those differences are, they will have enough of a common understanding of the basic point of production or exchange that they can agree to rank at least some systems of production and exchange as superior to others. In particular, it would be rational of them to aim for a set of rules by which, all other things being equal, people can produce and exchange goods and services with more predictability rather than less, and at the cost of fewer resources rather than more. But as we mentioned in Chapter 6 , efficiency is enhanced, not reduced, when certain background conditions of ethical behavior are satisfied, such as basic honesty and a tendency to keep promises, both of which are required for a minimum of trust to be the rational attitude to adopt in business transactions. A common interest in efficiency will, therefore, induce free individuals to consent to ethical rules such as these.

In addition, knowing that people engage in business for a variety of motivations in pursuit of a range of goals, the contractors will rationally want to protect their ability to achieve whatever ends they may set themselves when they engage in business transactions in the actual world. On the one hand, this will lead them to agree, as in Rawls's account, on an expansive set of rights. On the other, they will care about people's ability to do business in ways consistent, within limits, with whatever moral and cultural beliefs they may hold. Donaldson and Dunfee are right, therefore, to assert that agreement in the original position will treat "economic activity that is consistent with the cultural, philosophical, or religious attitudes of economic actors [as] preferable to economic activity that is not."[162]

RIGHTS REVISITED: SHAREHOLDERS VERSUS STAKEHOLDERS

The salient problem for rational contractors gathering behind a veil of ignorance is that they do not know where in the real economic world—as participants of which economic community and as occupants of what role within that community—they will find themselves. What is in their actual interest is hidden from them; they know neither what they may want nor which opportunities will be available to them to pursue what they want. They therefore have reason to agree on rules that will protect their individual interests, whatever these may turn out to be. Agreeing to safeguard a certain inviolability of individual choice requires them to endorse a set of individual moral rights and corresponding perfect duties. For, as we have seen, neither consequentialism nor traditional moralities that reject the notion of individual rights can provide such a safeguard. And it would be irrational for the parties in the original contracting situation to expose themselves to the risk of ending up in a position where the majority may benefit from sacrificing them or their interests for the sake of the greater (that is, the majority's) good.

Clearly, then, a social contract for business must endorse parts of the fundamental human rights as commonly enumerated. It must, for example, ban business activities that wantonly or knowingly cause deaths or subject people to forced labor. But we hardly need a social contract theory of business ethics to tell us that one must not kill or enslave for profits. Such rights and duties follow not from a consideration of rules for economic transactions; they come from the more fundamental social contract exercise in which the parties in the original position must decide on the basic constitutional rules for life in common. Murder is not wrong because it is bad for business (although it is), but because all rational parties would agree to rules prohibiting it in a social contract for society. However, the flip side of this is that some other commonly listed "rights" would probably *not* be part of a general agreement about political and social justice. In Rawls's original position, there would seem to be little reason for rational contractors to agree on including the U.N.'s idea of a right to periodic holidays with pay in the

---

[162] Donaldson and Dunfee, *Ties that Bind*, p. 28.

fundamental rules of political justice. Could, instead, anything like it be required by business ethics? If so, it would not, unlike respect for life and liberty, be because it was in any case required by the broader social contract.

This is where the social contract approach as a theory of *economic ethics* comes into its own: in its analyses of moral rights as they pertain specifically to business. One such analysis concerns whether the indisputable requirement to respect fundamental human rights means that *all* business activities that contribute to death or captivity are immoral—examples range from weapons manufacturing to the provision of services such as food or laundry to prisons. This is an example of a question we can address by considering how the contracting parties relate the rights and responsibilities as they apply to business to the broader social contract that governs society's political and social life at large. A plausible argument would hold that since the fundamental principles of political justice must allow proper authorities both to fight wars and detain prisoners in the appropriate circumstances, the contractors setting the rules for economic transactions would agree that business may contribute in profit-making ways to such activities when the latter are exercised with legitimate authority. This yields the plausible conclusion that companies may supply the armed forces or police authorities of a just society—but that they retain a duty to judge whether the forces they abet act within the bounds of authority defined by the just use of such powers. In certain cases the argument could support a moral duty not to do business with unjust states. More generally, it suggests that the original contractors must consider with some nuance what are the respective roles of business and government.

When parties to a social contract for business take special interests in the rights and duties relevant *for business*, they will do so not only in the passive sense of determining how such rights and duties are circumscribed by the wider social contract that should govern political society. In the original position they will also positively recognize that some rights and duties are more crucial than others to their ability to carry out business efficiently. This makes it rational for the hypothetical contractors to place *more* weight on those particular rights and duties when applied to business than they would give the same rights and duties if they were agreeing on rules for social interaction more generally. It stands to reason, for example, that rational contractors care particularly about their ability to enter and exit whatever sector or industry that they may see fit, and do business with whomever they choose. They would, therefore, agree to include a right to free association both of business owners (to set up a company for whatever purpose, as long as it is not immoral) and of workers (to organize in a union). They would also be particularly concerned to secure their control of what they produce or acquire in the course of doing business, so they would endorse a robust system of private property rights. And they would worry about situations such as Akerlof's "market for lemons" that we discussed in Chapter 6 , in which suspicions of dishonesty make people eschew Pareto-improving transactions. Thus, they would endorse a strong moral right to information and a corresponding moral duty of disclosure, if only for efficiency reasons.

The insight that rational contractors will take particular care in the original position to lay down rights and duties that affect the efficiency of business interactions allows us to sketch how a social contract approach to business ethics can resolve some of the dilemmas we have encountered earlier on.

Shareholders versus stakeholders debate

The social contract approach sheds new light on the controversy with which we started, between the two extreme views of "shareholder primacy" and "stakeholder theory." The hypothetical contractors' concern with a right to association for the purpose of doing business lends support to Milton Friedman's argument that shareholders have a moral right to managers' loyalty (even if such a right is not recognized by the law). For, in the original position, rational contracting parties will surely want to protect their ability, once the veil of ignorance is lifted, to pool their capital with others, hire a manager to deploy that capital on their behalf, and secure their managers' commitment to manage this capital in their interests. The mechanisms by which this commitment can be made would have to be specified in some detail—for example, does buying shares in a company whose founders gave it a charitable as well as a profit-making mission constitute acceptance of the founders' original goals for the company? But the natural presumption seems to be that a manager's moral duty is indeed to act as an agent of the company's founders and their successors and pursue their interests as they define them.

This, however, does not come close to justifying the conclusions of a full-fledged shareholder primacy view. Even if the contractors in the original position want to impose on managers a moral duty to owners, they will also place constraints on the kinds of business activities the owners may morally engage in. Some of those limits will follow from the fundamental moral rights enshrined in the broader political social contract—one may not kill or enslave in the pursuit of profit. Others will follow from the particular interest the social contractors have in protecting rights and duties of special importance to efficient business. Thus, if the right to free association is the foundation of shareholders' claims, it will also have to be protected for employees, since in the original position it is unknown who will be shareholders and who will be employees. Managers' duty to do what shareholders want, therefore, does not extend to prohibiting workers from organizing; indeed, it would be morally wrong to prohibit it.

At the same time, this does not entail giving all "stakeholders" an equivalent claim on managers' loyalty. A better description of what it is rational for the hypothetical contractors to agree on is a managerial duty to pursue shareholders' interests in ways *consistent with shareholders' own moral duties*. In other words, even as the social contract approach to business makes it a manager's duty to pursue shareholders' interests, it limits the actions by which the managers may morally do so, because *shareholders* are also under moral obligations regarding how they may have their capital deployed.[163] What are these obligations? They evidently include all the perfect negative duties subsumed under the requirement not to violate the rights of others in the conduct of business. As for imperfect duties such as charity, however, shareholders do not necessarily violate them by not using the companies they own to discharge it: Individual shareholders may choose to fulfill their imperfect duties privately. This suggests that the social contract for

---

[163] Thus a social contract theory of business ethics lends supports to Kenneth Goodpaster's analysis of the "stakeholder paradox" (see Chapter 2).

economic interactions must specify a rather nuanced set of managerial duties. On the one hand, it must require managers to respect the rights of all stakeholders, regardless of what shareholders may demand, and even if it reduces profits. On the other, managers must avoid using corporate resources for non-profit-maximizing purposes that can only be justified as *imperfect* duties. For those cases, hypothetical contractors wishing to preserve their ability to discharge imperfect duties in the manner of their choosing would have reason to set down rules requiring explicit shareholder approval in advance.[164]

Guidant and the disclosure of product defects

Envisaging their possible role as consumers, rational contractors in the original position will want to protect their ability to pursue their goals as efficiently as possible through their consumption choices. That is a reason for them to enforce in the social contract for business strong moral duties of disclosure of product defects on the part of producers—and especially strong ones when the defects threaten fundamental life goals, of which health is clearly one—even beyond what the law may require. Note, in particular, that for rational parties trying to reach agreement on a social contract, the utilitarian argument we sketched in Guidant's defense in Chapter 5 is unimpressive. The contractors are better able to protect their interest in rationally pursuing whatever goals they autonomously choose if, in the original position, they settle for individual rights to information rather than a manufacturer's duty to maximize the aggregate expected well-being of the population or even just of its customer population. Do the hypothetical contractors have any contrary reason to limit this duty of disclosure? Since they also consider how the proposed moral terms for economic interactions will affect their prospects as producers, they will avoid a moral duty of disclosure that is too onerous and of little use to consumers. But it is significant that they would have no reason to curtail a moral duty of disclosure simply to secure a company's advantage over competitors, since they do not know which company they belong to. In Guidant's case, therefore, it is hard to see how rational contractors behind a veil of ignorance would consider it relevant that revealing the defect in a case such as Guidant's may hurt consumer demand for the company's products or unfavorably alter the terms of its planned merger. This suggests that a fully developed social contract theory of business ethics would conclude that Guidant ought to have disclosed the defibrillator defect voluntarily.

---

[164] This basic distinction—between compulsory negative perfect duties (which managers must fulfill because shareholders may not free them from the obligation to do so) and imperfect duties (which they may not fulfill on shareholders' behalf unless the shareholders want them to)—leaves open the interesting logical possibility of positive perfect duties. Beyond not violating other people's rights, are shareholders ever required to actively do something to help others, and to do so through their company? If so, that is presumably a duty rational contractors in the original position would indeed agree to impose on company managers. It is not easy, however, to identify positive perfect duties—perfect duties tend to be negative. One candidate, however, is the *duty of rescue*: the moral obligation to extend help when one is uniquely or best placed to do so. This may apply to pharmaceutical companies—including Merck in the case of river blindness. See Thomas Dunfee, "Do firms with unique competencies for rescuing victims of human catastrophes have special obligations?" *Business Ethics Quarterly*, 16(2), 2006, pp. 185–210.

RELATIVISM REVISITED: SOCIAL CONVENTIONS AND MORAL FREE SPACE

We concluded our earlier discussion of social and cultural conventions about right and wrong by saying that they were not self-justifying. The fact that everyone (within a community) acts in a certain way, or even that everyone (within a community) believes that it is right or morally required to act in a certain way, does not make it right to act in that way. Conventions may be mistaken. And yet, we recognized that local practices, cultural traditions, and social conventions cannot simply be dismissed out of hand; their content matters for what morality commands. This is particularly true for social roles that come with normative standards built into them that, while not self-justifying, are not necessarily unjustified. On the contrary, the least experience with the diversity of the human experience suggests different rules may indeed apply, morally speaking, in different cultural contexts. Realizing this does not require us to accept any alleged moral equivalence of national cultures—not just because such moral equivalence does not follow from an admission that cultural practices matter (that is the logical mistake of cultural relativism), but because there is nothing special about *national* cultures. There are social conventions specific to all human groups, each with their own "culture" and social practices, and each with (sometimes slightly, sometimes drastically) different normative implications. Such groups may be defined, for example, by their members' age, gender, or similarity of tastes or experience—or by what is of particular relevance to us: their professional activities or their role in economic interactions. Local normative conventions exist within companies and even subdivisions of companies; within industries; and within professional roles across industries (lawyers working for the legal departments of different companies may share more normative conventions with each other than with their nonlawyer colleagues). Just as we should ask how cross-national cultural differences matter to how it is moral to behave, so we should ask the same of cultural differences between industries or companies. The normative conventions within a Microsoft and a Google, for example, may be sufficiently different that a moral theory must take seriously the question whether different behaviors are morally required by Microsoft and Google employees, either within their respective firms or toward outsiders.

Donaldson and Dunfee illustrate the point in the case of markets for different commodities. The "communities" of traders in each commodity market are remarkably similar except for the material they trade and, it turns out, their normative conventions:

> When it is clearly understood within the international rice market that bulk rice sellers do not expect to provide an exhaustive list of the rice's defects to purchasing agents, then purchasing agents know that they must either prod sellers to provide more information or check the rice themselves. On the other hand, when international rubber buyers know that sellers will voluntarily disclose information about product defects, then they need not check the rubber themselves . . . [In] the rubber market, failure of full disclosure would be unethical; but in the rice market it would not be.[165]

---

[165] Donaldson and Dunfee, *Ties that Bind*, p. 124.

It is surely sensible for a theory of business ethics to accommodate the intuition that such community-specific conventions matter for what it is morally right to do. At the same time, however, it must stay clear of the swampy territory of relativism and explain when communcal conventions should be rejected and their normative claims ignored or even opposed. But the social contract approach is very well suited to solve this apparent dilemma. For just as the contractors in the original position will consent to a set of rights and duties that participants in economic life must comply with universally, they may also rationally decide that some areas of morality should be left blank in the social contract and so to speak *delegate* to real communities the task of filling in these blanks with their own conventions. There are at least three reasons why the contractors may choose in this way to leave the social contract, within limits, indeterminate and open what Donaldson and Dunfee call "moral free space" for communities to furnish with their own conventionally established communal norms.

The first is related to that social convention of special normative force: the law. Since the parties agreeing on a social contract for economic life will rationally circumscribe it by the broader and more fundamental social contract for the entire political system, the rules of business ethics must generally be in a subordinate relationship to the more basic rules of political justice. Those rules lay down the moral authority of the law by setting out the basic principles that legal and political systems must satisfy, and the extent of our moral duty to obey laws passed in ways that satisfy those principles. Since the political social contract will not specify in detail the content of laws—in fact it must specify as part of people's political rights a certain freedom to shape the law to their preferences—there is also an inherent indeterminacy in what a social contract approach for business ethics can specify, beyond a general duty on those engaged in business to obey laws promulgated by just legal systems. Thus, the general moral presumption must be that business ethics requires obeying whatever local laws require. We may think of this as a rational decision by parties in the original position to establish a *division of moral labor* between business and government: Some of the more fundamental rules for social interaction will be left for the legitimate governments to determine, and it will be incumbent on business to respect those decisions.

In some cases, this will support the excuse sometimes offered by business people: "We don't make the law"—that is, there is no moral duty on business beyond the standards that government decides business should be held to. But this cannot always be so, for reasons we have mentioned in earlier chapters. The government may fail to fulfill its duty; the political or legal system may itself be illegitimate (according to the social contract theory of political justice itself); or there may be reasons for not using legislation to enforce certain behaviors that business ought nevertheless to adopt. Whether these cases apply will hinge on an argument about what, if anything, it would be rational for the contractors in the original position to agree that business should do in different cases of government not "filling in the blank." One may doubt, for example, whether the rule of law in Ecuador during Texaco's oil operations would satisfy the standards of a just social contract—and if it did not, simply having complied with legal requirements may not suffice to justify the environmental damage Texaco is alleged to have caused. (Contractors behind a veil of ignorance, not knowing whether they are oil company shareholders or Amazonian forest-dwellers, would rationally consent to a duty to protect others against environmental damage.)

Another intriguing example occurs in an industry that claims special role-related permissions for itself, even in regards to the law, namely the press:

Time, Inc. and journalistic ethics

In the investigation of the leak of CIA covert operative Valerie Plame's name to the press in 2004, Special Counsel Patrick Fitzgerald subpoenaed two journalists, Judith Miller of the *New York Times* and Matthew Cooper of *Time* magazine, demanding to see their notes from interviews with sources in the governments. Citing journalistic ethics and its requirement to protect sources, they refused. Miller went to jail until she received her source Lewis Libby's permission to hand over her notes. In the case of Matthew Cooper, it was his employer, Time Inc., that physically possessed the notes. Ought Time to have given them up (as it eventually did)?

It seems that contractors in the original position will wish (in circumscribed situations) both to permit civil disobedience and to encourage a role ethics for journalists that requires source confidentiality and permits publishing the truth against the government's will. Both provisions are rational to include in a social contract because the parties will realize that a government may overstep its legitimate authority, and an independent and informed citizenry is necessary to keep it within the bounds of justice. The contractors could rationally conclude that the most secure way to protect the social contract itself is to allocate different roles to different groups: While the government's role is to pass laws, others, such as journalists, have the role of documenting whether the government does what it should. It is, therefore, at least plausible that it was morally permitted, and perhaps even morally compulsory, for Miller as an individual journalist to refuse to comply with the subpoena even though she in one sense broke the law by doing so.

Time Inc., however, is not an individual journalist, but a subsidiary of Time Warner, a publicly traded corporation. Some argue that though journalistic ethics might justify civil disobedience by journalists, it does not allow a *company* to break the law, and that a corporation, moreover, has an obligation to shareholders not to jeopardize their pecuniary interest. In the social contract approach, the question must hinge on whether this differentiation between individual journalists and the companies that employ them is one the parties behind the veil of ignorance would find persuasive. We may well think that they would not. For in considering the need for civil disobedience and the role of journalists, the parties will clearly find that holding a government accountable must take priority over economic efficiency concerns. A just government is not only intrinsically of first moral importance but itself a great contribution to an efficient business environment. That priority is not affected, it seems, by whether journalists work for independent newspapers or for large conglomerates. *If* what matters most is the function of holding government accountable, *and* source confidentiality is a prerequisite for fulfilling that function, then it is not a stretch to imagine that contractors behind the veil of ignorance would want to see that role played by whomever is involved in newsgathering, whether those are individuals or companies.

The notion of a moral division of labor between the government and business leads to a second reason why the contractors in the original position will leave moral free space for social conventions, and in particular for the conventional norms built into social roles, to "fill in" with more detailed moral rules than can be specified in the original position. We have already recognized that efficiency is enhanced by ethical behavior, and that this gives the contractors a strong reason to agree on rules that limit self-interested conduct. But there are many possible sets of rules—of allocations of rights and duties—and many of them may be equally efficient. As Donaldson and Dunfee's illustration from commodity markets suggests, it may sometimes be a matter of indifference in what degree of detail a seller has a duty to volunteer unsolicited information about defects in a commodity and what is left to the buyer's prudential self-interest to inquire about, as long as all parties know what to expect. It is the function of custom and convention to entrench mutual expectations, so maximum efficiency may be secured simply by having *some* convention in place that is obeyed, regardless of what the convention says (in this example at least). In the original position, therefore, it would be rational for contractors to leave it open how much information a commodity seller must volunteer, and simply rely on the conventions that appear within the community of traders for each commodity to spell out the specific balance between a duty of disclosure and *caveat emptor*. What they would agree on, however, is a rule that whatever convention emerges ought, morally speaking, to be followed unless it clashes with more fundamental moral rules.

Similarly, it may not be strictly necessary for the efficiency of our economic interaction that the duties and permissions conventionally attaching to professional roles such as lawyer, doctor, or journalist are precisely what they happen to be in our society. They could conceivably be quite different and still divide moral responsibilities efficiently. What matters is that roles are well specified, so that everyone within the relevant community knows what to expect. Again, therefore, the contractors in the original position have reason to leave open the exact ethical requirements for those in professional roles, allowing these to be specified by conventions evolving within the professions themselves, which could vary across countries or time periods.

The third reason why the social contract for business will leave moral free space is due to the nature of the original position itself. Ensuring that the bargain is a fair one requires much of the contracting parties' local knowledge to be hidden by the veil of ignorance. But this also makes it impossible for the contractors to be very specific in the terms they consent to. The overall principles that are to govern economic interaction will have to be "thin," abstractly setting out basic rights and duties and perforce leaving a large degree of indeterminacy in their concrete implication for "thickly" described real-world dilemmas. What, for instance, can business ethics say generally about relationships between bosses and employees? The hypothetical contractors may agree that (a) hierarchy is necessary for efficient production; and (b) any hierarchical structure should be coupled with appropriate attitudes of respect both from subordinates toward their superior and vice-versa; but (c) what "respectful" behavior means in terms of concrete action is so culturally contingent that it would be silly to set out a universal list of actions that count as appropriately respectful. Similarly, what responsibility do employers have for accommodating employees' family lives? Again, it seems that rational contractors would choose to leave this to be influenced by social conventions on family structure and its role in society.

These three facts—the importance of law; the multiplicity of efficient divisions of moral labor; and the limited concreteness of fundamental abstract principles—give the contractors reason to leave "moral free space" in the social contract for business. Two points, however, must be noted. First, moral free space is free in the sense that communities may legitimately develop differing social conventions (which may vary also in how much of the moral free space they fill—what range of activities they regulate). It is not "free" in the sense that the rules are not morally binding. In the original position, it is rational for contracting parties to delegate the task of specifying the concrete content of rights and duties to social convention, but it is also rational for them to grant these conventions the moral force of the social contract itself. Although it would be arbitrary or impractical to specify the detail in the original position, it is no less true that rational contractors will want the specific rules to be followed, whatever they happen to be (subject to the exception discussed below). The prime importance of convention, after all, is that it can coordinate people's expectations and, therefore, their behavior; and it often matters very little what precisely people coordinate on doing whereas it matters enormously that they coordinate on *something* (consider the convention of driving on the one or the other side of the road). Thus, once a convention has been established—whether by conscious collective choice, tradition, superstitions or whatever other means—it can become morally compulsory to comply with it. We may justify this claim by direct appeal to a simple principle of fairness—if you willingly engage in a system of (otherwise arbitrary) set of rules and benefit from others' compliance with those rules, you owe it to them to likewise comply—or, more strongly, by noting that it would be rational for parties to a social contract to consent to such a principle.

But second, contracting parties in the original position would agree that socially created conventions are binding only if they satisfy certain criteria. Even for communities, moral free space is not a moral free-for-all. Put differently, no social contract theory would issue in relativism. Culture-specific variations in norms are only granted the moral force of the social contract justification if the contractors behind the veil of ignorance can plausibly expect them to fulfill their interest in efficiency and satisfy the basic rights and duties that will be agreed on in the original position. That, however, will not always be the case. If economic conditions change, so may the efficiency of a convention—thus, a social convention in favor of periodic holidays with pay may make them a moral requirement in economically advanced societies without the same applying in poor ones. Some social conventions may contravene the fundamental rights and duties conferred by the social contract (either as a matter of political justice or as a necessity for flourishing economic life), which Donaldson and Dunfee call "hypernorms." Since hypernorms are agreed on explicitly by the contractors in the original position, they necessarily take moral precedence over social conventions filling in moral free space, because the moral free space is delimited precisely by what hypernorms leave unspecified. So it is morally wrong for business to violate hypernorms, no matter how engrained a part they may be of local business practice. That the 'Ndrangheta's organized crime may be deeply bound up with local traditions in Calabria does not morally justify its dumping of nuclear waste off the Calabrian coast.

Thus the social contract approach to business ethics can accommodate social conventions without slipping into relativism because it subjects them to two tests. First, do the conventions in question conflict with the substantive universal rights and duties recognized in the social contract ("hypernorms")? If so, the conventions themselves are morally illegitimate; there is no moral duty to obey them and there may be a moral duty to resist or overturn them. Second, even if the conventions are compatible with the substantive terms of the social contract, do they provide an efficient specification of the moral free space left open in the original position? If so, there is a moral duty to obey them—even though other conventions should be obeyed whenever they perform the same function in other contexts. If not, there is no moral duty to obey the social conventions in question on the grounds of business ethics (although there may be other moral or nonmoral reasons to do so—not the least of which is good manners).

By showing that the contracting parties have good reason, when they settle terms for business ethics in the original position, to take an interest in communities' ability to form their own normative conventions, the social contract approach demonstrates that ethical reasoning can generate new insights from theory without giving up a sensitivity to local understandings of ethics as practiced in the world. In Donaldson and Dunfee's version, the social contract theory of business ethics marries social contracts at two levels—the theoretically derived "macrosocial" contract, specified by free and equal parties behind the veil of ignorance, and actually existing "microsocial" contracts—normative social conventions that enjoy local respect and ground mutual expectations of coordinated conduct. It is because it combines abstract and concrete norms in this way that Donaldson and Dunfee call their theory "Integrative Social Contracts Theory."

PARTIAL COMPLIANCE THEORY

The analysis we have pursued in this book has aimed at determining what people in business ought, morally speaking, to do. But even as we have developed a principled approach to answering that question, we have so far mostly ignored the pressing problem lurking under the surface of our reasoning, despite its salience to any practical attempt to do business ethically. Most people's tendency to do what morality requires of them is at best imperfect. The person with a practical interest in ethics as a guide to action can be forgiven for thinking that a moral theory of business may accurately specify the ideal moral conduct and yet be completely useless, because the ideal it presents is unattainable. Now this complaint could mean several things, and how it needs to be answered depends on which interpretation we choose. On the one hand, it could be that morality turns out to demand *too much*; more than any ordinary mortal can be expected to comply with. But while some moral theories may be guilty of this—we have, in particular, pointed out the unreasonable selflessness entailed by utilitarianism—there is good reason to think that the social contract approach goes free of this criticism. The parties in the original position do, after all, know the basic facts about human nature; it will not be rational for them to agree on terms that it is constitutionally impossible for humans to satisfy. Besides, that a moral theory sets out an ideal is not in itself a strike against it. The point of normative statements is, after all, to assert what ought to be, not what actually is.

There is, however, a different and altogether more powerful interpretation of the complaint. It is that, humanity being what it is, anyone who strives to act ethically will always find herself in a world where others do not—whether because they are less morally motivated than she, or because even those with the best intentions do not always have the strength of will to do the right thing. Can morality require ideal behavior in a world that falls sorely short of ideal? Some have argued that it can: Immanuel Kant infamously claimed that one must always tell the truth, even to a murderer at the door who is asking where his intended victim is hiding. But this is absurd. In Kant's example, it is right to mislead the murderer and wrong to tell the truth. The general point is that whether others breach *their* duties is relevant to what *our* duties must be. Immoral conduct by others may alter what morality requires from us (for example, from telling the truth to lying when the murderer is at the door). This is why, in Williams's examples of Jim and the Indian and George and the chemical and biological weapons, although the unappealing choice (shooting the one Indian and taking the CBW research job) is not obviously right, it is also not obviously wrong.

But from asserting, reasonably, that our duties may change in response to transgressions by others it does not follow that morality ceases to obligate because others violate its rules. Rather, what we ought to do when others do not do what *they* should do is itself an ethical question, the answer to which must be justified by moral reasons. A deviation of actual conduct from the ideal of universal ethical behavior, inescapable as it may be, is no departure from the realm where morality applies. It is, rather, a subset of morality—by far the largest subset and the only one of ultimate practical relevance to us, but nonetheless part of moral theory. It is the part covered by *partial compliance theory*—the theory of what morality requires in a world that only partially complies with it—as opposed to the *ideal compliance theory* with which we have been concerned throughout most of the book.

There were good reasons for postponing our discussion of partial compliance theory until the end. One is that although ideal compliance theory may be less relevant for practical decision making (because the conditions for it to apply are unrealistic), ideal compliance theory is logically prior to partial compliance theory in the order of reasoning. It is impossible to say what a partial compliance theory of ethics commands without knowing the requirements of the corresponding ideal compliance theory—if only because partially compliant behavior cannot even be defined without reference to the ideal behavior that it violates. There is also a pragmatic reason for developing ideal compliance theory in detail first. Its arguments are likely to be simpler, and once they are fully understood, their implications for partial compliance can be derived by considering specific departures from ethical behavior one at a time.[166]

In consequentialism, this distinction rather vanishes. Since all that consequentialism tells us is to produce the best outcomes available to us, it treats as immaterial whether the causal mechanisms we have to take into account involve others doing what *they*, according to consequentialism, ought to do. This is a necessary feature of the theory, since if the goodness of outcomes contains *all* the information that matters morally, then by definition whether or not the causal path to achieving the best possible outcome passes through transgressive acts by others does not matter for the moral rightness of *my* action. (This is why utilitarianism must see Williams's thought experiments as easy cases.) That social contract theory, by contrast, need not flatten its moral analysis in this way is another argument in its favor. We finish with two examples of the kinds of partial compliance considerations the original contractors may take into account.

Deception as self-defense

In our discussion of whether deception can ever be justified in business, two principal arguments stood out. Against Carr's claim that deception is justified because it is

---

[166] The natural model here is scientific inquiry, where, say, it is more constructive to calculate the equations describing an object's movement in a vacuum before determining the effect of air resistance.

sometimes a requirement for success stands the Kantian argument that deception is always immoral because it manipulates the rational agency of others, thus treating them as a mere means instead of respecting them as free persons with the right to pursue their own goals. Note that the *premises* of these two arguments are not incompatible. It may well be true that deception is sometimes necessary to succeed in business *and* that (even so) it is manipulative. The contractors in the original position must take both claims into account when setting the terms of the social contract for business.

Carr's empirical claim typically seems plausible in partial compliance situations. If it is impossible to succeed in an industry without deception (and not just for an individual company that is less competitive than its rivals), it tends to be because deception is the general practice, so that even companies that would thrive without being deceptive if *no* companies were deceptive must choose between deception and failure. The parties in the original position can ignore this possibility when deciding *ideal* compliance terms in the social contract—that is, the rules that everyone ought to follow provided everyone else is also following them. But the contractors may also want to lay down rules about how business people should behave in *partial* compliance situations—when others do, wrongly, engage in deception. Now, they will be wary of rules that justify "immoral equilibria" where everyone acts unethically (according to ideal compliance rules) just because others do. But they will also want to limit the costs to any individual decision maker of choosing to comply with morality, and, in particular, they have reason to prevent that one can only comply by being a "sucker" whom the noncompliant easily take advantage of. They will, therefore, seek to include in the social contract means for business people to defend themselves from falling prey to the wrongdoing of others.

This is not, of course, unique to business ethics. When agreeing on the broader social contract for morality, the parties will, for example, include a ban on violence yet make an exception for violence in self-defense to protect against the violence of others. Alan Strudler has proposed that the same reasoning applies to deception. In negotiations, bargainers will try to find out their counterparties' reservation prices, and sometimes the only reaction to probing questions that does not reveal this information is a deceptive one. Strudler suggests that morality must permit this, for your purpose in asking me probing questions when we negotiate is to use the information you obtain to harm my interests, and, moreover, you try to keep me in the dark about similar information regarding yourself. In self-defense, Strudler argues, I may do the same, provided I follow the normal moral requirements on self-defense, such as choosing actions that are proportionate with the threat and avoid harming innocent bystanders. Thus, I may use deception in business to prevent someone from finding out information about me which he would use to harm me (I may deceive to hide the lowest price I would be willing to accept) and which he has no right to have (I may not lie about the leaky roof of the house I am trying to sell, which the vendor does have a right to know about). But that does not mean I may deceive customers just because my competitors deceive their customers. If Strudler's analogy between deception and violence can be sustained, it suggests contractors behind a veil of ignorance will make similarly regulated self-defense exceptions for cases of partial compliance.

Corruption

Was such a self-defense argument available to Lockheed (see Chapter 4)? The company did defend its actions by saying that other companies were doing the same. Kotchian's argument can charitably be paraphrased as pointing out that this was a situation of partial compliance, and that morality in such situations permits behavior that under ideal compliance conditions would be immoral. But this kind of argument is likely to be given short shrift by the parties in the original position. For unlike deception in negotiations, the harm from corruption is inflicted on *third parties*—in Lockheed's case, on Japanese taxpayers who have to pay more than necessary for the planes because of self-serving politicians. Whereas the social contractors may find it rational to permit someone to deceive a competitor to the extent necessary to stop the competitor from harming him, it is hard to see what reason they could have to permit harming third parties in order not to lose out to competitors also harming third parties. Unlike dissimulating against a counterpart in negotiations, therefore, corruption will probably violate business ethics under the social contract approach even in partial compliance conditions.

CONCLUSION

This brief survey of how a social contract approach can be applied to business ethics strengthens the claim that opened the chapter: that social contract theory is a particularly promising approach to moral reasoning in business. The social contract approach can rescue much of what seemed plausible in the other theories we have scrutinized. But it also succeeds in rationalizing many intuitions which contradict those theories—and which put their adequacy in doubt because they are intuitions we cannot easily jettison.

Social contract theory is not without problems of its own. Its method of justification—that we ought to follow the rules we would have consented to in a hypothetical situation where did not know which rules would put us at an advantage or disadvantage relative to others—may strike some as too weak a conception of rational consent and autonomy on which to build the edifice of a comprehensive moral theory. Those who do not put much store in individual consent at all, needless to say, will find it even less convincing. Then there is the question of those incapable of rational consent, whose interest may not be respected by a theory built on what free and rational individuals consent to. Those who may be thought vulnerable in this respect include the mentally incapacitated—though how they are treated may rarely be subject to managerial decision making—but also nonhuman animals, whose treatment is very much at the center of many businesses essential to society's functioning.

These are important objections, which those who find social contract theory to be a plausible method for making moral decisions will have to confront. The social contract approach nevertheless captures in a system of simple principles an impressive range of moral thinking. A *theory* of moral reasoning by itself yields few answers, of course. For that, the reasoning must actually be *done* in the face of the concrete challenges one may face. The true test of the social contract approach, or any other theory of business ethics, is whether it can help business people move from the denial or confusion that recognitions of moral dilemmas often trigger, toward a more stable reflective equilibrium. Whether it has contributed to their ability do so is, of course, also the test of this book.

Summary of the Argument in This Chapter

John Rawls used his social contract approach to derive principles of political and distributive justice for the "basic structure" of society. But the justificatory strategy of social contract theory—which argues that a principle is justified if all those affected by it would consent to it if they did not know how a choice among principles would affect them individually—is equally applicable to other moral questions. So we can ask: "What are the rules for business conduct that all participants in commercial life would consent to if they had to agree on a social contract for business behind a veil of ignorance that hid from them knowledge that is arbitrary from a moral point of view?" The resulting moral principles that business practitioners must comply with—a *social contract theory of business ethics*—can be said to respect rational autonomy because they are what free and equal individuals would rationally agree to.

The precise content of those principles will depend on how the original contracting position is designed. Donaldson and Dunfee's theory includes in the original position all participants in economic transactions, excluding from their knowledge which *economic community* they are a part of but not their personal preferences or moral beliefs. Other specifications may be more defensible, but all social contract approaches to business ethics will share some general traits. One is a robust set of fundamental rights, with special importance given to those rights particularly conducive to the ease and efficiency of business transactions (freedom of person and association, rights to property, and rights to information). Another is that it would be rational for contractors to leave open some *moral free space* which each economic community—not just countries or regions, but industries, professions, companies, and unions—can "fill up" with their local normative conventions, or *microsocial* contracts. These will be morally binding provided they do not violate the overarching universal rights and duties laid down in the overall *macrosocial* contract that is explicitly agreed in the original position.

Thus the social contract approach manages to unify, within a single appealing justificatory system, a wide range of the arguments we have made throughout the book. It justifies individual moral rights. But it also provides a foundation for the importance to our moral thinking both of social roles specifically, and social conventions more generally, because of the moral free space which the social contract "delegates" to local economic communities. At the same time, it avoids the trap of cultural relativism, because it sets out and justifies limits on moral free space and the conditions that community-specific norms must satisfy to be morally valid. It also provides a systematic approach to *partial compliance theory,* which deals with the moral rules governing how to behave when others violate morality (as opposed to *ideal compliance theory,* which sets out the right thing to do provided everyone complies with the rules). Social contract theory—rich in plausible implications, metaphorically congenial, and theoretically appealing in its fundamental respect for autonomy—is as far as this book can bring its readers toward reflective equilibrium in moral reasoning for business.

Suggestions for Supplementary Material

Two short yet tremendously instructive books on moral philosophy that inspired the writing of this one are Bernard Williams' wonderful *Morality: An introduction to ethics* (Cambridge: Cambridge University Press, 1972), and James Rachels' *The Elements of Moral Philosophy*, which was published in its 6th edition by McGraw-Hill in 2010. In addition, this appendix gives references to texts cited in each chapter of the book, which some readers may want to investigate in detail, as well as to other related material not cited in the text. In most cases, the philosophical material is listed first, then case studies. Many of the texts are collected in Thomas Donaldson and Patricia Werhane, *Ethical Issues in Business: A Philosophical Approach*, 8th ed. (Upper Saddle River, NJ: Pearson, 2008) as well as in the original sources. All Internet links are accessible as of November 2010.

CHAPTER 1

The philosophical theory in this chapter draws significantly on Williams' *Morality: An introduction to ethics*, in particular chapters 1, 2 and 4. John Rawls explains reflective equilibrium in sections 4 and 9 of *A Theory of Justice* (Cambridge, MA: Harvard University Press, 1971); the concept receives an accessible treatment in the Stanford Encyclopedia of Philosophy on http://plato.stanford.edu/entries/reflective-equilibrium/. A classic text of moral skepticism is J. L. Mackie's *Ethics: Inventing Right and Wrong* (Harmondsworth and New York: Penguin Books, 1977).

For case material, the "Parable of the Sadhu" is available as a film in addition to the *Harvard Business Review* article cited in the text. So is *The Corporation*, which entertainingly (if tendentiously) argues that public corporations are designed to be amoralistic and that they exhibit all the clinical traits of psychopathy. The arguments surrounding U.S. internet companies' behavior in China are fascinatingly put on display in "The Internet in China: A tool for freedom or suppression?", the transcript of a joint hearing before the U.S. House of Representatives Committee on International Relations, 15 February 2006 (http://www.foreignaffairs.house.gov/archives/109/26075.pdf).

CHAPTER 2

The main poles in the shareholder vs. stakeholder controversy are well known. The *locus classicus* is the debate in the development of U.S. corporate law between legal scholars Adolph Berle and E. Merrick Dodd in the pages of the *Harvard Law Review*. See Berle, "Corporate Powers as Powers in Trust," *Harvard Law Review*, 44 (1931) and Dodd, "For Whom Are Corporate Managers Trustees," *Harvard Law Review*, 45 (1932). The modern protagonists are Milton Friedman, who gave his basic argument in "The Social Responsibility of Business is to Increase Its Profits," *New York Times Magazine*, 13 September 1970, and R. Edward Freeman, one of whose many statements of stakeholder theory is "A Stakeholder Theory of the Modern Corporation," in Tom Beauchamp and Norman E. Bowie, *Ethical Theory and Business*, Seventh Edition, Upper Saddle River, NJ: Pearson Prentice Hall, 2004, pp. 55–64. Kenneth Goodpaster's discussion of the "stakeholder paradox" in the inaugural issue of *Business Ethics Quartlerly* is highly instructive, as is Freeman's retort in the same journal. See *Business Ethics Quarterly* 1(1), 1991, for Goodpaster, and 4(4), 1994, for Freeman. Michael Jensen's utilitarian stakeholder theory is defended in his "Value maximization, stakeholder theory, and the corporate objective function," *Business Ethics Quarterly*, 12(2), 2002, pp. 235–47.

In the daily press, shareholder primacy was dissected in a *Financial Times* editorial article titled "Shareholder value re-evaluated" on 15 March 2009. A case study of Merck and the Mectizan decision is Kirk O. Hanson and Stephen Weiss, "Merck and Co., Inc: Addressing third-world needs," Harvard Business School case study 9-991-021, 1991. The Mectizan donation program is described in detail (from Merck's perspective) on http://www.mectizan.org.

CHAPTERS 3 AND 4

Aristotle developed his virtue ethics in *Nichomachean Ethics*. A modern treatment of the virtues is Alasdair MacIntyre's thought-provoking *After Virtue* (Notre Dame, IN: University of Notre Dame Press, 1981). The ethics of roles have a long pedigree; Montaigne discusses them in the *Essays*. Bernard Williams discusses goodness and roles in *Morality*, chapters 5 and 6. The best current book-length treatment is Arthur Applbaum, *Ethics for Adversaries* (Cambridge, MA: Harvard University Press, 1999). Academic articles on the general topic of role-relative ethics include Gerald Cohen, "Beliefs and Roles," *Proceedings of the Aristotelian Society*, 1996–7, pp. 17–34; Michael Hardimon, "Role Obligations," *Journal of Philosophy*, 91, 1994, pp. 333–63; and John Simmons, "External Justifications and Institutional Roles," *Journal of Philosophy*, 93, 1996, pp. 28–36. Robert C. Solomon applies virtue-ethical reasoning to business ethics specifically in the article cited in the text ("Corporate roles, personal virtues: An Aristotelean approach to business ethics," *Business Ethics Quarterly*, 2(3), 1992, pp. 317–339). An excellent overview of relativism and its problems is James Rachels, "The Challenge of Cultural Relativism," chapter 2 of *The Elements of Moral Philosophy*; see also Williams, *Morality*, chapter 3.

The Kate and Lucy example is inspired by Joseph L. Badaracco, Jr. and Jerry Useem, "The Analyst's Dilemma," Harvard Business School case 9-394-056, 1993. Most professional associations publish a code of professional ethics; two are the American

Medical Association's code of medical ethics (http://www.ama-assn.org/ama/pub/physician-resources/medical-ethics/code-medical-ethics.shtml) and the American Bar Association's model rules of professional conduct (http://www.abanet.org/cpr/mrpc/mrpc_toc.html). Harvard Business School students recently proposed an ethics oath for MBA graduates based on the hippocratic oath (http://mbaoath.org/). Hannah Arendt famously chronicled and analyzed Adolf Eichmann's court trial for *The New Yorker*. Her reports are published in book form in *Eichmann in Jerusalem: A Report on the Banality of Evil* (New York: Viking, 1965).

CHAPTERS 5, 6, AND 7

The classic introductions to utilitarianism are Mill's *Utilitarianism* and J.J.C Smart and Bernard Williams' excellent *Utilitarianism: For and Against* (Cambridge: Cambridge University Press, 1973). Allen Buchanan's *Ethics, Efficiency, and the Market* (Totowa, NJ: Rowman & Allanheld, 1985) covers notions of efficiency in detail. Rachels' *Elements of Moral Philosophy*, chapters 7 and 8, give an introductory overview of utilitarianism, including the rule-utilitarian form. Amartya Sen provides a nuanced look at what Smith's theory implies for ethics in "Does Business Ethics Make Economic Sense?" *Business Ethics Quarterly*, 5(1), January 1993. A good dissection of the confusions arising from the multiple uses of the term "utility" is John Broome, "Utility," *Economics and Philosophy* 7, 1991. Much ink has been spilled on the Trolley Problem; a good exposition is Judith Jarvis Thomson, "The Trolley Problem," *The Yale Law Journal* 94(1985). Jonathan Glover's *Causing Death and Saving Lives* (Harmondsworth and New York: Penguin Books, 1977) is a wonderfully engaging philosophical discussion of trolley problems, hospital cases, and other thought experiments. J.J.C. Smart's attack on rule-consequentialism is in his "Extreme and restricted utilitarianism," *Philosophical Quarterly* 1956. Waheed Hussain's argument on the lack of a personal sphere under conequentialist justifications of profit maximization is laid out in his paper "Profit maximization and the boundary problem" (http://lgst.wharton.upenn.edu/whussain/papers.htm).

Some examples of corporate reports that justify "doing good" because it will increase profits are the BASF 2001 Social Responsibility Report, PepsiCo's 2004 *Sustainable Advantage* report, and MacDonald's 2006 Worldwide Corporate Social Responsibility Report (all available on http://www.corporateregister.com). The circumstances surrounding Guidant's discovery of the defective defibrillator are detailed in Martin E. Sandbu, *Dicing with death? A case study of Guidant Corporation*, 2009 (available on http://www.martinsandbu.net/guidant). The film *Wall Street* remains an entertaining morality tale about the ethics of profit maximization. *The Economist*'s survey on CSR was published on 22 January 2005. Texaco's travails in Ecuador are summarized in Denis G. Arnold's case study "Texaco in the Ecuadorian Amazon," (available in Tom Beauchamp, Norman Bowie and Denis Arnold, *Ethical Theory and Business*, 8th ed., Upper Saddle River, NJ: Prentice Hall, 2008). Both sides of the Texaco-Ecuador story are described in Sheila McNulty, "An Amazonian publicity battle", *Financial Times*, 19 January 2010 (http://www.ft.com/cms/s/0/5abf2c72-0499-11df-8603-00144feabdc0.html). Robert Frank's article, which gives more examples than the ones analyzed in the text, is "Can Socially Responsible Firms Survive in a Competitive Environment?" in David Messick and Ann Tenbrunsel, *Codes of Conduct: Behavioral Research into Business Ethics* (New York: Russell Sage Foundation, 1996). Dostoyevsky's

Crime and Punishment contains Raskolnikov's utilitarian justification of murder. The Plasma case is written up by T. W. Zimmerer and P. L. Preston as "Plasma International," available in Robert D. Hay, Edmund R. Gray, and James E. Gates (eds.), *Business and Society: Cases and Text* (Cincinatti: Thomson South-Western, 1976) and reprinted in Donaldson and Werhane, *Ethical Issues in Business*, 8th ed., pp. 156–7. The thought experiments about Jim and the Indians and about George and the CBW lab are in Williams' "A critique of utilitarianism," his contribution to the Smart and Williams book cited above.

CHAPTER 8

The conceptual material in this chapter draws heavily on Feinberg, "The Nature and Value of Rights," *The Journal of Value Inquiry*, 1979. Mill's discussion of rights and justice can be found in chapter 5 of *Utilitarianism*, and Bentham's disparagement of them in his *Anarchical Fallacies*.

As for examples of rights declarations, the historically most important ones are the United States Declaration of Independence, France's Declaration of the Rights of Man, and the United Nations Universal Declaration of Human Rights. For Google in China, see the reference to the Congressional Committee hearing under Chapter 1. For Guidant, see Chapter 5. For Kate's Dilemma, see Chapter 4.

CHAPTER 9

The "Asian values" debate has largely been waged in speeches and magazine articles (although see Chapter 4 for relevant philosophical expositions of relativism). An overview can be found in Matt Steinglass, "Whose Asian values?"*The Boston Globe* 20 November 2005. Mahathir bin Mohamad's Senate House speech is available on http://www.pmo.gov.my/ucapan/?m=p&p=mahathir&id=1584. Lee Kuan Yew's remarks are in Fareed Zakaria, "Culture Is Destiny: A Conversation with Lee Kuan Yew," *Foreign Affairs* 73(2), March/April 1994. Amartya Sen has criticized the Asian values argument in a number of articles including "Human Rights and Asian Values," *The New Republic*, 14 and 21 July 1997, the longer version of which is his identically titled 1997 Morgenthau Lecture on Ethics and Foreign Policy, published by the Carnegie Council on Ethics and International Affairs. Sen's eulogy of the Universal Declaration of Human Rights on its sixtieth anniversary ("The Power of a Declaration," *The New Republic*, 4 February 2009) is well worth reading. Dworkin's discussion of Chinese criticisms of rights is in *The New York Review of Books* 49(14), 26 September 2002 (available on http://www.nybooks.com/articles/15692).

Levi Strauss & Co.'s global sourcing and operating guidelines are available on http://www.levistrauss.com/library/levi-strauss-co-global-sourcing-and-operating-guidelines, and two case studies of the company's decision are available as Lynn Paine and Jane Katz, "Levi Strauss & Co.: Global Sourcing (A/B)," HBS case numbers 9-395-127/9-395-128, 1994. For the Internet companies in China, see the reference to the Congressional Committee hearing under Chapter 1. For a discussion of sweatshops, see Ian Maitland, "The Great Non-Debate over International Sweatshops," *British Academy of Management Annual Conference Proceedings*, September 1997.

CHAPTER 10

The treatment of Kantian moral theory in the text is largely an exegesis of Kant's *Groundwork for a Metaphysics of Morals*. There are of course a variety of applications of Kant's theory to business problems beyond the ones considered in the chapter, but for job security, two useful articles arguing opposite sides of the debate are Tara J. Radin and Patricia H. Werhane, "Employment at Will, Employee Rights, and Future Directions for Employment," *Business Ethics Quarterly*, 13(2), 2003 and Richard A. Epstein, "In Defense of the Contract at Will," *University of Chicago Law Review*, 34, 1984. For corporate communication, details on the example of the juice carton wording can be found in Ivan Penn, "Orange juice labels: pulp fiction?" *St. Petersburg Times*, 25 August 2007 (http://www.sptimes.com/2007/08/25/Business/Orange_juice_labels__.shtml.) A general philosophical critique of advertising practices from the perspective of personal autonomy is Roger Crisp, "Persuasive Advertising, Autonomy, and the Creation of Desire," *Journal of Business Ethics*, 6, 1987, pp. 413–418.

CHAPTER 11

The technical and philosophical issues of distributive justice referred to in the chapter are mostly covered in the references given in the footnotes there. For moral desert in the market, see Hsieh's article ("Moral Desert, Fairness and Legitimate Expectations in the Market", *Journal of Political Philosophy*, 8(1), 2000), but also Samuel Scheffler's work on desert more generally. For libertarianism, Robert Nozick, *Anarchy, State, and Utopia*, is the *locus classicus*. The main points of Rawls' justice as fairness are introduced in his *Theory of Justice*, chapters I, II, and III.

A wealth of material exists on the incessantly astonishing world of executive pay. Details about the example used in the text is available in the 2006 ExxonMobil proxy statement (SEC Schedule 14 information, available from http://www.sec.gov). Newspaper articles on the topic are readily found. *The Economist* published a largely positive survey of executive pay on 20 January 2007. The *Financial Times* interactive feature "Oil and gas chief executives: are they worth it?" lets users to compare pay with a range of variables (http://www.ft.com/ cms/s/0/190f9e7c-bd8d-11de-9f6a-00144feab49a.html). For more detailed research, the Corporate Library (www.thecorporatelibrary.com) is an important source; the *New Yorker* featured an article on this institution and its co-founder Nell Minow in its 12 October 2009 issue (David Owen, The World of Business, "The Pay Problem", available on http://www.newyorker.com/reporting/2009/10/12/091012fa_fact_owen). In 2005, Ed Woolard, former DuPont CEO and chair of the New York stock exchange's compensation committee, gave an entertaining and scathing critique of executive pay practices in a speech to the 2nd Annual Executive Compensation Conference (available on http://www.compensationstandards.com/nonmember/EdWoolard_video.asp; the transcript is on http://www.compensationstandards.com/nonmember/EdWoolard_transcript.asp).

CHAPTER 12

The book-length treatment of Integrative Social Contracts Theory is Thomas Donaldson and Thomas Dunfee, *Ties that Bind: A social contracts approach to business ethics* (Boston,

MA: Harvard Business School Press, 1999). See also the references to Rawls for Chapter 11. Strudler's arguments on deception can be found in Alan Strudler, "Deception Unraveled," *The Journal of Philosophy*, CII(9), September 2005, pp. 458–473.

The dilemma facing Time Inc. in the Valerie Plame affair is described in news reports including Adam Liptak, "Judge Warns Reporters They Face Jail in a Week," *The New York Times* 30 June 2005, and "Time Inc. to Yield Files on Sources, Relenting to U.S.," *The New York Times* 1 July 2005. Some of the arguments around Time's decision are rehearsed in "Judith Miller goes to jail," the *New York Times* editorial article from 7 July 2005 and in Frank Rich, "We're Not in Watergate Anymore," *The New York Times* 10 July 2005. The allegations that the 'Ndrangheta mafia dumped toxic waste are outlined in Guy Dinmore and Eleonora de Sabata, "Italian police close in on 'toxic' shipwreck," *Financial Times*, 21 October 2009.

INDEX